LIVES OF THE MASTERS

Gendun Chopel

TIBET'S MODERN VISIONARY

Donald S. Lopez Jr.

Shambhala
BOULDER · 2018

Shambhala Publications, Inc.
4720 Walnut Street, Boulder, Colorado 80301
www.shambhala.com

FRONTISPIECE: A photo that Gendun Chopel sent to his mother after his arrival in India in 1934.

9 8 7 6 5 4 3 2 1

FIRST EDITION
Printed in Canada

♾ This edition is printed on acid-free paper that meets the
American National Standards Institute z39.48 Standard.
♻ This book is printed on 100% postconsumer recycled paper.
For more information please visit www.shambhala.com.

Distributed in the United States by Penguin Random House LLC
and in Canada by Random House of Canada Ltd

Copyright page continued on page 278.

Contents

Series Introduction

BUDDHIST TRADITIONS are heir to some of the most creative thinkers in world history. The Lives of the Masters series offers lively and reliable introductions to the lives, works, and legacies of key Buddhist teachers, philosophers, contemplatives, and writers. Each volume in the Lives series tells the story of an innovator who embodied the ideals of Buddhism, crafted a dynamic living tradition during his or her lifetime, and bequeathed a vibrant legacy of knowledge and practice to future generations.

Lives books rely on primary sources in the original languages to describe the extraordinary achievements of Buddhist thinkers and illuminate these achievements by vividly setting them within their historical contexts. Each volume offers a concise yet comprehensive summary of the master's life and an account of how they came to hold a central place in Buddhist traditions. Each contribution also contains a broad selection of the master's writings.

This series makes it possible for all readers to imagine Buddhist masters as deeply creative and inspired people whose work was animated by the rich complexity of their time and place and how these inspiring figures continue to engage our quest for knowledge and understanding today.

—Kurtis Schaeffer, *series editor*

Preface

THIS IS my sixth book about Gendun Chopel. I had not intended to write so much about him. I began with his controversial treatise on Madhyamaka, *Adornment for Nāgārjuna's Thought*, a work generally disavowed and despised by Gelukpas and embraced and beloved by Nyingmapas. I decided to translate this difficult text—a text that others had begun but never finished—in the hope of bidding a fitting farewell to the Geluk scholasticism in which I had been trained at the University of Virginia in the 1970s. I was using the first edition of his collected works, published only in 1990, in three volumes, not in India, but in Lhasa. As I was leafing through volume 2 each day to get to the text, I would come across poems and stories that often seemed more interesting than the philosophical fine points of the affirming negative[1] and the nonaffirming negative[2] that I was translating. That eventually led me to the challenging task of collecting his poetry, much of it found in stray volumes where poems had inspiring titles like "Miscellany Number 2."[3] I published the poems with Tibetan and English on facing pages in a book called *In the Forest of Faded Wisdom*.

The more of Gendun Chopel's works I read, the more I wanted to translate; with each reading I understood how misunderstood Gendun Chopel has been for so long. Much of what you hear about Gendun Chopel when speaking to Tibetans are stories: about the time at Gomang when he dressed up like an illiterate *dop-dop*, the monastic equivalent of the Hell's Angels, and defeated a *geshé* on the debating courtyard; about the time he got dead drunk, took off all of his clothes, and then drew an elaborate and beautiful figure without lifting the pencil from the paper; about the time he put his cigarette out on the forehead of a Buddha image and then debated with some monks about whether the Buddha feels pain; about the time he laughed in the face of a powerful Tibetan aristocrat who praised Gendun Chopel's translation of the Pāli classic, the *Dhammapada*, as a "blessed tantra of the Buddha." As entertaining as these anecdotes are, they are only that.

My point, and it is certainly a banal point, is that one learns a great deal about an author by actually reading what they wrote. To do that, we need to translate the author's works. However, this is more easily said than done with authors like Gendun Chopel, who wrote so much. And it is clear that he wanted to be remembered for his writings. In fact, he thought that that was all he would be remembered for. As he wrote in a poem:

In my youth, I did not take a delightful bride;
In old age, I did not amass the needed wealth.
That the life of this beggar ends with his pen,
This is what makes me feel so sad.

If I was to do justice to Gendun Chopel, if I was to have the courage of my convictions, I could not just translate his contested work on Madhyamaka, much of which was constructed from a student's notes after he died. I could not just translate his poetry. I would have to translate the work that he considered his greatest contribution to Tibetan letters, a work that is over six hundred pages long. This is his *Gtam rgyud gser gyi thang ma*; even its title is hard to translate. When Gendun Chopel's works are discussed, one often sees this book referred to as his "travel journals." But this is because so few have read it; scholarship has focused almost exclusively on the first chapter and its list of Sanskrit manuscripts that Gendun Chopel and the Indian scholar Rahul Sankrityayan had discovered during expeditions in southern Tibet in 1934 and 1938. The distinguished Tibetan scholar Thupten Jinpa expressed interest in doing a co-translation of this work, something neither of us had tried before. The result was a fat book called *Grains of Gold: Tales of a Cosmopolitan Traveler*.

Gendun Chopel was also a remarkable artist, but few of his works—watercolors and pencil sketches—had ever been published. Drawing on the lectures from a conference held at the Trace Foundation's Latse Library in New York in 2003 to celebrate the centennial of his birth, I published *Gendun Chopel, Tibet's First Modern Artist*, which included many of his extant paintings and sketches. Most recently, Thupten Jinpa and I have produced a new verse translation of his famous, and infamous, work on erotica, the *Treatise on Passion*, published as *The Passion Book: A Tibetan Guide to Love and Sex*.

I was surprised to be invited to contribute a volume on Gendun Chopel to Shambhala Publications' Lives of the Masters series for two reasons. First, Gendun Chopel did not consider himself to be a master or, at least, he lamented that he was not considered one. In dividing his poetry into thematic sections for *In the Forest of Faded Wisdom*, I called one section "Teachings of a Master without Disciples" and another "Laments of an Unknown Sage." In one of his poems, he wrote:

> Spread upon the ground, this pauper's precious treasure,
> Gathered by a scholar as he wandered through the realms,
> Is no match for the rich man's golden dharma,
> Passed down in whispers from ear to ear.

And at the conclusion of his famous essay on Buddhism and science (reproduced in full in the second part of this volume), he tells his fellow Tibetans, "Please do not think that I am a dullard, believing immediately in whatever others say. I too am rather sharp-witted. In matters related to [the Buddha's] teaching, neither have I found disciples to whom I can expound the dharma nor have conditions been suitable for me to establish a monastery; I am not capable of those great deeds. My concern for the dharma is not less than yours." Here, he not only confesses that he is not a master, but he also anticipates his complicated legacy among his compatriots. Long before he was hailed as a prescient culture hero, he was despised as a traitor, an apostate, and an atheist. Even today, his fame derives largely from his poetry and his paintings. He is rarely counted as a Buddhist master.

I am sometimes asked by Western Buddhists why Gendun Chopel is considered an important Buddhist thinker if he died young from complications of alcoholism. It was Gendun Chopel's fate to confront the madness of modernity like no Tibetan before him, to be portrayed not in the warm tones of the *thangka* painting but in the starkness of the black and white photograph. Perhaps we know too much about him to imagine him to be a Buddhist master. I would ask readers to keep that question in mind as they read through the pages of this book.

Gendun Chopel

Introduction

On August 25, 1945, Gendun Chopel wrote this letter in cursive Tibetan script to the Russian Tibetologist George Roerich:

> To my old and dear dharma friend George,
> I assume that you are in good health and that your projects are flourishing. I arrived in Lhasa a little while ago and am well. In a few months, I will be returning to India. Please tell me what is happening with the book about emptiness that we wrote in English. Here, one of my aristocrat friends very much needs the books that Madame Blavatsky wrote herself as well as the first two books of Ouspensky. Please send me a letter clearly stating the price and the address.
>
> I have a friend named Chodrak who is a *lharampa* geshé of Sera Je. His birthplace is Buryatia in Mongolia. His knowledge of all of the traditional sciences and philosophies is unrivaled. He is serving as the tutor to many aristocrats here. He was invited to America by Bernard through Tsarong but was unable to go. Because he knows a little Russian and his Mongolian is excellent, he thought that his Russian would improve if he came to your place. Please tell me clearly what you think of his idea. When you write to me, you can send it to this address or through Tsarong.

Deliver to Amdo Gendun Chopel, Lhasa Chusin Shargyu
c/o Dharmaratna
Gyaling Chogpa
Gyantsé, Tibet

Arriving in Lhasa after many years, it seems like a new Lhasa. There are many people who have modern attitudes. There are even many who are interested in the system of Trotsky. Hearing that I had just arrived from India, in just a month's time I have been invited to the homes of various aristocrats who ceaselessly ask amazing questions. Everyone likes to talk about the fourth dimension.

Thank you for sending the letter that was sent from Amdo from Gyalsé through you.

I don't have any other news.

With best wishes, respectfully,
Gendun Chopel
August 25, 1945

There is a great deal to say about this letter. In the course of the pages that follow, we will encounter all of the people he mentions: George Roerich, with whom Gendun Chopel collaborated on the translation of the *Blue Annals* and son of the famed Russian Theosophist Nicholas Roerich; Geshé Chodrak (1898–1972), the Mongolian monk and friend of Gendun Chopel and author of a famous Tibetan dictionary, a work that some claim was in fact written by Gendun Chopel; Theos Bernard, the self-proclaimed "White Lama," who tried, and failed, to bring Gendun Chopel to America; Tsarong, a favorite of the Thirteenth Dalai Lama and an important aristocrat during the minority of the Fourteenth Dalai Lama.

It is clear from the letter that Gendun Chopel has business with Roerich. He wants to know the status of the book on emptiness that they wrote together in English; this undiscovered text is one of several holy grails among his oeuvre. He needs to buy books. And he wants to send his friend to study at Roerich's Urusvati Himalayan Research Institute in the Kulu Valley.

However, here we are concerned with the tone of the letter. Gendun Chopel has just arrived back in Lhasa after twelve years in South Asia. Much has changed in the city that he left in 1934. Many people have become "modern;" some are even interested in Trotsky. There seems to be great interest in the various mystical religions of the day. He has a friend who wants to buy books by Madame Blavatsky (1831–1891), the founder of the Theosophical Society; Gendun Chopel specifies the books that she wrote herself (as opposed to those written by her disciples), presumably *The Secret Doctrine* (1888) and *The Voice of the Silence* (1889). He also wants books by the Russian mystic and teacher of George Gurdjieff (1866–1949), P. D. Ouspensky (1878–1947), author of *The Fourth Dimension* (1909). Of course, the person in Lhasa who knew the most about Trotsky, who knew about Blavatsky and Ouspensky, was Gendun Chopel himself; he likely learned about them while living with the Roerich family in Kulu.

Lhasa at the time was a city of about thirty thousand inhabitants, with Drepung and Sera, two of the "three seats" of the Geluk sect, each with some ten thousand monks, on its outskirts. News of his return must have spread quickly. And so he was the toast of the town of the new Lhasa, being feted each night for the past month in the homes of Tibetan aristocrats. Still, he was eager to return to India. He was only forty-two. He still had much to do.

But Gendun Chopel never left Lhasa. A year after he wrote this letter, he would be arrested, flogged, and imprisoned. Six years later, he would be dead. As we shall see in the pages that follow, the reason for his arrest remains yet another of the many unanswered questions about the life of Gendun Chopel. It is clear, however, that several of the aristocrats who were so happy to have him in their homes were also happy to have him locked in the prison at the foot of the Potala.

A host of problems face the biographer of Gendun Chopel. The most obvious of these are the dates of the major events of his life, a problem rarely encountered for a figure who lived and died in the twentieth century. In various accounts of his life, one finds birth dates ranging from 1894 to 1905. Although he died in 1951, the day and month are variously reported. It was generally thought that he returned to Tibet early in 1946, but the letter above makes it clear that he had been in Lhasa since at least July of 1945. It is not known exactly when he was arrested, how long he spent in two different jails, or when he was released. And as we shall see, there is no end to theories about why he was arrested in the first place; he himself would put forth several.

In some ways, it seems appropriate that the standard conventions of the genre of biography would remain elusive for a figure who, throughout his life, was so unconventional, who called all manner of conventions into question. The most famous line from his most controversial work is the refrain, "I am uncomfortable about positing conventional validity."

It is therefore difficult to provide a conventional biography of Gendun Chopel, one that provides an accurate account of the various periods of his life. We know relatively little about his youth and early training in the monasteries of his native Amdo, ending with his time at Labrang Tashikhyil. After he left Labrang—for reasons that remain unclear—we have some reminiscences from his fellow monks at Drepung monastery, but these were collected long after his death, mostly from monks who had followed the Dalai Lama into exile. His twelve years in India are largely undocumented by others. It was during this time, however, that he wrote all but one of his most famous works; it is difficult to determine with precision where he was during this period. Ironically, the densest documentation of Gendun Chopel's life is only of his final years, especially the years (or year) after his release from prison, when he was as infamous as he was famous.

Indeed, unlike other important figures in Tibetan history, he was a man who made his name abroad, his life beginning and ending with the two most consequential foreign invasions in Tibetan history. He was born in August 1903, four months before British troops, under the command of Colonel Francis Younghusband, crossed the border into Tibet. He died in October 1951. On September 9, he was lifted from his deathbed to watch the troops of the People's Liberation Army march into Lhasa.

In the pages that follow, I will strive to provide as much chronological specificity as possible. However, as may be fitting for perhaps the greatest Tibetan writer of the twentieth century, this will be largely a literary life of Gendun Chopel, drawn from his own writings. Again, unlike other important figures in the history of Tibetan Buddhism, he did not compose an autobiography, a *namtar*. Near the end of his life, one of the few disciples who remained loyal after he was released from prison asked him, in the traditional Tibetan way, to compose his autobiography. Rather than do so with a lengthy work characteristic of the genre, he responded spontaneously, with a four-line poem:

A virtuous family, the lineage of monks, the way of a layman,
A time of abundance, a time of poverty,
The best of monks, the worst of laymen,
My body has changed so much in one lifetime.

A Note on Tibetan Transliteration

All Tibetan terms found in the main body of this book have been transliterated phonetically. Wylie transliterations can be found in the notes section.

The Biography

A monastic assembly at Labrang monastery

CHAPTER 1

Tibet

GENDUN CHOPEL was born in the village of Shopong in the valley of Sermojong in the district of Rebkong in Amdo, the northeast province of the Tibetan cultural domain. Recent consensus has placed his birth on August 14, 1903. His father, Alak Gyalpo (also known as Alak Belden) was an incarnate lama and *māntrika*[4] of the Nyingma or "ancient" sect of Tibetan Buddhism. He was an accomplished scholar of a genre of texts called the Heart Essence of the Great Expanse (Longchen Nyingtik). His mother was named Pema Kyi.

Some years prior to his birth, his parents were visited by a prominent Nyingma lama known as Dodrak Tulku or "the tulku of Dorje Drak," an abbot of Dorje Drak monastery in Lhasa (his name was Rigdzin Jigmé Sonam Namgyal). Before he departed, he told them that he would be reborn as their son, leaving behind his ceremonial hat as an omen. His parents and their toddler daughter later made the long pilgrimage from Rebkong to Lhasa. Gendun Chopel was conceived during the journey. Upon reaching Lhasa, his parents visited Dorje Drak monastery, where they learned not only that the tulku who had visited them had died, but that the monks believed that the child Pema Kyi carried was his next incarnation; the abbot had left a letter predicting that his incarnation would arrive at the monastery after his death. Although the monks urged the future parents to remain in Lhasa until the child was born, they decided to begin the journey back to Amdo. They knew that if the child was a girl it would be considered inauspicious, and if it was a boy, the monastery would insist that the child remain there for his education. Before they reached their home village, Gendun Chopel was born, near the birthplace of Tsong kha pa (1357–1419), the famous "founder" of the Geluk sect. His double affiliation to Nyingma and Geluk would continue throughout his life.

His birth name was Rigdzin Namgyal. Although he was never formally invested with the title, Gendun Chopel was regarded as the incarnation of Dodrak Tulku and was known by that name. Indeed, his identity as the incarnation of the abbot was confirmed by two prominent lamas who visited Rebkong when he was a young child, the renowned "treasure discoverer"[5] Sogyal Lerap Lingpa (1856–1926) and the Third Dodrupchen Jigmé Tenpé Nyima (1865–1926).

Gendun Chopel's father taught him spelling, grammar, and poetry, beginning at the age of three. He also learned many prayers by heart. At the age of eight, he studied (in Tibetan translation) the standard handbook on Sanskrit poetry, the *Mirror of Poetry* (*Kāvyādarśa*), composed in the seventh century by the Indian poet Daṇḍin, a work that he would return to throughout his life. Some time during this period, his father died. After his death, he continued to study at the nearby Nyingma hermitage of Yama Tashikhyil, founded by the renowned Amdo lama Shabkar Tsokdruk Rangdrol (1781–1851), which had some fifty resident monks and lamas. Around the age of fourteen he entered a local Geluk monastery of some six hundred monks, called Ditsa, where he was ordained as a Buddhist monk with the ordination name Gendun Chopel. *Gendun* is the Tibetan translation of *saṃgha*, the community of monks; *chopel* means "spreading the dharma." According to some accounts, he was ordained by the great Amdo scholar Gendun Tenzin Gyatso. However, he died in 1912 and thus would have been dead if Gendun Chopel was born in 1903 and came to Ditsa at the age of fourteen.

At Ditsa, he studied Buddhist logic for three or four years, developing a reputation as an excellent debater. It was from his time at this monastery that he came to be known as "Ditsa Slim," a nickname by which he was known among his fellow Amdo countrymen throughout his life. Despite his ordination as a monk of the Geluk sect, he returned to Yama Tashikhyil on several occasions to receive instructions in the Heart Essence of the Great Expanse.

Some time around 1923, he moved to Labrang Tashikhyil, one of the six great Geluk monasteries of Tibet, with some four thousand monks, where he completed his studies of logic and epistemology and began studying the taxonomy of the Buddhist path, known as "perfection" because it is said to be the hidden teaching of the perfection of wisdom (*prajñāpāramitā*) sūtras.

During his subsequent studies in Lhasa, Gendun Chopel was notorious among his fellow monks for never seeming to study. But it is clear that he read widely and deeply throughout his life, a habit that he seemed to have developed at an early age. A common ceremony for generating merit in a Tibetan monastery is to have the entire canon of the words of the Buddha recited. The one hundred eight volumes are taken from their place in the temple and distributed among the monks in the assembly hall. They all then begin to read aloud, not in chorus but in cacophony; each monk takes a different portion of a volume and reads it at the top of his lungs until every page of canon has been spoken. During one such ceremony, Gendun Chopel was observed quietly reading the text that had been given to him to recite.

Indeed, his prodigious knowledge of Buddhist literature was noted throughout his life, from the time of his childhood. When he was later asked how he acquired the remarkable capacity to remember whatever he read, he said that when he was a small child, he had a dream in which a shower of the syllable DHĪḤ—the root syllable of Mañjuśrī, the bodhisattva of wisdom—fell from the sky and covered his entire body. From that point on, he had the ability to remember whatever he read after a single reading.[6]

Status in the Geluk academy, however, was not gained by study but by debate, using the choreographed gestures for which the Geluk is so famous. Gendun Chopel's fame as a skilled debater, gained at Ditsa, continued at Labrang. It was considered particularly impressive if a monk was able to successfully defend a position that is traditionally refuted by what is regarded as the orthodox position. Gendun Chopel was once able to defend the Jain position, rejected by Buddhists, that plants have consciousness, a topic that he would return to in his essay on science (see pages 204–209). At Labrang he met an American missionary, Marion Griebenow (1899–1972), whose remarkable photographs provide some sense of monastic life during Gendun Chopel's time there.[7] His mother and sister apparently warned him about spending too much time with the American and his family, fearing that Gendun Chopel's hair would turn blond and his eyes would turn blue.

Although the ability to hold unorthodox positions on the debating courtyard is revered by Geluk monks, this is not to say that there is no demand for orthodoxy. Each of the monastic colleges has its own set of textbooks, which present what is regarded as the correct position on myriad points of Buddhist doctrine. At Labrang, the monastic textbooks had been composed by Jamyang Shepa (1648–1721), one of the luminaries of the Geluk sect and the founder of the monastery. Gendun Chopel is said to have criticized some of his positions, earning him the opprobrium of a number of influential monks, who labeled him a *thanyepa*,[8] a term that he would come to use to refer to himself. The term has a range of meanings, from "lover of words" to "rhetorician" to "sophist." In this last sense, it refers to someone who is skilled in words but has little appreciation or interest in their deeper meaning. This latter term of abuse was directed at Gendun Chopel.

His time at Labrang was brief, some four years. The reason for his departure, probably in 1927, is unclear. As with many key moments in his life, multiple explanations have been provided. Some say he was expelled from the monastery for his critical remarks about the positions set forth in the monastic textbooks. Other sources say that he was expelled for making mechanical toys, often identified as some kind of boat. Still others say that he insulted some senior monks by pointing his feet at them (a profound insult) during an assembly. After his return from India, Gendun Chopel provided yet another reason. The monks were performing an elaborate fire ceremony to propitiate the wrathful protector deity of the monastery, the Lord of Death Yama, known as Damchen Chogyal. At one point in the ceremony, the officiating monk tied a black ribbon around his forehead. He looked to Gendun Chopel like a Hui Hui, that is, a local Chinese Muslim, causing him to laugh uncontrollably, considered poor form during a tantric ceremony. That night he had a dream that a wild yak was chasing him. He took this as a sign from Damchen Chogyal that he should leave the monastery.[9]

Although it was not mentioned by Gendun Chopel, his time at Labrang was a turbulent period for the region, with almost constant warfare between Tibetan tribes and Muslim Hui militias between 1922 and 1928. The monastery itself and the neighboring town came under repeated attack by Hui armies. The main incarnate lama of the monastery, the Fifth Jamyang Shepa, was forced to flee in 1925, not returning until 1927; during one offensive in 1926, Hui soldiers turned their machine guns on fleeing monks.[10]

Regardless of the reason for his departure, Gendun Chopel left Labrang Tashikhyil, later writing a poem in which he bitterly criticized the monastery for banishing a studious monk while corrupt monks were allowed to stay (see pages 146–147 for the complete poem):

Rather than banishing to distant mountain passes, valleys,
and towns
Those who take pride in studying the books of Ra and Se,
Would it not be better to banish to another place
Those proudly selling meat, beer, and tobacco?

After leaving Labrang he returned to his home village. Some months later he bid farewell to his mother, his sister, and his village, never to return. Accompanied by an uncle and a cousin, he joined a caravan of two hundred travelers for a four-month trek to Lhasa. On the sixth day of the month of the dragon (the third month of the Tibetan calendar) in the year of the Earth Dragon (1928), the caravan set out from Kumbum, about seventy-five miles east of Rebkong, the great Geluk monastery built at Tsong kha pa's birthplace.[11] Some seventeen miles farther east is the village of Taktser, where the Fourteenth Dalai Lama would be born in 1935.

Upon his arrival in Lhasa, Gendun Chopel initially stayed at the home of a merchant named Gonchok Norbu before entering Drepung, one of the "three seats" of the Geluk sect in Lhasa and the largest monastery in the world, having at that time some eleven thousand monks. There, he became a member of Gomang college. Not long after his arrival, his cousin was killed in an accident. Gendun Chopel wrote a poignant poem lamenting the death of his childhood companion (see pages 151–152).

The monastic colleges of the Geluk monasteries were divided into houses, which provided living quarters, meals, and instruction to monks from a particular geographical region. Gendun Chopel joined one of the Amdo houses, called Lubum. There, he studied with the most famous scholar of the house, and one of the most prominent Geluk intellectuals of the day, Dobi Sherab Gyatso (1884–1968), a man of wide interests and progressive political views. Their relationship apparently began well, but deteriorated when Gendun Chopel once again criticized the positions taken by Jamyang Shepa in the monastic textbooks of the college that Gomang used, the same ones that Gendun Chopel had criticized at Labrang. When he attended Sherab Gyatso's lectures, the two would fall into heated arguments, so heated that he eventually refused to address Gendun Chopel by name, calling him only "the madman." Gendun Chopel would later declare that he learned nothing from Sherab Gyatso; other times he would speak of him with great respect. Although he stopped attending lectures, Gendun Chopel would still frequent the debating courtyard to confound his fellows, often challenging the best students while disguised as one of the illiterate *dop-dop*; these were the "monk police," something of a cross between an American college fraternity and the Hell's Angels motorcycle club. Nonetheless, while at Drepung, he seems to have completed the curriculum on the "five texts" of the Geluk academy, the curriculum he had begun years ago at Ditsa: the *Adornment of Realization* (*Abhisamayālaṃkāra*) of Maitreya, the *Commentary on Valid Knowledge* (*Pramāṇavārttika*) of Dharmakīrti, the *Entrance to the Middle Way* (*Madhyamakāvatāra*) of Candrakīrti, the *Treasury of Knowledge* (*Abhidharmakośa*) of Vasubandhu, and the *Discourse on Discipline* (*Vinaya Sūtra*) of Guṇaprabha.

Unless monks came from wealthy families or had a local patron, they needed to support themselves during their years of study. Gendun Chopel supported himself by working as an artist, painting murals in the homes of aristocrats and portraits of their children. He soon came to the attention of Pabongkha (1878–1941), the most powerful Geluk lama of the day. He had seen a black and white photo of the Thirteenth Dalai Lama that Gendun Chopel had hand-painted and asked that he make a painting of himself. Gendun Chopel wrote a poem on the back that incorporated Pabongkha's name:

Your sphere of kindness is perfect,
Upholder of the teaching, source of joy, crown ornament.
The light of your deeds shines upon the golden realm.
Lord of the all-pervading ocean of Victors.[12]

On May 19, 1934, the Indian scholar Rahul Sankrityayan (1893–1963), who was making his second visit to Tibet, arrived in Lhasa. Although only forty at the time, he was already a distinguished Sanskritist and an active figure in the independence movement, having served a six-month term in a British prison. He was a member of the Communist Party of India. In 1936 he would help to found the All India Kisan Sabha, the peasant movement of the Communist Party. He had first come to Tibet in 1929, making his way to Lhasa, disguised as a pilgrim from Khunnu. Once in Lhasa, he stayed at the home of a Nepalese merchant Dasaratan Sahu, moving eventually to Drepung, spending a total fourteen months in Tibet.[13] He then traveled to Sri Lanka, where he was ordained as a Buddhist monk in 1930. In 1934, Rahul Sankrityayan returned to Lhasa, seeking to photograph or copy the many Sanskrit manuscripts preserved there. However, he needed a guide to lead him through the great libraries of the monasteries of southern Tibet and to negotiate with the abbots for permission to explore their often musty contents. He first went to Sherab Gyatso for help. Sherab Gyatso himself was too exalted a figure to accompany the foreigner on his expedition, but he recommended two younger scholars for the task, the Mongolian monk Geshé Chodrak of Sera monastery and Gendun Chopel.

Despite his apparently desultory participation in the monastic curriculum, it seems that by 1934, Gendun Chopel was just completing the courses needed to participate in the examinations for the rank of *lharampa* geshé, the highest academic title among the Geluk. In a letter to Sankrityayan, he asked that their departure be delayed long enough for him to complete the examinations on

Vasubhandhu's *Treasury of Knowledge* and Guṇaprabha's *Discourse on Discipline*, the final two of the "five texts" of the Geluk curriculum. He apparently completed the examinations but did not remain in Lhasa to sit for the geshé examination. Nonetheless, in India, he would refer to himself as a geshé; several of his essays in *The Maha-Bodhi* are signed "Lama Geshe Chömpell." Translating the second part of Gendun Chopel's name ("spreading the dharma") into Sanskrit, in his own writings Rahul Sankrityayan often referred to him as "Geshe Dharmavardhana."

In his autobiography *My Journey Through Life* (*Meri Jeevan Yatra*), Rahul Sankrityayan described their first meeting:

> On June 20, I met the Amdo artist for the first time at Drepung. Geshe Dharmavardhan was introduced to me by this name. At that time I was unaware that this slightly built, slender, simple person was a formidable scholar of Tibetan literature and philosophy, a gifted artist, a poet of a high order, and a generous-hearted idealistic man. Since then over many years I got to know Dharmavardhan closely and became his great admirer. [. . .]
>
> On that first day we only conversed. There was no indication then that Dharmavardhan will accompany us. I have written in my diary: "He has a great knowledge of literature and dialectics, has made a study of the *Pramāṇavārttika*. He also remembers many sutras of the *Sārasvat* [the Sanskrit grammar *Sārasvatavyākaraṇa* by Anubhūti Svarūpācārya]. Thus, he is not merely a painter. He wishes to come to India. Why not take him along on the trip to Samye?"[14]

Here is how Gendun Chopel explained what happened: "From the time I was a child I have wondered again and again whether I would be able to go to India just once. Having been at Drepung monastery for about seven years after arriving in central Tibet, I met a *paṇḍita* by the name of Rāhula who had come to Tibet. He encouraged me to go [with him]. This was a wish come true, and we set out. First, the *paṇḍita* and I went on a pilgrimage to places such as the Phenpo region and Radreng. In our spare time, I began to study a little Sanskrit with the *paṇḍita*. He had a lot of money and knew about as much Tibetan as a seven-year-old child. He was under the protection of some Lhasa aristocrats, so we were able to examine closely the sacred objects of the various monasteries, such as Radreng."[15]

They visited a number of important monasteries, including Shalu, Ngor, and Sakya. The first chapter of Gendun Chopel's *Grains of Gold* offers a detailed account of their travels, listing the scores of Sanskrit manuscripts they discovered.[16] In the course of his account, he laments the fate of many of the manuscripts:

> Some religious-minded sentient beings said that keeping mixed up scriptures brings bad luck so they threw them in the rubbish heap in the cellar, causing all the texts to be wasted. Even in India, it is extremely difficult to find even a few pages of ancient texts written on palm leaves; how sad that there is so little regard for this kind of precious treasure [in Tibet]. Similarly, some of the faithful have stolen pages from a text that is complete to make a protection amulet. They have torn the page of a book into little pieces and eaten it, saying that this is a blessing. They have offered them as texts to be placed inside statues and reliquaries. Thus [these ancient texts] are nowhere to be seen today. These people damage the continuity of the Buddha's teaching and still boast about this to others.[17]

At some point during their travels, Rahul Sankrityayan invited Gendun Chopel to join him as he returned to India. Gendun

Chopel agreed. They crossed the border from Tibet into Nepal on November 10, 1934. Arriving in Kathmandu, they began going through the manuscripts they had collected and showing them to the great Sanskrit scholar Hemaraja Sharma, royal preceptor at the Nepalese court. Both Sankrityayan and Gendun Chopel describe showing him a fragment of Dharmakīrti's *Commentary on Valid Knowledge*, checking the Sanskrit manuscript against the Tibetan text to determine what portions were missing. They remained in Kathmandu for almost a month before proceeding to India. Gendun Chopel wrote in *Grains of Gold*, "From Nepal, going southwest and crossing the pass called Chandragiri, we soon encountered the Indian railway line. So on the eighteenth day of the winter month of *rawa* of my thirty-second year, I drank the water of the Ganges. During the entire winter of that year I stayed in Pāṭaliputra [Patna], with a sense of sadness, like that of an insect who has fallen into the middle of a lake."[18] In the traditional Tibetan calendar, *rawa* is the first of the three winter months, the tenth month of the lunar calendar. The date that Gendun Chopel gave would be December 5, 1934. He was now in India.

S. K. Jinorasa and Gendun Chopel

CHAPTER 2

India

GENDUN CHOPEL'S twelve years in South Asia would prove to be the most important and productive in his life. All but one of his most famous works (the notorious *Adornment for Nāgārjuna's Thought*) would be written there, including the work that he considered his magnum opus, *Grains of Gold: Tales of a Cosmopolitan Traveler*. In this and his other prose works of the period, his autobiographical comments are occasional; from these—and from various letters that have survived—we gain some sense of where he went and what he thought about the world that he encountered in South Asia, a world with both a classical past and a colonial present. A better sense comes from the many poems that he wrote during this period. In this chapter, we will consider where he went, what he saw, and whom he met. Those encounters, and the meaning he found in them, were made possible in many ways from his mastery of two languages: Sanskrit and English. He would esteem one and disparage the other. In a poem for his friends at Labrang, his monastery in Amdo, he wrote:

> With the years of my youth passing away
> I have wandered all across the land of India, east and west.
> I have studied Sanskrit, most useful,
> And the useless language of the foreigners.[19]

Both, however, would prove essential.

In Buddhist literature, it is said that there are "five sciences" that a bodhisattva must master: grammar, logic, medicine, the arts, and the "inner science" of Buddhist doctrine. These were studied in the great monasteries of all the major sects of Tibet. Here "grammar" means Sanskrit grammar; there was a long tradition of the study of Sanskrit in Tibet, beginning especially with the great translators of the "later dissemination" of the dharma that began in the eleventh century. The extent to which Tibetan scholars of the early twentieth century could read, and especially compose, Sanskrit is not clear. In *Grains of Gold*, Gendun Chopel, having learned Sanskrit properly in India, repeatedly mocked the linguistic skills of his compatriots. Nonetheless, even before he began receiving Sanskrit lessons from Rahul Sankrityayan during their expedition, Gendun Chopel had gained some knowledge of the language, its grammar, and its poetic conventions. As noted in the previous chapter, Pandit Rahul was impressed to learn upon meeting Gendun Chopel that he had memorized several passages from Anubhūti Svarūpācārya's *Sārasvatavyākaraṇa*, a simplified version of Pāṇini's grammar composed in the thirteenth century that had been translated into Tibetan by Tāranātha. Gendun Chopel's knowledge of Sanskrit would improve markedly during his time in India. English would prove more difficult. But as his notebooks and letters attest, he learned to read and write quickly.

As Gendun Chopel reports, the first city that he visited in India was Patna, built on the site of the ancient city of Pāṭaliputra, the old capital of Magadha and capital of the emperor Aśoka. Rahul Sankrityayan apparently went there in order to deposit the materials he had collected during the expedition at the Bihar and Orissa Research Society, which had been founded in 1915. Patna is the capital of the state of Bihar, which derives its name from the Sanskrit *vihāra*, or "monastery." The region is so named because there were once many Buddhist monasteries there; Bodh Gayā, Vulture Peak,

Nālandā, and Vaiśālī are all located in Bihar. Rahul Sankrityayan took Gendun Chopel on a tour of these sites, the first of several visits during his time in India; the notes that he took would become the basis for his *Guide to the Sacred Sites of India*, published in 1939, with an expanded edition in 1945.[20]

The travel guide[21] was a well-established genre of Tibetan literature, and Gendun Chopel knew many of its more famous works.[22] His, however, was different, strongly influenced by the Maha Bodhi Society (discussed below) in both its inspiration and its content.[23] For example, he made use of English-language sources, including translations of the accounts of the Chinese pilgrims Faxian (337–422) and Xuanzang (602–664). He recommends that Tibetan pilgrims visit modern museums. Among the museums he recommends is the Lahore Museum, the site of the scene in Kipling's *Kim* where the British curator (based on the author's father, Lockwood Kipling) instructs the Teshoo Lama (that is, the Tashi Lama or Paṇchen Lama) in Buddhist art. Gendun Chopel provides modern maps that he himself drew. He also provides railway and bus routes with instructions on where to get off and how much to pay, noting that he is giving fares for the least expensive seats and that fares are subject to change. Tibetans would not recognize the Hindi names of the sacred sites that they knew from Buddhist texts, so he provides phonetic renderings of them, underlined in his text to make them easy to find. He also provides the names in English with capital letters, which could be compared with station signs. Thus, for those who wished to make a pilgrimage to Dhānyakaṭaka (Drepung in Tibetan), where the Buddha is said to have taught the *Kālacakra Tantra*, he writes, "From Calcutta to Kha-rag pur (KHARAGPUR), Be-za-wa-da (BEZWADA), and then Gun-tur (GUNTUR) [by rail], and then 1 *rupee* by motorcar from there, one reaches Dhanakoṭa (Drepung). However, those hoping for great things will not see anything there."[24]

Elsewhere in the text he clearly sets forth his methodology, one that would be familiar to a modern scholar. He writes, "Thus, with regard to those sacred places that were determined and identified above, in writing about this I have put questions to scholars who have fully examined the annals of the past, I have carefully compared those to the unmistakably ancient histories of Tibet, and I have identified what is being referred to. I have never boasted, 'I think it is and so it is.' Thus, there is no need to have even the slightest doubt."[25]

Yet he is writing for an audience familiar with a different kind of travel journal, derived from different kinds of sources. Traditional Tibetan travel guides regaled the reader with all manner of wonders, wonders that Gendun Chopel knew about from his reading but did not encounter in his travels. They also included information about distances and locations that he found to be demonstrably false. For example, he notes that Tibetan sources state that the distance between Gayā and Bodh Gayā is a five-month journey when in fact it is a seven-mile walk or, as he says, "the time it takes [before stopping] for a hot cup of tea."[26] Yet these guides were often the works of great saints who were regarded as enlightened masters. How could they be wrong? In both his *Guide to the Sacred Sites of India* and *Grains of Gold*, he resorted to a standard element of tantric discourse, "pure vision," to explain them. Thus, in the travel guide he writes, "Some adepts went there in pure visions, serving as the source of a few stories that describe many wondrous sights; it is most inauspicious to wonder whether these sacred sites are real or not. Because pure visions are seen when one's karma is pure, we must only pray to have them; how could our ordinary perceptions be a source for correcting visions? When one attains an apparitional body, one is able to travel to buddha fields through the eye of a needle. In that case, we who bear the burden of never being free, day and night, from this corporeal mass of flesh and blood are not worthy to even seek it, much less condemn it."[27]

At the same time, he is often highly critical of his gullible compatriots. He writes, "When some other pilgrims arrive at an unfamiliar site and see an amazing temple, they identify it as this or that place of the Buddha. That talk spreads from one to another and a famous place arises. This is happening many times every year."[28] Later in the text, he again admonishes Tibetan pilgrims, arguing for his own veracity while remaining doubtful that anyone will believe him:

> Thus, apart from the difficulty of identifying these sacred sites, because one can rely on modern railroads, motorcars, and so forth, there is no difficulty at all in the actual mode of travel. Those who only have unreliable histories of India in their ears have doubts about everything because of the difference between the crash of thunder heard with the ears and the small drum seen with the eyes. This is the starting point of nothing other than incessantly deceptive stories about things like the real and false Bodh Gayā and the large and small Vārāṇasī. This India of today is certainly the real India; one need not doubt that these sacred sites are the real ones. Furthermore, I am not some gullible fool who believes everything he hears. I am a discerning beggar who is naturally intelligent and who has spent this human life in learning. Thus, one need not have any of the three qualms about anything that I say here: that is it mistaken, that it has no textual source, or that it is confused. For the majority of the human race, if you explain something that is difficult in an easy way, they do not believe you and are dismissive. If you explain something easy in a difficult way, you are counted as a scholar and they believe you. Thus, nothing can be done."[29]

After their brief tour of the sacred Buddhist sites of Bihar, Rahul Sankrityayan departed for an extended trip abroad that would take him to Japan, Mongolia, and the Soviet Union. Left alone in the Land of the Noble Ones, Gendun Chopel went north toward Tibet. Their route from Tibet to India in 1934 had taken them through Nepal. However, the traditional route to India for Tibetans—whether pilgrims, merchants, or exiles—was south through Sikkim down to Darjeeling or Kalimpong, both in West Bengal. Prosperous merchants in the wool trade and a number of Tibetan aristocrats had estates there. The Sikkimese practiced Tibetan Buddhism and spoke a dialect of Tibetan called "the language of the Rice Valley."[30] Gendun Chopel, having learned upon his arrival that Sanskrit was not the spoken language of India, decided to travel to a region where there were many who spoke his native tongue. During his time in India, it seems that, following a longstanding practice of the British, he often escaped the heat of the Indian plains by retreating north to Darjeeling and Kalimpong in the summer and venturing south for his various travels around the subcontinent during the winter months.

He seems to have gone first to Darjeeling, where he befriended a Sikkimese named S. K. Jinorasa. Despite the prevalence of Tibetan Buddhism in his homeland, he had been ordained as a Theravāda monk in Sri Lanka. He was not unique in this regard. Another Sikkimese, the half-brother of Kazi Dawa Samdup—the translator of *The Tibetan Book of the Dead* and someone esteemed by W. Y. Evans-Wentz while pitied by Alexandra David-Neel—was also ordained as a Theravāda monk and spent his life in Sri Lanka, where he became a renowned poet, known as S. Mahinda (for Sikkimese Mahinda).

Jinorasa had founded the local branch of the YMBA, the Young Men's Buddhist Association. Gendun Chopel was in need of both financial support and knowledge of English. Jinorasa was able to provide both, hiring him to teach at the YMBA and offering him lessons in English. Eventually, together they would translate Śāntideva's *Introduction to the Practice of Enlightenment* (*Bodhicaryāvatāra*) (whether the entire text or just the ninth chapter is not clear) into English. Also during this period, he is said to have collaborated with a Roman Catholic nun on the translation of Dharmakīrti's *Commentary on Valid Knowledge*. These titles appear in the long list of lost works of Gendun Chopel.

Indeed, translation would be one of Gendun Chopel's primary preoccupations during his time in South Asia, making translations from Tibetan into English (which he seems to have done to support himself in most cases), but far more important in his mind, making translations from Sanskrit into Tibetan, just as the great translators—the *lotsāwas*—of the earlier and later disseminations of the dharma had done a millennium before. Thus, from the time of his arrival he seems to have devoted a great deal of energy to the study of Sanskrit, not to translate or retranslate Indian Buddhist works but to translate the jewels of classical Indian literature, both religious and secular. From his earliest letters in India he expresses his desire to translate *Śakuntalā* by Kālidāsa, a poet he esteemed above all others. For example, in a letter written in English to Rahul Sankrityayan from Sikkim on February 7, 1936, he writes, "And still I long most to translate *Śakuntalā* with the help of your honor, and I can promise to make it as beautiful a line as a great Tibetan poet has done, and never defile your bright fame." He would make an abridged translation of the Indian epic the *Rāmāyaṇa*[31] and would translate four chapters of the famous *Bhagavad Gītā*.[32] In his *Treatise on Passion* (discussed below), he says that he consulted over thirty works of Sanskrit erotica, listing eight by name, including the *Kāma Sūtra*. He would also compile a Sanskrit-Tibetan lexicon that he called *Treasury of Sanskrit*.[33] During his sojourn in Sri Lanka, he would translate the *Dhammapada* from Pāli into Tibetan. He would come to take special pride in his skills as a Sanskrit translator, as is clear in this poem:

> Recognizing my own home, familiar from so long ago,
> And finding the remnants of my deeds from former lives,
> How can I show my joy in translating anew, at long last,
> This scripture of the perfect Buddha?
>
> They say that today there is in Magadha
> After a gap of eight hundred years in India
> A late-coming translator [from Tibet]
> Who can actually read the Sanskrit treatises.[34]

We do not know how he selected these works for translation. We know, however, that he had been preceded by other translators, not from Sanskrit into Tibetan but from Sanskrit into English. One notes that each of the works that Gendun Chopel selected for translation into Tibetan was already something of an Orientalist classic, certainly famous within the Indian tradition in its own right, but exalted further by having been translated into English by a British scholar decades before: Charles Wilkins's *Gīta* (1785), Sir William Jones's *Śakuntalā* (1789), Ralph T. H. Griffith's *Rāmāyaṇa* (1870–1874), and Sir Richard Burton's *Kāma Sūtra* (1883).

The *Dhammapada* also fell into this category, having been translated by F. Max Müller and published in 1881 in the tenth volume of his Sacred Books of the East series. Despite its modern fame, the *Dhammapada* was unknown in Tibet (although a similar work, the *Udānavarga*, was well known). During Gendun Chopel's time in India, Buddhist modernists of the Maha Bodhi Society were seeking to promote the *Dhammapada* as the representative book of Buddhism just as the *Bhagavad Gītā* was being promoted by

Hindu modernists.[35] Thus, Gendun Chopel's decision to translate the text into Tibetan, following in the wake of Rahul Sankrityayan's translation of the text into Hindi in 1938, should be understood as motivated by this movement.[36]

From the time of his arrival in India, Gendun Chopel had money troubles; his lack of funds and his lack of a steady source of income would be a consistent theme in his letters during his time in South Asia. Apparently because he lacked the necessary funds to remain in Darjeeling, Jinorasa took him to his hometown of Chakung in Sikkim, about eight miles north of Darjeeling. In a letter written from there to Rahul Sankrityayan on December 15, 1935, in the capital Tibetan script,[37] he said, "I would like to go to Magadha but I have not been able to go this year. Why? [Here, he switches into English.] A poor man cannot do anything." Writing to him again on January 14, 1936, again in Tibetan, he seems in despair. Jinorasa has gone to Calcutta and he is alone. He has no reason to remain in India. He would like to visit places like Ajanta, Mathurā, and Sanchi, but he does not have any money. He has no wish to return to Tibet (by which he means central Tibet), but he has a strong wish to return to his homeland (by which he means Amdo). However, he has no money and, he says, "Only money is the GOD of the world." He writes "GOD" in English.

It appears that Gendun Chopel did not receive a response from his friend. In January 1936, Rahul Sankrityayan was recovering from typhoid fever while planning another expedition to Tibet in search of more Sanskrit palm-leaf manuscripts. He set out for Nepal on February 16. Gendun Chopel was apparently unaware of Pandit Rahul's plans; he likely would have accepted an invitation to join the expedition. Rahul Sankrityayan remained in Tibet for almost a year, crossing the border into Sikkim on November 4. Shortly after his return to India, he traveled to the Soviet Union to teach Sanskrit at Leningrad University. With time on his hands, Gendun

Chopel began working on his translation of the *Rāmāyaṇa* from Sanskrit into Tibetan in 1936.

His fortunes and spirits would improve when he moved to Kalimpong, some thirteen miles to the east of Darjeeling. There he met the Tibetan Christian, Dorje Tharchin (1890–1976), better known as Tharchin Babu, who would remain Gendun Chopel's devoted friend for the rest of his life. He was the founder and editor of *Mirror of the News from Various Regions*,[38] known simply as *Melong* ("mirror"), the only Tibetan-language newspaper of the day (apart from one published by Christian missionaries in Ladakh);[39] it was published between 1925 and 1963. Gendun Chopel would first appear in the pages of *Melong* in a brief news item in the April–May 1935 issue: "The Indian paṇḍita named Rahula who went to Tibet last year has recently gone to Japan. The Amdo geshé who came with him from Drepung, who is very skilled in such things as grammar as well as painting, has now gone to Darjeeling. We have heard he is living at Dotsug."[40] In the years ahead, Gendun Chopel would publish a number of essays and poems in *Melong*; his first poem to appear there was called "Alphabetical Poem Expressed Sincerely in the Common Language," published in the October 16, 1936, issue (see pages 155–156). A heartfelt obituary of Gendun Chopel, written by Tharchin, would appear on the front page of the December 1, 1951, issue.

Perhaps in 1937, Gendun Chopel shifted his base to Kalimpong, working with Tharchin on a Tibetan dictionary. It was during this period that Gendun Chopel first learned of the Tibetan manuscripts from the dynastic period that had been discovered in 1908 in the Library Cave at Dunhuang by the French scholar Paul Pelliot (1878–1945). In 1931, his colleague, Jacques Bacot (1877–1965), brought photographs of some of the manuscripts to Kalimpong and requested the assistance of Tharchin in reading them. In 1937, Tharchin in turn showed them to Gendun Chopel, who was able to provide assistance.[41] Years later, Gendun Chopel would make use of these manuscripts when writing his unfinished history of the Tibetan dynastic period, the *White Annals*.[42]

Kalimpong and Darjeeling were the first stops in India on the trade routes from Tibet, and the caravans would carry mail. Gendun Chopel seems to have remained in touch with his family in Amdo and with his friends at Labrang and Drepung. In 1937, he learned that his erstwhile teacher Sherab Gyatso would be sailing to China from Calcutta and arranged to meet him there. In Sherab Gyatso's hotel room they again got into a heated debate, this time over the shape of the earth. According to traditional Buddhist cosmology, the world is a disk floating in space, with a rim of iron mountains enclosing a vast ocean. In the center of that ocean is Mount Meru, surrounded by four continents, each of a different shape, in the cardinal directions. To the south is a triangular island called Jambudvīpa, the abode of humans. Gendun Chopel, having learned something of astronomy, tried to explain to him that the world is round. (A similar debate had occurred in Sri Lanka in 1873 between a Buddhist monk and a Christian cleric.) However, Sherab Gyatso would not relent, slapping the table and saying, "I will make it flat." Gendun Chopel warned his teacher that if he said such things in China, not even a dog would approach him. At that point, Sherab Gyatso slapped Gendun Chopel in the head. Seeing that the other people in the room were becoming alarmed, the teacher and student explained that they always acted that way when they were together. The next year, Gendun Chopel would publish an essay in the June 28, 1938, issue of *Melong* entitled "The World Is Round or Spherical," complete with a map of the round world that he had drawn himself (see pages 135–137).

In September 1936, Gendun Chopel had made the acquaintance of an American, leading to perhaps the greatest case of "what if" in the history of Tibetan Buddhism in the West. His name was

Theos Bernard (1908–1947). He was the nephew of Pierre Bernard (1875–1955), a rather notorious yoga teacher and head of the Tantrik Order of America, referred to in the tabloid press as "Oom the Magnificent." Theos shared his uncle's interest in yoga and tantra, traveling to India in September 1936. Proceeding from Calcutta to Darjeeling, he met Jinorasa and Gendun Chopel at the YMBA. Bernard seems to have been immediately impressed by Gendun Chopel. In Calcutta the following February, he invited him to a dinner that included Charles Lindbergh, Anne Morrow Lindbergh, Francis Younghusband (who had led the British invasion of Tibet in 1903), David McDonald (the long-serving British Trade Agent for Tibet), and Sherab Gyatso, who was on his way to China.[43] Someone should write a play about that evening.

Bernard studied Tibetan in Kalimpong with Tharchin Babu (and briefly Geshé Wangyal, who would found the Lamaist Buddhist Monastery of America in Freewood Acres, New Jersey, in 1958) but was particularly impressed with Gendun Chopel, hoping to invite him to America to work with him on his studies of the Tibetan Buddhist canon. With the assistance of Tharchin and the approval of British officials, Bernard was given permission to visit Tibet, arriving in Lhasa on June 24, 1937. His time there, and the many Tibetan texts he collected, made him all the more convinced of the need to bring Gendun Chopel to America. He returned to the US, where he completed a PhD at Columbia University (with a dissertation on yoga) and, referring to himself as "the White Lama," published an account of his time in Tibet, *Penthouse of the Gods*. With the assistance of his lover, the Polish opera star Ganna Walska (he would become her fifth husband in 1942), Bernard acquired property in Santa Barbara, California, where he planned to establish Tibetland, a translation and study center. Gendun Chopel was to be the resident lama.

While Gendun Chopel was in Sri Lanka (as discussed in the next chapter), Theos Bernard, with the assistance of Walska's attorneys, began the difficult process of procuring a visa; Bernard was sufficiently hopeful that he booked passage for Gendun Chopel on a ship scheduled to depart from Calcutta on August 3, 1941, bound for San Francisco. However, the visa was denied. Gendun Chopel, waiting in Darjeeling, had decided to return to Amdo if he was not able to go to America. However, he agreed to stay in Darjeeling for another year, with support from Bernard, in the event that the visa would be approved. Jinorasa wrote to Bernard:

> In conclusion I must write to you again something about Geshe Chho-phel La. I must tell you that he is the greatest Tibetan scholar I have ever met with in my life and he is one of the few rare best scholars in Tibet so you must not miss him by all means to help you in your Great Work if you really want to do real research works in Mahayana Buddhism. If you do miss him I doubt very much whether you will again get another man like him. So do not miss him by all means. I shall do my best to keep him here till the war ends.[44]

With America's entry into the war in December 1941, Gendun Chopel was never able to accept Theos Bernard's invitation to come to America. However, in 1942, he would receive an invitation from another foreigner.

Although based in Kalimpong, Gendun Chopel seems to have traveled often. Thus, at some point during this period, he spent six months studying Sanskrit at Kashi Vidyapith (today called Mahatma Gandhi Kashi Vidyapith) in Vārāṇasī; founded by Gandhi in 1921, it was the first modern university established in India and was one of the first that was not under the administration of the British.

In 1936, Rahul Sankrityayan organized another, and larger, expedition to Tibet, to Shalu, Sakya, and Ngor; a number of Indian monks had visited the area during the thirteenth century and he knew from his trip in 1934 that there were many Sanskrit manuscripts there.[45] In May 1938, he made another trip, his fourth. This time, Gendun Chopel returned to Tibet with him. Before their departure, however, Sankrityayan took him to Shantiniketan, the college that had been founded by Rabindranath Tagore (1861–1941) in 1921, funded in part by the Nobel Prize in Literature that he had won in 1913. There, they met the aged Tagore himself, who offered Gendun Chopel a teaching position at Shantiniketan. He declined.

During the four-month expedition to western Tibet, the party stopped in Shigatsé, where they encountered Jamyang Shepa (1916–1947), the fifth incarnation of the founder of Labrang Tashikhyil monastery and the most important incarnate lama of the monastery. He had been a child during Gendun Chopel's years there and knew of his reputation. Jamyang Shepa invited Gendun Chopel to a private audience, where he invited him to return to Amdo. He declined.

In addition to the various figures who played important roles in Gendun Chopel's life during his years in South Asia, there was also an important organization: the Maha Bodhi Society.

In 1886, the British journalist Edwin Arnold (1832–1904), who in 1879 had published his best-selling verse biography of the Buddha, *The Light of Asia*, visited Sri Lanka. He had recently been to Bodh Gayā, which was under the control of Hindu priests, as it had been for centuries. Shocked by the sad state of what he called "the Buddhist Jerusalem," he recounted his experience in the *Daily Telegraph*, noting that when he had asked a Hindu priest whether he might pick a few leaves from the sacred Bodhi tree, the priest replied, "Pluck as many as ever you like, sahib, it is nought to us."[46]

During a meeting with a group of Sri Lankan Buddhists, Arnold called for two of the most sacred sites of Buddhism—Bodh Gayā, the site of the Buddha's enlightenment, and Sarnath, the site of his first sermon—to be placed under Buddhist administration. Among those present at the meeting was Anagārika Dharmapāla (1864–1933). He would go on to be the most famous Buddhist of the *fin de siècle*. Educated in the Roman Catholic academies of Colombo, in 1880, he met the founders of the Theosophical Society—Helena Petrovna Blavatsky and Henry Steel Olcott—when they visited Sri Lanka to help revive Buddhism (or Buddhism as they understood it). He would join the Theosophical Society in 1884. In 1882, he read *The Light of Asia* and decided to become a Buddhist renunciant. Prevented by a childhood leg injury from becoming a Buddhist monk, he wore robes and called himself an *anagārika*, or "wanderer."

Dharmapāla was able to visit Bodh Gayā himself in 1891, where he was shocked to see the state of decay of the most sacred Buddhist site of India. That same year, he founded the Maha Bodhi Society, which called on Buddhists from around the world to work, among a host of other aims, for the restoration of the four great sites of the life of the Buddha (the sites of his birth, enlightenment, first sermon, and his passage into nirvāṇa) to Buddhist control, a goal that was only achieved in the case of Bodh Gayā in 1949, long after Dharmapāla's death.[47] Nonetheless, with the financial support of Dharmapāla's family and a headquarters in Calcutta, the Maha Bodhi Society was the major Buddhist institution in India during Gendun Chopel's years there. He would become a devoted member. Between 1939 and 1941, he published five short essays and four poems, all in English, in the society's journal, *The Maha-Bodhi*, where he was called Lama Gedun Chompell, Lama Geshe Chompell, and Lama Geshe Chompell of Tibet.[48] Both his *Guide to the Sacred Sites of India* and his translation of the *Dhammapada* were published by the Maha Bodhi Society. His trip to Sri Lanka was likely facilitated and supported by the society. His last appearance in the journal of the Maha Bodhi Society was in the

August 1941 issue, where there is an article called "Lama Geshe Chompell." It begins:

> Lama Geshe Chompell, with whom our readers are already acquainted, has returned from his sojourn in Ceylon. He gives us a very pleasing account of the landscape beauty of the "Pearl of the Southern Seas" as well as of the hospitality with which the Sinhalese people treat strangers. He has an invitation from an American Tibetan Scholar to visit New York, which journey, though not without danger, he seems willing to undertake. During his stay in Calcutta he has given us a glimpse into the inner life of the strange land of snow, as well as of its ancient literature....[49]

Gendun Chopel's time in Sri Lanka is the subject of the next chapter.

It was upon his return from Sri Lanka that Gendun Chopel learned that Theos Bernard's attempt to bring him to America had failed. Unable to travel to Tibetland, Gendun Chopel decided not to return to Tibet, accepting an invitation from the Russian Tibetologist George Roerich (1902–1960) to come to his family's center in the Kulu Valley in Himachal Pradesh, not far from Dharamsala, where the Fourteenth Dalai Lama would reside after he came into exile in 1959. Roerich, who had been trained in London, Harvard, and Paris, was the son of Nicholas Roerich (1874–1947) and Helena Shaposhnikova (1879–1955). Both parents were remarkable figures.

Prior to the Russian Revolution, Nicholas Roerich was a well-known painter as well as a set designer, designing the sets and costumes for Stravinsky's *The Rite of Spring*, choreographed by Nijinsky, which premiered in Paris in 1913 and drew jeers from the audience on opening night. Helena Roerich had translated Madame Blavatsky's *The Secret Doctrine* into Russian and claimed to be in constant communication (often through séance and automatic writing) with Master Morya. Along with Master Koot Hoomi, Morya was one of the "mahatmas" with whom Madame Blavatsky was in psychic communication. It was likely during his time at the Roerich's Himalayan Research Institute at Urusvati, as they called their estate in Kulu, that Gendun Chopel learned about Blavatsky, whom he describes at some length in *Grains of Gold* (see pages 202–204) and whose books he requested from George Roerich in his 1945 letter from Lhasa.

After the Russian Revolution, the family traveled widely, with extended stays in London and New York, where Nicholas Roerich was feted as an artist and where the couple promoted what they called Agni Yoga (also called "Living Ethics"), a philosophy that they said had been transmitted to them by Master Morya; the Master Building at 310 Riverside Drive in Manhattan is named after Master Morya and was built to serve as an international center for the arts and for teaching Living Ethics.

In the years between the wars, Nicholas led an expedition to Central Asia from 1925 to 1928 (which attempted but failed to reach Lhasa) and an expedition to Manchuria and Mongolia in 1934–1935. Although the expeditions included both scientific and artistic projects, their ultimate destination was Shambhala, the utopian Buddhist kingdom described in the *Kālacakra Tantra*. The true goal of the expeditions—apparently announced by Master Morya—was to establish a Theosophical-Buddhist theocracy in Central Asia, with Nicholas Roerich in the role of potentate. The second expedition was sponsored by Henry Wallace, a supporter of Roerich who was then Secretary of Agriculture under Franklin D. Roosevelt; he would also serve as Vice President during his last term. Wallace's presidential aspirations in 1948 would be derailed when his letters to Roerich, which began "Dear Guru," became public.

Perhaps Nicholas Roerich's greatest public success was the Treaty on the Protection of Artistic and Scientific Institutions and Historic Monuments—known to history as "the Roerich Pact"—signed in a ceremony in the Oval Office on April 15, 1935. The treaty was meant to protect important cultural and artistic works in times of war; buildings that housed such works would fly the "Banner of Peace," designed by Roerich.

In 1929, the family had established the Himalayan Research Institute in what is today Himachal Pradesh. This became their primary residence during the Second World War and until Nicholas Roerich's death in 1947. After that, Helena and George Roerich moved to Kalimpong, where they remained until Helena's death in 1955, after which George returned to Russia where he died suddenly in 1960.

In 1942, his plans to go to America thwarted, Gendun Chopel accepted George Roerich's invitation to Urusvati. Roerich was seeking his assistance in translating the *Blue Annals*,[50] a massive history of Tibetan Buddhism composed by Gö Lotsāwa (1392–1481). It is primarily a lineage history, setting forth the lines of transmission—who received which teachings from whom—for the numerous sects and subsects of Tibetan Buddhism as they existed in the fifteenth century, with capsule biographies and vignettes about hundreds of Indian and Tibetan figures; it contains over five thousand Tibetan personal names, in addition to all manner of place names and book titles. In the 1940s, it would have been impossible for a European scholar to translate it. Yet the translation of the *Blue Annals* would be completed in 1946 and published in Calcutta in 1949. Near the end of the introduction, George Roerich writes, "It has been a source of much satisfaction to me that I was able to discuss the entire translation with the Rev. dGe-'dun Chos-'phel, the well-known Tibetan scholar, and I gratefully acknowledge here his very helpful guidance." Only the name "George N. Roerich" appears on the title page. It is likely, however, that Gendun Chopel did much more than "discuss the entire translation" with Roerich, and there is some evidence that he resented his treatment in Kulu. His close friend Rakra Tethong (1925–2012) reports that a particularly pungent passage in one of Gendun Chopel's most famous poems is a reference to Roerich:

> The talents of a humble scholar seeking only knowledge
> Are crushed by the tyranny of a fool, bent by the weight of
> his wealth.
> The proper order is upside down.
> How sad, the lion made servant to the dog.[51]

Whatever hard feelings Gendun Chopel may have harbored, quite justifiably, against George Roerich, their friendship does not seem to have been irreparably damaged. Gendun Chopel's letter to Roerich from August 1945 makes it clear that their collaboration had continued and that they were on good terms. Indeed, Gendun Chopel seems to have won the admiration of a range of foreign scholars, beginning with Rahul Sankrityayan, who was immediately impressed with the young monk he met in 1934. Once in India, he would win the respect of Jinorasa and the staff of the Maha Bodhi Society. He assisted the great French scholar Jacques Bacot (although it seems that he never met him in person). Theos Bernard wanted to bring him to America. It is noteworthy that the list of Gendun Chopel's known foreign friends and collaborators does not include British names. His father had been involved in the aftermath of the incursion of British troops into Tibet in 1888, which left many Tibetans dead on the battlefield, and his friend and mentor Rahul Sankrityayan was imprisoned by the British on several occasions, the first time in 1922. He certainly shared his views of the British with Gendun Chopel, who presents a scathing critique of colonialism in the final chapter of *Grains of Gold* (reproduced in full in part 2). His views of the British also appear in a poem:

Lacking the oil of compassion that benefits others,
Those skilled in the arts, with the sorcery of electricity,
Show the crooked path to honest humans.
Beware thc race of golden-haired monkeys.[52]

Let us return to an earlier period in Gendun Chopel's time in India and to a different collaboration. In January 1936, Gendun Chopel had written to Rahul Sankrityayan in despair. Because he was destitute, he was unable to visit places mentioned in the ancient texts, such as Ajanta, Mathurā, and Sanchi. Three years later, in January 1939, he would compose the colophon of one of his most famous works. It reads:

> This *Kāmaśāstra* by Gendun Chopel—who traveled across the ocean of our own and others' sciences, eliminating misconceptions about the passion of desire through hearing, thinking, and experience—was completed in the latter part of the middle month of winter in the Tiger Year [January 1939] in the great city of Mathurā in Magadha near the banks of the glorious Yamuna River, while the radiance of a summer dawn was descending in the house of Gaṅgādeva from Pañcāla, a companion in the same practice.[53]

Gendun Chopel's years in India were not a time of unremitting deprivation, melancholy, and loneliness.

When the lives of Tibetan lamas are written, whether by themselves or by others, there is generally little about their erotic lives apart from often formulaic references to the practice of sexual yoga and the use of the tantric consort (*sangyum*, literally "secret mother"), a practice said to be essential, for example, for the discovery of treasure texts (*terma*).[54] This is not the case with Gendun Chopel, in part because, as a figure of the twentieth century, we have reports of those who knew him. The more important reason, however, is that he was one of only two figures in the history of Tibetan Buddhism to write a book about sex. The other author was the great Nyingma master, and monk, Jamgön Mi pham (1846–1912).

As we have seen, apart from where he studied when and praise for his skills as a poet and debater, we know relatively little about his life before he came to Lhasa in 1927. However, we can assume that he maintained his monastic vows; in the bitter poem written after he left Labrang cited above, he contrasts himself with "impure monks."[55]

He clearly gave up his monastic vows, including the vow of celibacy, prior to the composition of his *Treatise on Passion*, which he completed in 1939. A friend who saw him in Lhasa shortly before his departure for India reports that he was not wearing his monk's robes.[56] This could suggest that he had renounced his monkhood before he left Tibet. The photograph of him taken in India in 1936 (which he sent to his mother in Amdo) also shows him in lay dress, as do the photos taken on a brief expedition back to Tibet in 1938, the year that he completed his treatise. There is a photograph of him wearing the robes of a Theravāda monk, perhaps taken during his visit to Sri Lanka in 1940–41, but a poem from his time there suggests he had given up his monastic vows years before.

> Although the dress of a monk has long disappeared
> And the practice of monastic discipline has left no trace,
> This meeting with the assembly of elder monks
> Must be the fruit of a deed in a former life.[57]

Elsewhere, he writes that "the unwanted tax of the monk's robe is left in the ashes."[58]

During his time in South Asia, he seems to have had an active erotic life, based both on what he says himself in his *Treatise on*

Passion and what his friends reported in the many stories that are told about him.[59] He had a series of lovers and frequented the brothels of Calcutta. In a poem written about his time in India, he alludes to a love affair:

Wandering like a deer from the realm of six ranges
To arrive in a distant kingdom of unfamiliar humans,
There I lost my heart to a glamorous fickle woman.
A wretched son who has forgotten his kind parents,
    I am sad.[60]

However, it is the *Treatise on Passion* that provides the clearest insight into his erotic life and his attitudes on sexuality. Here we find the exuberance of a man in his mid-thirties discovering the joys of sex, joys that had been forbidden to him for so long during his years as a monk. He writes, "As for me, I have little shame and great faith in women." In his treatise, women are not sources of male pleasure (or tantric realization); they are full partners in the play of passion. As he writes:

This passion that arises so naturally
In all men and women without effort,
Is covered by a thin veil of shame.
With just a little effort, it shows its true face, naked.

The second section of this book includes a number of passages from the *Treatise on Passion*. We will quote only the final passage, what would be the dedication of merit in a traditional Buddhist text. Here, he offers prayers not to the Buddha and to the lineage of his lamas, but prayers for three of his lovers, a Tibetan, an Indian Hindu, and an Indian Muslim. He also offers a prayer for all people, not that they achieve buddhahood, but that they find sexual pleasure. Although the *Treatise on Passion* is often called Gendun Chopel's "sex manual," it is much more than that. It does offer detailed and explicit instructions for lovemaking. However, it has two other aims. First, as a student of classical Indian literature, Gendun Chopel knew that one of its genres that had not been studied in Tibet was erotica. He therefore made a careful study of a number of Sanskrit works on the subject and then composed his own in Tibetan, drawing heavily on those works, and composing his text in some of his most beautiful poetry. His other aim might be called political. Having lived so long as a monk, Gendun Chopel had witnessed firsthand the hypocrisy of the vow of celibacy; in the *Treatise on Passion* he often mocks it. As a tantric practitioner, he understood the importance of sexual yoga and the role of bliss in the path to buddhahood. He knew, however, that such states were available only to the spiritual elite. The bliss available to the rest of us is achieved through orgasm. He thus presents sexual pleasure as a human right, one that no institution—whether church or state—should restrict. As he writes at the end of the *Treatise on Passion*:

> May all humble people who live on this broad earth
> Be delivered from the pit of merciless laws
> And be able to indulge, with freedom,
> In common enjoyments, so needed and right.

Among Gendun Chopel's writings from his time in India, the *Treatise on Passion* was the most notorious. A manuscript copy that he sent back to Lhasa is said to have at once aroused and scandalized the aristocrats who read it. However, his greatest work from his time in India, indeed, the greatest work of his life—in terms of size, in terms of scope, and in terms of the brilliance of his scholarship—is *Grains of Gold: Tales of a Cosmopolitan Traveler*. It has not achieved the fame of works like *Guide to the Sacred Sites of India*, *Treatise on*

Passion, or *Adornment for Nāgārjuna's Thought* because it is so long, because it was not published in Tibetan until 1990, and because it was not translated into English until 2014. Gendun Chopel states in the colophon that he is sending it back to Tibet from Sri Lanka, which he left in 1941. However, there are references in the text to dates subsequent to that, suggesting that the version he sent in 1941 was not the final version. The titles of the seventeen chapters provide only a hint of the remarkable contents of the text:

1. First, How I Set Out from Lhasa
2. General Formation of the Land of India and How It Acquired Its Name
3. How the Lands Were Given Their Names
4. The Snow Mountains of the North and Analysis of Related Issues
5. What the Famous Places of the Past Are Like
6. On Men, Women, Food, Drink, and Various Apparel
7. Identification of Various Species of Flowers and Trees and How to Recognize Them
8. Writing Systems of Various Regions of Past and Present
9. On the Linguistic Rules of the Tibetan Language
10. The Inscriptions of the Dharma King Aśoka Carved on the Rock Face of Mount Girnar
11. The Gupta Dynasty
12. The Pāla Dynasty
13. From 1,600 Years after the Passing of the Buddha to the Present
14. On the History of Siṅghala
15. On the Conditions and the Customs of the Tibetan People in Ancient Times
16. The Religion of the Tīrthikas
17. Conclusion

Grains of Gold is often described as Gendun Chopel's "travel journals." This is a great disservice to this carefully crafted and meticulously researched work of scholarship. It may be that it is often referred to with that term because it begins that way. The first chapter describes the expedition of Gendun Chopel and Rahul Sankrityayan to the monasteries of central Tibet in search of Sanskrit manuscripts. Because Gendun Chopel provides lists of scores of texts they discovered, this chapter is one that has been most read by scholars who are seeking to supplement Sankrityayan's own lists in the articles he published in the *Journal of the Bihar and Orissa Research Society*. However, *Grains of Gold* contains so much more, with the chapter titles sometimes masking the content. Thus, chapter 3 includes a discussion of Indian Buddhist art and iconography, with Gendun Chopel noting the apparent "aniconism" of early Indian Buddhism in which images of monks and deities are common but the Buddha himself is not depicted. Chapter 5 includes a discussion and condemnation of the caste system. Chapter 6 includes what is likely the first discussion in the Tibetan language of nineteenth-century race theory. In this same chapter he also recounts the life of the Buddha drawn from the sources employed by European Indologists, sources largely unknown in Tibet (especially from Pāli), noting points of divergence from Tibetan versions on several key scenes in the traditional biography. Chapter 8 and chapter 9 deal with linguistics, ranging from a discussion of the origins of writing to the exploration of a number of questions about the Tibetan language itself, including the development of the writing system based on an ancient Indian script, the modern gap between spoken and written Tibetan, and the relationship between Sanskrit and Tibetan. In chapter 10, he translates some of the famous rock edits of the emperor Aśoka. Although the story of Aśoka was known in Tibet, the rock edicts were not; they had only been deciphered by James Prinsep of the East India Company in 1837.

Gendun Chopel explains that one of his purposes in writing *Grains of Gold* is to recount what has happened in South Asia since the thirteenth century, the last period of sustained Tibetan contact with India. Chapters 11, 12, and 13 form a continuous history from the Gupta Dynasty to the present; chapter 12 contains the most extensive discussion of Islam available in the Tibetan language at that time. The lengthy chapter 14, on Sri Lanka, is discussed in the next chapter of the present volume. Chapter 15 deals with ancient Tibetan history, serving as a kind of prolegomenon for the *White Annals*. Chapter 16, another long chapter, includes a range of Hindu myths drawn largely from Gendun Chopel's study of the *Viṣṇu Purāṇa* and the *Bhāgavata Purāṇa*. The final chapter, simply called "Conclusion" (included in its entirety in part 2) contains a scathing critique of European (and especially British) colonialism, a lengthy discussion of the compatibility of Buddhism and science, and Gendun Chopel's considered opinions of such "new religions" of India as Theosophy and the teachings of Sri Ramakrishna.

In addition to writing what would be published as over six hundred printed pages, Gendun Chopel also painted over two hundred watercolors that he intended as illustrations. During the Cultural Revolution, all but twenty-seven were lost.[61]

Grains of Gold concludes with this poem:

> Walking with weary feet to the plains of the sandy south,
> Traversing the boundary of a land surrounded by the pit of dark seas,
> Pulling the thread of my life—precious and cherished—across a sword's sharp blade,
> Consuming long years and months of hardship, I have somehow finished this book.

Although there is no one to beseech me
With mandates from on high or maṇḍalas of gold,
I have taken on the burden of hardship alone and
written this,
Concerned that the treasury of knowledge will be lost.

Though terrified by the orange eye of envy
In the burning flame of those bloodthirsty for power,
Accustomed to the habit of gathering what I have learned,
My mind is attached to reasonable talk.

If it somehow enters the door of a wise person intent on
learning,
Then the fruit of my labor will have been achieved.
For the smiles of the stupid and the approval of the rich,
I have never yearned even in my dreams.

When this ink-stained body's need for food and drink is
finished,
When this collection of bones—its thread of hope for gain
and honor snapped—is scattered,
Then may the forms of these letters, a pile of much learning
amassed through hardship,
Reveal the path of vast benefit in the presence of my unseen
friends.[62]

In 1945, after almost twelve years of wandering, his weary feet would take him back to Tibet, where he would be greeted by the friends he had not seen for so long. And he would encounter those bloodthirsty for power, their orange eyes burning with envy.

CHAPTER 3

Sojourn in Ceylon

AMONG GENDUN CHOPEL'S twelve years abroad, one of the most fascinating periods is his time in Sri Lanka. He devotes a lengthy chapter to Sri Lanka in his *Grains of Gold*, a chapter that is highly regarded by Tibetan readers, so much so that it has been published as a freestanding work. Many of Gendun Chopel's surviving watercolors derive from his time there. According to his own account, he spent almost sixteen months there. As with so many events in his life, exactly when those sixteen months occurred requires some triangulation.

In a letter from Gendun Chopel to Sankrityayan, dated December 29, 1943, he says, "I have been touring Ceylon for the last two years. I was invited to visit America but could not undertake the journey because of the war."[63] As noted in the previous chapter, Gendun Chopel published some of his English-language poetry in *The Maha-Bodhi* in August 1941. The editor's preface states, "Lama Geshe Chompell, with whom our readers are already acquainted, has returned from his sojourn in Ceylon." In his account of his visit, he describes what is clearly the dedication of the Ruwanwelisaya stūpa in the ancient capital of Anuradhapura. He writes:

> Then, the Buddhists of Burma collectively sent as a gift a top ornament [for the stūpa], a piece of crystal one cubit long adorned with many large pieces of diamond and ornamented with gold, altogether worth 200,000 rupees. Beginning on

> the fifteenth day of the fifth [lunar] month, a festival was held [for installing] the top ornament, which lasted for a month. Most of the laypeople from the entire island as well as all of the monks gathered for this. It was said that such a great festival had not taken place for many generations. Many people even came for the event from faraway Buddhist kingdoms like Burma, Siam, and Cambodia. I was also there by chance, and it became known that even people in the land of Tibet had heard about it and someone had come. If at the time people [in Tibet] had not even heard of the stūpa itself, how could they have heard about its festival?
>
> On this occasion the stūpa was covered up to its peak with a rainbow of electric lights of five different colors. In the four directions, there were [lights] in the appearance of the Buddha in the four postures. Out of the empty sky resounded stanzas from the sūtras and various melodies, and from out of the clouds, airplanes flew and, circling it clockwise, rained white flowers down upon the stūpa as they circled. Various modern miracles as these were displayed. I think that the Buddha himself would have been astonished if he saw all of this.[64]

The dedication of the stūpa took place on June 17, 1940. Thus, if we assume that he was back in India by July 1941, a month before the announcement of his return in *The Maha-Bodhi* in August, and we accept his rather precise calculation that "I stayed for one year and a few days less than four months," he would have arrived in Sri Lanka as late as May 1940, about a month before the dedication of the Ruwanwelisaya stūpa.

Regardless of how long he stayed, by his own reckoning, he was one of the first Tibetans ever to visit the island. Or, as he writes, "Thus, although there had been a few visits to this island by Tibetan

Gendun Chopel dressed in the robes of a Theravāda monk

lamas in the past through their magical power, among those who have not attained the power of magical emanation, I think I am one of the earliest [Tibetans] to arrive here."[65] There is much to say about his time in Sri Lanka. Here we will focus on his reports and reflections on Buddhism. We must recall that Gendun Chopel had recently been a monk and a Tibetan Buddhist monk, meaning that he would have held not only the *prātimokṣa* vows of a monk—shared, with slight variations, with monks of the Hīnayāna—but also Mahāyāna bodhisattva vows and Vajrayāna tantric vows. His time in Sri Lanka allows us to witness what happens when vehicles collide.

Every day for centuries Tibetan monks have recited the so-called coarse infractions[66] of the tantric vows, some of which include "relying upon an unqualified consort and entering into union without the three perceptions; showing secret substances to the unqualified and arguing in the offering assembly (*gaṇacakra*); giving a wrong answer to a question from the faithful and staying seven days in the abode of a *śrāvaka*."[67] These vows are kept by a great many Buddhist monks in Tibet and are vows that Gendun Chopel himself would have taken. The infractions of the tantric vows listed here all fall within the stereotypical view of tantric practice as being concerned above all with sex and secrecy, except for the last: "staying seven days in the abode of a śrāvaka."

A śrāvaka is literally a "listener" in Sanskrit; it is a common term for a disciple of the Buddha, deriving from an Indian culture in which religious truths were heard rather than read. The term took on a more specific meaning in the Mahāyāna, coming to mean a monk who follows the Buddhist path in order to become an arhat. Thus the path of the śrāvaka (together with the path of the *pratyekabuddha*) constitute for Tibetans the Hīnayāna, the polemical term often euphemistically rendered as "lesser vehicle" but which in fact means the "base vehicle" or the "vile vehicle." The vehicle of the śrāvaka and the vehicle of the pratyekabuddha are the first two of the three vehicles (the third being the bodhisattva vehicle) that the Buddha describes in a number of Mahāyāna sūtras. In the *Lotus Sūtra*, for example, he declares that there is only one vehicle, the buddha vehicle, and that his teaching of the three vehicles was but an expedient device (*upāya*).

Thus, the vehicle of the śrāvaka is not a path that a Mahāyāna monk would be encouraged to follow. But why would tantric practitioners in India take a vow not to stay with a śrāvaka for seven days? Over the many centuries of the history of Buddhism in India, śrāvakas constituted the majority of Buddhist monks. In the polemics of the Mahāyāna schools, śrāvakas were those who denied that the Mahāyāna sūtras—and, of course, the Buddhist tantras—are the word of the Buddha. Furthermore, they saw the bodhisattva as a being who appears but rarely in cosmic history, rather than as the destiny of all sentient beings. To stay with a śrāvaka would be to risk conversion; Mahāyāna texts speak of bodhisattvas of "indefinite lineage" who abandon the bodhisattva path to follow the much shorter and easier śrāvaka path.

The Tibetan scholar and translator Chak Lotsāwa (1197–1264) reports that when he walked through the gates of the monastery at Bodh Gayā with a copy of the *Perfection of Wisdom in Eight Thousand Stanzas* on his back, he was stopped by a Sinhalese monk who asked him what text he was carrying. Chak Lotsāwa replied, "It is the *Perfection of Wisdom*." The monk replied, "You are a good monk; the Mahāyāna text you are carrying on your back is not good. Throw it in the river. This so-called Mahāyāna was not spoken by the Buddha. It was fabricated by a clever man named Nāgārjuna."[68] Thus there may have been good reason for tantric practitioners in India to limit their contact with śrāvakas.

But what would the prohibition against seven days with a śrāvaka have meant in Tibet? For students of doxography,[69] Vaibhāṣika and Sautrāntika were the two Hīnayāna schools. However, they were scholastic categories and had never been established in Tibet. Among the "five texts" that Gendun Chopel had studied as part of the geshé curriculum, the last two were Hīnayāna: the *Treasury of Knowledge*, which set forth Sautrāntika positions and critiqued Vaibhāṣika positions, and the *Discourse on Discipline*, which set forth the monastic code of the Mūlasarvāstivāda, a Hīnayāna school whose rules governed Tibetan monastic life.

At the same time, all Tibetan monks professed to follow the path of the bodhisattva. There were, in short, no official śrāvakas in Tibet, and with the demise of Buddhism in India, the possibility of Tibetan contact with śrāvakas there was significantly curtailed. Yet the path of the śrāvaka was studied assiduously in the monastic curriculum, not only in the *Treasury of Knowledge* and the *Discourse on Discipline* but in the "perfection"[70] curriculum based on the

Adornment of Realization, where the structure of the Hinayāna path was studied in a number of contexts, including that of the "twenty members of the saṃgha."[71]

During his South Asian sojourn, Gendun Chopel would spend many more than seven days with a śrāvaka. We thus might try to imagine what his knowledge of Sri Lanka might have been prior to his arrival on the island in 1940. From his own monastic training in Tibet, he would have regarded the monks of the island as followers of the Hīnayāna. This would mean, in turn, that they did not accept the Mahāyāna sūtras (and certainly not the Buddhist tantras) as the word of the Buddha. The monks would be śrāvakas, each seeking to achieve the nirvāṇa of the arhat for himself, each lacking *bodhicitta*, the aspiration to attain buddhahood for the welfare of others. They would furthermore deny the existence of such fundamental constituents of the Mahāyāna path as the ten bodhisattva stages (the *bhūmis*) and the three bodies of a buddha (the *kāyas*), as well as buddha fields or "pure lands." They would hold that there is not ultimately one vehicle to enlightenment but three, each culminating in a nirvāṇa that is the cessation of mind and body. Gendun Chopel would have studied all of these doctrines during his years at Labrang and Drepung, and he would have studied their Mahāyāna refutation. He would find these doctrines embodied in the Theravāda monks of Sri Lanka.

However, for Gendun Chopel, Sri Lanka would not simply be an abode of the Hīnayāna; it was also a powerful place of tantra. The island of Lanka, at least in its mythological form, is well known in Tibet. In ancient India, Lanka and its inhabitants evoked images of demons and mythic subjugation, most famously in the *Rāmāyaṇa*, and these same associations continued in the Tibetan imagination. Southern India in general (depicted most famously in the *Karaṇḍavyūha Sūtra*), and Lanka in particular (as depicted, for example, in the *Laṅkāvatāra Sūtra*), was a land filled with dangers.

Lanka also came to be associated with the teachings of the Buddhist tantras. In the influential account of the subjugation of Maheśvara by Vajrapāṇi, the island had become so evil and threatening to the welfare of the world that it was necessary to reveal the teachings of the tantras in order to subjugate its demons; the Buddha, in the form of Vajrapāṇi, taught the tantras atop Mount Malaya.[72] In some accounts, Padmasambhava's Copper-Colored Mountain is located in Lanka.[73] Thus Gendun Chopel arrived in Sri Lanka expecting to meet both śrāvakas and *mahāsiddhas*. He would meet many of the former and would express his dismay at not finding any of the latter.

His view of the Hīnayāna and of Sri Lanka would become complicated after his arrival in India, where, for the first time, textual passages read in Tibet would somehow come to life in Sri Lanka. As we have seen, one of his first friends and supporters in Darjeeling was the Theravāda monk Jinorasa. Rahul Sankrityayan would have told him about his own time in Sri Lanka, where he had taught in 1927–28 and where he was ordained as a Theravāda monk in 1930; he had translated the *Dhammapada* into Hindi for the Maha Bodhi Society in 1938. By the time of Gendun Chopel's arrival in Sri Lanka, he had already published the first edition of his *Guide to the Sacred Sites of India* and had learned of the work of the Sinhalese activist Anagārika Dharmapāla, whom he praises for his efforts to wrest Bodh Gayā from the Hindus and restore it to Buddhist control. Indeed, after having spent almost six years in British India, he welcomed the chance to leave it. As he wrote in the chapter on Sri Lanka, "Today, Magadha, the home of our forefathers, is under the control of the Hindus as the wife and the British as the husband; it is not a pleasant place and has been made uninspiring."

Gendun Chopel was now in another British colony, but one where the majority of the people were Buddhist, and he clearly felt the solidarity of the co-religionists. His allegiance to the Buddhist cause is evident in his description of the famous Pānadure Debate in 1873 between the Buddhist monk Guṇānanda (whom Gendun Chopel mistakenly calls Guṇaratna) and the Christian clergyman Rev. David de Silva. We note that at the end of the passage below, he alludes, as he does so often, to the provincialism of his fellow Tibetans, who, he says, would have difficulty participating in such a debate. He writes:

> After that, due to the influence of the people of the hinterlands, different religions arrived as well. The Christian or the tradition of Mashika [Jesus] spread widely, and during this period the position of Buddhism became greatly weakened. At that point, an articulate monk named Guṇaratna, who had studied all the religious systems and was skilled in debate, made a wager with the Christian teachers and their religion and debated with them for many days.[74] He defeated them completely, and many thousands returned to the Buddhist side. There is a teacher, an elder named Dharmānanda, who is very advanced in years. He told me that when he was a child he had met this monk; the monk had rough arms and piercing eyes, such that if he looked at you, you felt frightened. There is also a record of the debate that they had at that time, which is quite amazing. Although there do not appear to have been debates on the essential points of the view [of no-self and emptiness], the arguments of the opponents are presented on the basis of a knowledge of modern science. Thus, I think it would have been extremely difficult for people like us [Tibetans] to make a response.[75]

The first publication to appear from Gendun Chopel's time in Sri Lanka was his translation of the *Dhammapada* from Pāli into Tibetan, a project in which he collaborated with his teacher, the monk Dhammānanda of Asgiriya monastery in Kandy. It would be published in Gangtok in 1946 (after his return to Tibet) as part of the Anagarika Dharmapala Trust Publication Series. In his colophon to the translation, Gendun Chopel writes:

> A Sthaviran of Siṅghala,
> A Sarvāstivādin of the Snowy Range;
> Disciples protected by the same Teacher,
> Sole remnants of the vanished eighteen schools.
>
> Sugata's word, endowed with four seals,
> Sthaviran scripture, passed down by stages,
> I made this epistle, a pleasing pearl-handled cane,
> Arrive in the realm of snowy mountains.[76]

The non-Mahāyāna schools of Indian Buddhism are often referred to, following Bhāviveka, as "the eighteen schools" (although there were certainly more). One of these was the Sthavira Nikāya, the "school of the elders," which the Sinhalese regard as the Indian antecedent of the Theravāda (Pāli for Sthaviravāda, a term that does not seem to appear in Indian sources). Thus, Gendun Chopel's teacher Dhammānanda, from the Tibetan perspective, was a member of the Sthavira school. The monastic code of another of the eighteen schools, the Sarvāstivāda, the "school [that asserts that] everything exists," (in fact, a branch of that school, called the Mūlasarvāstivāda), was adopted in Tibet. Thus, although he had given up his monk's vows by the time he arrived in Sri Lanka, Gendun Chopel called himself "a Sarvāstivādin of the Snowy Range."

But nothing is simple in the life and works of Gendun Chopel. We should not, therefore, be surprised to learn that his relations with the Theravāda monks of Sri Lanka evoked a range of reactions from him, from heartfelt admiration, to frustration, to disdain. In the chapter on Sri Lanka in *Grains of Gold* and in reminiscences recorded by his friends, Gendun Chopel provides a number of vignettes from the days he spent with the Sinhalese monks. These vignettes offer some sense of his complicated relations with his hosts. When he followed the monks on their daily alms rounds, he felt as if he had been transported back in time and was in the presence of the first disciples of the Buddha. "Every day the monks went on their alms round, and I would go along to watch. Standing at the door of a layman's house, the older ones would recite the essence of dependent origination, saying, *ye dharma*. Not long after that, the laymen offered them hot and flavorful food that was ready to be eaten. As they left, walking in order, I thought, 'They are the sthavira Mahākāśyapa and the *āryan* Upāli. I alone am seeing this legacy of our compassionate teacher.' On many occasions, my eyes filled with tears, and I had to sit on the ground for a moment."[77] Indeed, he concludes the chapter on Sri Lanka with this poem about himself:

> Although the dress of a monk has long ago disappeared
> And the practice of monastic discipline has left no trace,
> This meeting with the assembly of sthavira monks
> Must be the fruit of a deed in a former life.[78]

But, as Gendun Chopel knew well from his study of the scriptures, even at the time of the Buddha, there had been good monks—such as the "group of five" who were the first to become arhats—and there were bad monks, such as the "group of six" who are credited with a wide range of violations of the *vinaya*, the code of monastic conduct. Gendun Chopel evokes the first group in the passage above; he evokes the second group here, in which he describes a different encounter:

> Once a good monk was walking through the middle of a field, and with an attitude of faith, I bought some fruit and offered it to him. He saw that there were still two *pana* [coins] in my hand and said, "You can still buy more." Having bought them, he made me carry them and we went on a little way. He received chickpeas from the farmers and obtained a large amount. Then, as we went he saw coconut bark and saying, "This is good for sweeping," made me carry a big bundle on my back, and we returned to the temple. I thought that all these monks live by the same dharma and the same path of [disciplinary] actions, yet when it comes to the way they display their greed, they are similar to that "group of six" in ancient times. Reflecting on this, I felt like laughing as well as a tinge of sadness.[79]

Gendun Chopel thus expresses a profound ambivalence toward the Theravāda monks; he develops warm friendships with several monks and a sincere admiration for the purity of their practice. Yet he is dismayed by their conservatism, saying at one point that the minds of the Sinhalese monks are "narrower than the eye of a needle" and notes, "In general, all these Siṅghala monks tend to hold only their own system to be supreme. With respect to the systems of others, regardless of how good or bad it may be, they tend to reject it completely without making distinctions."[80]

One way to avoid conflict would be to limit the topic of conversation to the monastic code; despite the large number of such codes in ancient India, they share much in common, such that a Sthaviran of Siṅghala and a Sarvāstivādin of the Snowy Range would have many topics to discuss. For example, as is well known, monks are not permitted to eat solid food after noon each day, although a "medicinal meal" is permitted in the evening; exactly what may constitute this medicinal meal is widely interpreted across the Buddhist world. While the rule against an evening meal is strictly observed in Sri Lanka, in Tibet it is generally ignored. Gendun Chopel reports a conversation on the topic:

> One time, I was having a conversation with another monk about eating in the evening. I explained that in Tibet there were no restrictions about that, and that it depended on the season and the locale; if one did not have some *thukpa* [Tibetan noodle soup] in the evening during the winter, it is harmful to the health. The monk said, "Oh, I know the rules about what is permitted and what is prohibited. Not being allowed to eat in the evening is very difficult. It is especially difficult for the new monks; some of them even eat cookies in secret." He then took some cookies out of his trunk and we had a nice time eating them together.[81]

Yet, the Buddhist solidarity he had hoped to find in Sri Lanka was constantly challenged by doctrinal and cultural differences, differences that became personal when the Sinhalese monks disparaged Tibetans and Tibetan Buddhism. In a poem that he sent back to the monks at Labrang, Gendun Chopel describes the views of the Theravāda monks about Tibet:

> They say that the Vajrayāna
> Is like the system of the *tīrthikas*.
> If they read a tantra, they would be hostile;
> If they saw a statue, they would be ashamed.
>
> In this assembly of monks of little learning,
> The majority say this:
> In Tibet, Śāntarakṣita

First established the Vinaya Piṭaka.
When they had to sit without chattering,
The Tibetans did not like the sūtras.

Then Padmasambhava
Arranged the offering and beat the horse [text missing],
He made burnt offerings, and did the dance.
And so, they say, Tibetans had faith in mantra.

They also say that though the Tibetan vinaya
Forbids killing, lying, stealing,
And doing harm to others,
When it comes to beer, women, and evening meals,
Doing whatever one likes is allowed.

They also say that a fox-fur cloak
Is the Mahāyāna monk's robe,
That a wooden bowl lined with silver
Is the Mahāyāna begging bowl.

There is much of this confused talk,
Saying that Tibetans and Tibetan pilgrims
Behave in crazy ways.

I say this to them:
"The vinaya scriptures in Tibet
Are all of the Śrāvaka Piṭaka."
I say this, but they do not think it's true.[82]

The immediate source for the monks' views of Tibetan Buddhism here are not immediately clear. One can imagine that Gendun Chopel's Sinhalese interlocutors had read some of the English-language works on Lamaism, which they seemed to trust over the testimony of a Tibetan scholar who had lived as a monk in several of the great monasteries of Tibet for some twenty years. One of thc works that the Sinhalese monks might have known was W. Y. Evans-Wentz's *Tibet's Great Yogī Milarepa*, first published in 1928. Apart from the Dalai Lama, Milarepa would likely have been the only Tibetan that a Sinhalese monk had ever heard of. They took the opportunity to ask their Tibetan guest about him:

> One time a monk said, "I have seen the biography of Milarepa, and he is an incredible practitioner of the dharma." I explained many things to him about Milarepa, and at one point the way in which the venerable Mila was a mantric yogin came out. The face of that monk immediately turned very dark. Then he said, "If that's the case, my faith in Mila has been damaged." I thought, "Alas! If I hadn't explained that to him, it would have been fine." I felt a tinge of regret that I was so talkative.[83]

Dismayed by the Sinhalese monk's rejection of Mahāyāna and of tantra, Gendun Chopel seems to have set out in search of them, or at least their remnants, on the island. Despite persistent efforts, he met with little success:

> Similarly, there are not even stories of the Mahāyāna masters who came to this land in the past, such as Āryadeva, Śāntipa [Ratnākaraśānti], and so on. Hoping to find the direct disciple of Śāntipa whom Buddhaguptanātha [a teacher of Tāranātha] said that he met in Kandy in Sri Lanka, I wandered around that region for more than a fortnight, but no one had even heard of him. At that time, he was said to

> have been about seven hundred years old; now he would be more than nine hundred years old. Or he must have passed away. Otherwise, I wondered why he would not grant an audience to the one Mahāyāna person who had come from Tibet. Similarly, no one seems to know the place where the sthavira Vajriputra resides, so if someone happens to travel here in the future, please look for him in the region of Mount Masdenatala [?]. . . . Nevertheless, everyone is familiar with the fact that in the past the Mahāyāna did spread here; this is even described at length in their annals. There is also a history of the Bodhi tree composed in the past by a layman named Guruḷugōmī who was a follower of the Mahāyāna. He is also said to have composed some commentaries on Mahāyāna sūtras.[84]

In the end, Gendun Chopel seems to have come to the conclusion, and one quite contrary to the Buddhist modernism of the day—both his day and ours—that cultural identity ultimately outweighs religious identity, that even though he and his Theravāda friends were both "sole remnants of the vanished eighteen schools," it was not necessarily in their mutual interests to spend a great deal of time together. He seems to have found a certain respite in Sri Lanka, despite the British colonial presence, from the oppression he felt in India, constrained on one side by the British husband and on the other by the Hindu wife. However, as we see in the concluding passage of his lengthy chapter on Sri Lanka in *Grains of Gold*, a chapter that he describes as a long conversation, he offers his view on the best way for Buddhists of different lands—in this case Sri Lankans and Tibetans—to proceed in the future, one that we might call friendship from a distance, celebrating their kinship as Buddhists without delving too deeply into their many points of contention:

During that time, I did not stay in one place, but wearing a cloak-like robe, I masqueraded as an *upāsaka*. Since I traveled constantly, I almost made a circuit of the entire island. I met with all the important monastic elders. Many times I felt a faith that brought tears to my eyes, mixed with deep sadness at having fallen to the ends of the earth. Walking through the forests without traveling companions, I was frightened by elephants, and once I even had to go for two days without finding food and water. For the most part, I wandered along the shores of the ocean, and because I stayed in fishing villages, I learned how to swim well, something that I did not learn to do until I was forty years old. I acquired many skills that I did not have before, like sucking the red legs of a crab and swallowing tadpoles. When I arrived at each monastery, the monks provided boundless help and support. In the towns, as the news spread that a new creature had arrived from the land of Tibet, the road became impassable because of all the people who came to see the sight. In brief, whatever kind of Buddhist pilgrim arrives on this island, they will not need to have the slightest hardship in finding food, clothing, and shelter.

Today, Magadha, the home of our forefathers, is under the control of the Hindus as the wife and the British as the husband; it not a pleasant place and has been made uninspiring. But now the time has come for us to ask Siṅghala, an island in the southern ocean, to take the place [of Magadha]. Thus we need to establish a relationship of identity between Vajradhara and Śākyamuni, a relationship of interdependence between the Sarvāstivāda and the Sthavira, and furthermore, a connection between the Mahāyāna of the north and the Hīnayāna of the south on the basis of the four seals that define a view as being that of the Buddha. Everyone needs to respect these sacred and profound connections. Yet those of the black begging bowl [the Sinhalese] are suspicious of everything, while those of the human leg-bone flute [the Tibetans] trample on everything. Regardless of who it is, each of the two [sides] has reached the peak of hardheaded stubbornness. Thus, for the time being, it is vitally important for both sides to live in a state of appreciation and affection for each other from our respective lands so that at least the recognition of our kinship in having the same Teacher and teaching will not be lost. Thus I have engaged in this long conversation [on the history of Sri Lanka].

> Although the dress of a monk has long ago disappeared
> And the practice of monastic discipline has left no trace,
> This meeting with the assembly of sthavira monks
> Must be the fruit of a deed in a former life.

This is just a song sung at the end of a [long] conversation.[85]

Rakra Tethong Rinpoche and Gendun Chopel after his return to Lhasa

CHAPTER 4

Return to Tibet

In 1945, apparently against the advice of some of his Tibetan and European friends, Gendun Chopel began the journey back to Tibet. As is clear from the letter to George Roerich that opens this volume, sent from Lhasa on August 8, 1945, all seemed well upon his return to his homeland after some twelve years away. In the month or so after his arrival in the capital, he was the toast of the town, receiving invitations to the homes of a wide range of aristocrats. He does not seem to have considered his return permanent; he wrote that he planned to return to India in a few months. His reasons for returning to Tibet, and for returning to Tibet when he did, are not known. Some say he was ordered by the British to leave India; others say he was invited to return by a tutor of the Dalai Lama. However, it is clear from a number of sources that one of his purposes was research.

As discussed in a previous chapter, in his first years in Kalimpong, Dorje Tharchin had shown him photographs of Dunhuang documents from the Tibetan dynastic period. In the wake of the An Lushan Rebellion, Tibetan troops captured Dunhuang in 781 and controlled it until 848. The Tibetan monarchy ended and the Tibetan empire collapsed in the wake of the assassination of King Lang Darma in 842. The Hungarian scholar (in the employ of the British) Sir Aurel Stein, the French scholar Paul Pelliot, and the Japanese scholar Count Ōtani Kōzui discovered thousands of folios of Tibetan texts in the Library Cave at Dunhuang, beginning in 1907.

The documents that Gendun Chopel studied had been collected by Pelliot and taken to Paris. Also during this period, Gendun Chopel learned about Tang Dynasty sources on Tibet from an 1880 article by the physician and amateur Orientalist Stephen Wootton Bushell (1844–1908) entitled "Early History of Tibet from Chinese Sources."[86] Gendun Chopel's interest in Tibetan history was likely enhanced by his work with Roerich translating the *Blue Annals* at the Himalayan Research Institute in Kulu.

It was perhaps during his time in Kulu that Gendun Chopel went to Lahul where he saw the famous statue of Avalokiteśvara called the Karsha Pakpa. Years later, he told his student Horkhang Sonam Belbar, "While I was returning to Tibet from India, on the road there were Buddhists and Hindus who were going to see the famous [statue] Karsha Pakpa Rinpoche. I went to see it and one day I slept in the presence of Pakpa. Pakpa is a statue that is white in color, made from marble, and one cubit tall. That night, in a hallucination that was like a dream, I dreamed that Pakpa Rinpoche said, 'Write a history; it is very auspicious. However, there will be an obstacle for you.' Pakpa Rinpoche wept. I also cried."[87]

He had learned a great deal about the history of India during his years there. Indeed, one of his stated purposes in writing *Grains of Gold* was to recount for his compatriots all that had happened in the Land of the Noble Ones since the time of the visits of the great Tibetan translators of the eleventh and twelfth centuries. However, his interest in history was not entirely antiquarian. The period between the world wars was a time of nationalist movements among the many European colonies in Asia, with native scholars, in some cases using the work of Orientalists, extolling the grandeur of their cultural heritage and recalling the times when Asian kingdoms were the conquerors rather than the conquered. Gendun Chopel was clearly inspired by this movement, coming to lament Tibet's loss of military might and even the memory of that might. And so he wrote in a poem:

> Compiling the available ancient writings
> Setting forth authentic accounts and clear chronologies,
> I have mustered a small degree of courage
> To measure the breadth and might of the first Tibetan
> realm.
>
> It is said that Tibet's army of red-faced demons,
> Pledging their lives with growing courage
> To the command of the wrathful Hayagrīva,
> Once conquered two-thirds of the earth's circle.[88]

Gendun Chopel knew that, apart from the Dunhuang documents, most records from the dynastic period of Tibet had been lost. However, an important source remained: inscriptions on stone monuments and pillars. At least one of his motivations for returning to Tibet was to visit these sites and document these sources, work that would be continued by Hugh Richardson (1905–2000), head of the British Mission in Lhasa. Gendun Chopel's research on the dynastic period would be cut short by his arrest in 1946, with the essays he had written up to that point later published by his student Horkhang as the *White Annals*.[89]

As is clear from his letter to Roerich and from the reminiscences of his friends, Gendun Chopel seems to have been something of a celebrity upon his return, gathering a circle of young disciples, to whom he taught poetry and grammar. This circle included two Nyingma lamas—Lachung Apo (also known as Sherab Gyatso, 1905–1975) and Dawa Sangpo (1916–1958). Lachung Apo reports in his biography of Gendun Chopel, written in 1972, that Gendun

Chopel came to visit him when he was recovering from a serious illness: "One day, when I was somewhat more lucid, he gave me a small book of Elephant Brand paper in which were written the words, beginning with, 'All of our decisions about what is and is not' and ending with the verse, 'I am uncomfortable about positing conventional validity.' He said, 'Look at this; it will keep you from sleeping.' It was a great help to me."[90] He reports that he and Dawa Sangpo later received lessons in Sanskrit poetics from Gendun Chopel, as well as in Madhyamaka philosophy:

> Then he gave Dawa Sangpo instruction in Madhyamaka. He had him take notes to supplement the small book he had given to me earlier.... At the end, when it had been completed and printing blocks had been carved by [the sponsorship of] Kashopa, he said to Dawa Sangpo, "Later, there is going to be controversy about this. The controversy will not occur until after I am already dead. If it occurs, it is all right. You must be careful. Do not forget the essential points I explained."
>
> He also said, "In order for human birth to have real meaning in this world, one must leave some imprint. In my own opinion, I thought that I must draw out some of the distinctive features of Madhyamaka and Pramāṇa. Now, I have done what is appropriate to suffice for the Madhyamaka."[91]

The book is his controversial *Adornment for Nāgārjuna's Thought*, published after his death and discussed in the next chapter. (A translation of the contents of the "small book of Elephant Brand paper" appears in part 2.)

In addition to his work on the *White Annals* and his teachings to his students, Gendun Chopel assisted the Sera geshé, Geshé Chodrak—the other monk that Sherab Gyatso had recommended to Rahul Sankrityayan in 1934 and whom Gendun Chopel recommends to Roerich in his letter—in the compilation of a Tibetan-Tibetan dictionary.[92]

On January 15, 1946, the Austrian mountaineer and former SS sergeant Heinrich Harrer arrived in Lhasa, together with his compatriot Peter Aufschnaiter. Eight months earlier, they had escaped from a British detention camp in Dehradun in northern India. Together, they would spend seven years in Tibet. On February 13, just a month after his arrival, Harrer made the following entry in his diary.

> At Geshila's [a Chinese from Shanghai, who escaped to Tibet and stayed at the Chinese mission] I met a Mongolian Lama, who spoke English and who is doing translations and who is also writing poetry. His name is Chömphel. He says that he translated for money the book about the last Lama for Bell. When it was printed it was sent to Canada. All this sounds rather strange, as one could scarcely assume that Bell would have given his name to a book he had not written himself. He tells us that the book had been written by another Lama in Tibetan and that [the Thirteenth Dalai Lama's] friendship with the Englishman was not mentioned even once, but always only with [*sku*] *drag* [aristocrats]. He himself is now writing a history of Tibet, which should be finished in the next months. Of course, it is written in Tibetan. He will bring me an English book about Gesar. It seems as if he is permanently living in Lhasa. He is earning his living with painting and also gets something from his books. He is a friend of Tucci and says that a student of Tucci has published a history on Tibet. He does not like Gould very much, because in his opinion he has published too many books on Tibet without knowing Tibetan.[93]

We learn a great deal from this diary entry. Six months after Gendun Chopel's letter to Roerich, he is still circulating in Lhasa society. He tells the Austrian that he has recently translated a biography of the Thirteenth Dalai Lama (who had died in 1933) from Tibetan into English, and that this translation had then been sent to Sir Charles Bell (1870–1945), the long-serving British political officer in Sikkim who had retired to Canada, where he wrote his famous biography of the Thirteenth Dalai Lama, *Portrait of the Dalai Lama*, published in 1946, a year after Bell's death. In the preface to his book, Bell refers to the text: "A biography of the late Dalai Lama was compiled under the orders of the Tibetan government. It was completed in February, 1940, between six and seven years after the Dalai Lama's death on December 17, 1933 and is entitled *The Wonderful Rosary of Jewels*.[94] The Regent was so good as to give me a copy of it, printed from the wooden blocks made in Tibetan style. Sir Basil Gould, the Representative of the Government of India in Tibet since 1935, kindly arranged for the translation of the relevant parts. This translation was supervised by my old friends Raja and Rani S.T. Dorji. This biography, which reached me after I had completed mine, deals with the Dalai Lama's life on typically Oriental lines."[95] Bell then goes on to disparage that style.

It seems, then, that the representative of the king of Bhutan in Kalimpong and his wife—Sonam Tobgye Dorji and Chuni Wangmo (who carried the titles "Raja" and "Rani" from the viceroy of India)—"supervised" the translation, but that the translation was done by Gendun Chopel and perhaps Dorje Tharchin, who knew Sir Basil Gould well.[96] The typescript of the translation resides today among Bell's papers at the British Library. The contributions of Gendun Chopel (and Tharchin) were not credited. In addition, we learn from Harrer that Gendun Chopel is writing his own history of Tibet. And we learn that he does not have a high opinion of the British, something that is eminently clear throughout his works.

In Harrer's diary, we read in an entry from November 26, 1946, some nine months after he met Gendun Chopel, "By the way, the Geshé from Amdo, who was imprisoned some time ago because of 'new fashions,' has also been whipped (sixty times). Allegedly he will be released soon."[97] What had happened during that time? Of the many mysteries and questions surrounding the life of Gendun Chopel, none is more contentious, and consequential, than the reason for his arrest and imprisonment. There are questions about when he was arrested, how long he spent in prison, and the conditions of his imprisonment. However, the question that looms over all others is why he was arrested.

Gendun Chopel seems to have been arrested in July 1946, hence Harrer's statement that he was "imprisoned some time ago." He was charged with passing counterfeit Indian rupees. The previous May, counterfeit currency had indeed been seized in the Kalimpong region. However, a search of Gendun Chopel's room in Lhasa revealed nothing apart from a list of Tibetan government officials and some notes on the Sino-Tibetan border. Among the many theories that are put forth concerning his arrest, all seem to agree that the charge was a pretext for something else.

Some have claimed that he was arrested because he had embarrassed a powerful member of the cabinet. This was Kashopa Chogyal Nyima (1903–1986). He had long been a supporter of Gendun Chopel. As a token of his gratitude, when Gendun Chopel completed his *Treatise on Passion* in 1939, he sent a copy to Kashopa. Upon his return, Gendun Chopel had been invited to the nobleman's home and was giving English lessons to his son. As discussed in the previous chapter, while he was in Sri Lanka, Gendun Chopel had studied Pāli and translated the *Dhammapada*, perhaps the most famous work, at least in the West, of the Theravāda tradition, from Pāli into Tibetan. On one of his visits to Kashopa's home, Gendun Chopel presented him with a copy of the translation. Kashopa said,

"The terminology of the tantras is unlike anything else." Gendun Chopel burst out laughing because the *Dhammapada* is not a tantra. According to some, this was enough to send him to prison.[98]

Others claimed he was a Russian spy. Such a charge was a remnant of the Tsarist days, when Britain and Russia vied for influence over Tibet as part of the Great Game. During this period, there were Buddhist monks who were Russian partisans, including the noted Buryiat scholar Ngawang Dorje (1854–1938), whose name was Russianized as Agvan Dorzhiev. But Stalin launched a campaign against religion in which the many Buddhist institutions in the Soviet Union, especially in Kalmykia and Buryatia, suffered greatly, especially in the Great Repression of 1937–1939. Gendun Chopel could only be considered a Russian spy in a particular flight of imagination, perhaps because he had collaborated with the expatriate Russian scholar George Roerich and lived at the estate of his father Nicholas in Kulu.

It appears that at least one factor that led to his arrest was his involvement (although the extent of his involvement remains a matter of debate) in what is known in English as the Tibet Improvement Party. Its logo, designed by Gendun Chopel, featured a sickle (clearly reminiscent of the Soviet hammer and sickle), a sword, and a loom (reminiscent of Gandhi's spinning wheel), with the name of the organization in both Chinese and Tibetan. In Chinese, it was Xizang Gemingdang. *Xizang* is a standard Chinese name for Tibet, literally meaning "western treasury." *Gemingdang* is usually translated as "revolutionary party." In Tibetan, however, the name was far more docile; it was called the Nub bod legs bcos kyi skyid sdug, which means the "Association for the Improvement of Western Tibet." In Tibetan, it is thus a friendly association rather than a political party, dedicated to improvement rather than to revolution. However, the otherwise innocuous Tibetan name is betrayed by the term *nub bod*, "western Tibet," a term that means nothing in Tibetan unless one knows the Chinese designation of the country.

The founder of the group, Rapga Pandatsang (1902–1976) was from Kham, a region that had long chafed under the rule of the government in Lhasa; his brother had led a failed revolt in 1934. Rapga was a great admirer of Sun Yat-sen, the founder of the Chinese Republic, and had translated some of Sun's writings into Tibetan. He had met with Chiang Kai-shek in Nanjing in 1935. Rapga envisioned Tibet as an autonomous state, organized along democratic lines and under the overall control of the Republic of China. Article Two of the Tibet Improvement Party agreement states, "Recently President Chiang has declared to allow autonomy of Tibet. According to this we must exert our efforts mainly for Liberation of Tibet from the existing tyrannical Government. Also we must act in the light of other progressive and democratic nations of the World and especially democratic Central Government of China for which all members of our party must work as men on the same boat."[99]

During his time abroad, Gendun Chopel had become increasingly critical of the government of Tibet and of the corruption and political machinations of the Geluk monasteries, and he likely found kindred spirits in the Tibet Improvement Party. He believed that major reforms were necessary in Tibet. He proposed, for example, that monks be paid salaries rather than being allowed to own estates and that they be required to study and be prohibited from engaging in commerce. His erstwhile teacher Geshé Sherab Gyatso had long been a political radical by Tibetan standards, admiring Mao and supporting his movement during the 1930s; he would meet a terrible fate, dying in 1968 after being beaten by Red Guards.

Yet others would claim that Gendun Chopel was a Communist. Rahul Sankrityayan was a proud Communist who had visited Moscow. Nicholas Roerich and his family had left Russia after the October Revolution, but he later reconciled with the Soviet

Union. Indeed, in the 1920s, he would proclaim an alliance between Buddhism and Communism to liberate Asia from foreign control, claiming that the identity of the two had been confirmed both by Tibetan lamas and Theosophical mahatmas.[100] Nicholas Roerich was approaching seventy when Gendun Chopel visited the family estate in Kulu in the early 1940s; in the years before the Second World War, he was repeatedly denied a visa to return to his native Russia, by then, the Soviet Union. His son George Roerich would return to the Soviet Union in 1957 at the personal invitation of Khrushchev, an admirer of his father's paintings. Gendun Chopel was thus clearly exposed to socialist and communist ideas, although it is unlikely he identified himself with the Soviet Communists, who were hated in Tibet for the devastation they had caused to Buddhist monasteries in the Soviet republics; there were many monks from Kalmykia and Buryatia at Drepung during Gendun Chopel's years there. Indeed, a monk from Drepung reported a conversation in which Gendun Chopel ascribed the origins of Marxism to the fact that Marx was always hungry and jealous of the rich, arguing that the Russian Revolution was the result of years of famine and could have been averted by food aid from Britain and America.[101]

Thus the degree of Gendun Chopel's involvement in the Tibet Improvement Party, and his own political beliefs more generally, like so many other elements of his biography, are in doubt. Indeed, although Gendun Chopel wrote on a remarkable range of topics, no overtly "political" writings have emerged among his extant works apart from the critique of European colonialism found in the final chapter of *Grains of Gold* (see page 195ff.). It may have been that he designed the logo of the Tibet Improvement Party simply because Rapga, knowing him to be a noted artist, asked him to do so.

Another of the reasons put forth for Gendun Chopel's arrest is that he drew maps of the Tibetan-Bhutanese border, returning to Tibet by an unusual route in order to do so. Some speculate that these maps were intended for the Kuomintang. Maps were indeed discovered when his rooms were searched at the time of his arrest. After his release, Gendun Chopel would provide a variety of explanations for his arrest, including one which involved his map-making skills. A friend of Gendun Chopel reported the account that he gave:

> While Gendun Chopel was in Calcutta, he got to know a Chinese man. Having gotten to know him, he asked him to make a map starting in Assam and Loyul to the east of India and ending in Nepal. He did not know whether it would be beneficial or harmful, but he made the map. It said things like, "the land is like this," "the bridge over the river is like this," "the households on the other side of the bridge are like this," "the police are like this," "the number of police at the place is like this." In many ways it was like an army map. It was not something vague; he made it absolutely clear. It fell into the hands of the British and they were at the point of arresting him. In the end they issued a notice that he was not permitted to remain in India. This is what he told me.
>
> He said that after he left for Tibet, the British sent a letter to the Tibetan government saying, "A Communist has left for Tibet." Everyone believed it and saying, "Gendun Chopel is a Communist," they put him in prison. This happened because of the evil intentions of the British. The main person was Kashopa and there were others.[102]

Gendun Chopel's suspicion that the colonial authorities considered him to be a Communist is confirmed in an intelligence report dated July 23, 1948—two years after he was arrested—by Harishwar Dayal, Political Officer of the Government of India in Sikkim, who wrote, "It is gathered from a reliable source that Gedun Chomphel, who is now in the custody of the Tibetan Government is a Communist and an agent of Soviet Russia, appointed by Pandit Rahul La [Sankrityayan]. It is said that he stayed with Pandit Rahul in India for some time and during that time they manufactured false Tibetan currency notes."[103]

In addition to the story of the maps, Gendun Chopel would provide another explanation for his arrest, one that placed the blame more squarely on the British, specifically on Hugh Richardson. Here, as reported by one of his students, Gendun Chopel alludes to his translation of the biography of the Thirteenth Dalai Lama:

> The one who "put a black hat on a white person" was the British representative named Richardson, who lives at Dekyilingka. Richardson talked to the Kashak [cabinet]. Why did he need to speak to them? When I went to British [India], I translated a book [into English]. It was a very good translation. At that time, because they knew that my English was very good, the British government repeatedly asked me to stay, saying they would give me a big salary. Because I did not stay, from that point, the British developed a strong dislike for me. Richardson is British. When he was asking me questions earlier, I was certain that as soon as he saw me he did not like me. Based on that, he talked to Kashopa and Surkhang. Kashopa and Surkhang talked to the Kashak. They made strange charges against me and I was arrested. The one who did that was Richardson.[104]

Regardless of the reason, by early 1946, several months after Gendun Chopel had arrived in Lhasa, the members of the Tibet Improvement Party were under surveillance by the British, who acquired copies of the bilingual (Chinese and Tibetan) membership applications that the party had had printed in Kalimpong; these copies were passed on to the Tibetan cabinet in Lhasa. In April, the cabinet requested that Rapga be arrested and extradited to Tibet, something that the British could not do since Rapga claimed Chinese rather than Tibetan citizenship. However, the residences of Rapga and six other members of the party were raided on June 19, 1946 on suspicion of espionage, revolutionary activities, and counterfeiting Indian currency. Rapga was deported, departing for China on July 22.

Thus, that Gendun Chopel was arrested in July does not appear to have been a coincidence. On January 4, 1946—about six months after Gendun Chopel's return to Lhasa—Hugh Richardson, British Representative in Lhasa, had written to Basil Gould, British Representative in Sikkim, "The [Tibetan] Foreign Bureau know all about Chomphel La. They say he is always demanding interviews with the Shapes [cabinet ministers], decrying Tibetan Buddhism as corrupt, praising the 'New Wisdom' (which seems to emanate from India), speaking in favor of Nazism and generally conducting himself in an eccentric way. For these reasons the Tibetan Government have had him watched. They say he is corresponding regularly with Roerich."[105] On July 11, 1946, J. E. Hopkinson, who had replaced Basil Gould as Political Officer in Sikkim, quoted Richardson's letter to the central intelligence office in Shillong in Assam.

Gendun Chopel's friends and admirers, who included members of the prominent Horkhang and Tethong families, do not report eccentricities, praising him instead for his learning and his skills as a poet and a *raconteur*. He seems to have conducted something of a salon, where conversation on modern politics was mixed with instruction on Sanskrit poetics. Despite the reports of the British, his friends never doubted his patriotism. Indeed, his primary project in his year in Lhasa prior to his arrest was his work on a history of Tibet, not a religious history (*chojung*, literally "the arising of the dharma" in Tibetan) but a history of the political system.[106] He had begun the project in India and had continued his research and writing in Tibet; he had been transcribing inscriptions from stone monuments outside the city on the day of his arrest.

And so it was that in late July of 1946, almost one year after his triumphant letter to Roerich, Gendun Chopel returned from the home of Trijang Rinpoche (1901–1981), tutor to the young Dalai Lama, to find two magistrates waiting at his door. They arrested him on charges of distributing counterfeit currency and took him to the courthouse jail of Lhasa, the Nangtseshar. A search of his rooms yielded a black box containing notes and papers connected with a number of projects. There were also various papers around the room, including information on the border area and a list of members of the government. Upon his arrest, Gendun Chopel informed the magistrates that when they searched his room, they would find all manner of papers—from copies of ancient manuscripts to notes written on cigarette wrappers—that were the basis of a history of Tibet. He asked that these not be disturbed. Although his room was sealed after his arrest, when he eventually returned to it, all of his papers, and his black box, were gone, and were never recovered. The fate of the black box has been yet another of the enduring mysteries about his life.

At the city jail, he was given a separate room on an upper floor and was allowed to receive food and bedding from friends, but he was interrogated repeatedly, especially about his relationship with Pandatsang, on one occasion receiving some fifty lashes. During the first months of his incarceration, Gendun Chopel continued his work on the *White Annals* (not knowing that the papers in his room had been lost) and also wrote letters and poetry. A letter that was received by Horkhang Sonam Belbar on the thirtieth day of the eleventh month of the Fire Dog Year (1946; hence early 1947) included a lengthy discussion of the dates of the Tibetan kings based on inscriptions. The letter begins, "It has been in my mind since the beginning that there would be obstacles to this history, but this obstacle is absurd. However, as Jetsun Mila said, 'If the instructions of the lama were not profound, why would the demons create obstacles?'"[107] He goes on to say that during his interrogation, he put forward his work on the history of Tibet as evidence of his patriotism. He is very concerned that the history be completed and published. Should he die before the book is finished, he provides a poem for Horkhang to place at the end of the unfinished manuscript.

With the luster of white loyalty to my race
Abiding in the center of my self-arisen heart
I have rendered a small service with my strength
To the king and his subjects of my snowy land.[108]

At the conclusion of the letter, he mentions that he has transcribed an ancient Tibetan poem that he had committed to memory. He asks that this poem be framed in glass after his death. He then exhorts Horkhang to continue to work on the history, which Horkhang would eventually publish as the *White Annals*. The letter concludes with this poem, addressed to Horkhang.

When this corpse-like body dies,
I will feel no regret;
Were these gold-like insights to die with it,
This would be a great loss.

Thus, undaunted by such flaws as depression,
Dejection, discouragement,
By the virtue of your efforts
May the royal lord be pleased.[109]

At the time of the New Year celebration of 1947, Gendun Chopel was transferred to the prison at Zhol at the base of the Potala. Rahul Sankrityayan and George Roerich made appeals to the Tibetan cabinet, requesting his release. They went unheeded, perhaps because of the tenor of their argument; they pleaded for clemency by explaining that a Communist takeover of Tibet was inevitable, at which time Gendun Chopel's friendship with China would prove useful. Indeed, Sankrityayan reports, "In the beginning of 1949, Shogang Shapé, the younger brother of an influential minister of the Lhasa government, came to India for some work. I met him and explained, 'It would be rare to find such a great scholar as Geshe la. You must ask him to write the history of Tibet. It will also benefit you, if you interact properly with him. Nobody can stop communism from entering Tibet. When communism actually enters Tibet, a friendship with this person will solve the problems of your country.'"[110] Recalling Gendun Chopel in his autobiography, Sankrityayan would remember him fondly:

> "Geshe" is a title given to a great scholar in Tibet and there was no doubt that he was a formidable scholar. He had made a deep and systematic study of Buddhist Logic and was a rationalist. He was a good poet and had an abundant knowledge of Buddhist literature and Buddhist tradition. Combined with this was his greatest trait: that he did not have any conceit about his learning and thought that he had grasped but a drop or two from the Ocean of Knowledge. He was an artist of the top order. In the houses of the nobility in Lhasa there may not have been many takers for his learning but his artistic talent was widely recognised. It was his love for learning that had caused him to forsake a life of ease and comfort. Like the other reincarnate lamas he too had the means to pursue the pleasures of the rich.

> Yet he abandoned the inheritance, the glory of his monastery and took the road to Lhasa in pursuit of learning. He continued his studies for many years at Drepung. Later on we were together for many years, though intermittently, as I had to travel alone in and out of the country for my other work. And then again how could I drag him with me into government jails? Yet this I must state that it is difficult if not impossible to find as learned, talented, sacrificing, cultured, idealistic, humane a person as Geshe in all of Tibet. Often my heart says that the two of us live and work together but it is not in our hands. Then only the recollection of sweet memories provides satisfaction.[111]

Conditions in the prison seemed to be lax. Gendun Chopel had visitors who brought him food and alcohol, received gifts of food from such eminent personages as the regent of Tibet and the tutor of the young Dalai Lama, and had a lover, a nomad woman from the north. He painted a picture of Tārā, later saying that she gave him solace during his imprisonment; he recited her prayer one hundred thousand times.

Like the date of his arrest, the date of Gendun Chopel's release from prison remains unknown, with one source stating, almost certainly incorrectly, that he served only one year.[112] According to some reports, including that of one of his jailers, he was released from prison as part of a general amnesty connected with the celebrations of the Fourteenth Dalai Lama's enthronement as Head of State, an event hastened by the invasion of Tibet by the People's Liberation Army. The enthronement took place on November 17, 1950. Thus, if Gendun Chopel was arrested in July of 1946, as several sources indicate, he would have served over four years in prison. If this date is correct, however, it means that he would have lived for only another eleven months after his release.[113] Whenever Gendun

Chopel was released from prison, he is said to have left this poem written on the mattress in the cell:

> May the wise regard as an object of compassion
> The small truthful child left all alone
> In the wilderness where the frightening roar resounds
> Of the stubborn tiger drunk on the blood of envy.[114]

The regent of Tibet at the time of his arrest was Taktra Rinpoche, whose name means "tiger rock." Yet, again, there is reason to doubt that the poem referred to the regent. Several people report that Gendun Chopel was something of a favorite of Taktra Rinpoche and that he even sent him "snacks" while he was in prison. In addition, this poem does not appear to have been a spontaneous *cri de coeur*; it appears in *Grains of Gold* and thus was likely composed years earlier.

Gendun Chopel was initially released into the custody of some monks from Drepung monastery, who allowed him to live in a building that the monastery owned in Lhasa. He lived there with a woman from Chamdo named Tseten Yudron and her young daughter, Gakyid Yangzom. By his own report and the recollections of those who visited him during his years of imprisonment, Gendun Chopel began drinking heavily while he was in prison; the alcohol was supplied by a prison guard and by his students. It seems that he drank heavily until his death. Friends and students describe him as often morose, feeling betrayed by the Tibetan aristocrats who had once been his patrons. The remainder of *Adornment for Nāgārjuna's Thought*, after the section written in his own hand that he had presented to Lachung Apo, likely derives from the notes that Dawa Sangpo took from Gendun Chopel's oral instruction; it was reported that after a few drinks he would have flashes of his former brilliance.

The government eventually provided him with rooms behind the

Jokhang, above the Ministry of Agriculture. The unfinished version of the *White Annals* had been assembled by Horkhang; Gendun Chopel was instructed by the government to complete the project and was provided with a subsidy to do so. However, he seems to have refused. In yet another portent of the gathering storm, he was also asked to translate British military commands from English into Tibetan. In 1951, his health began to fail.

Troops of the People's Liberation Army entered Lhasa on September 9, 1951. Too weak to get up, Gendun Chopel asked to be taken up to the roof to witness them march through the Barkor. At the beginning of October, he developed a severe cough and his body began to retain fluids, causing acute swelling (edema is one of the symptoms of advanced cirrhosis of the liver). Eventually unable to walk, he asked Lachung Apo to read him two poems, Tsong kha pa's *Praise of Dependent Origination*[115] and Mi pham's *Prayer to the Indivisible Basis, Path, and Fruit of the Great Perfection of Mañjuśrī.*[116] His double identity, Nyingma and Geluk, remained with him to the very end. Mi pham's poem begins:

> May I spontaneously achieve my aim without effort:
> The state of identity with Prince Mañjuśrī
> Arrayed in the mode of nonduality with the wisdom body
> Of the sugatas of the ten directions and four epochs, together
> with their sons.
>
> Through the faith that sees the primordial protector,
> the glorious lama
> As identical to the *dharmakāya*
> May the blessings of the intention of the true lineage enter
> my heart
> And may I achieve the empowerment of the skill in
> awareness.

Because it abides primordially, may I see, by the power of the lama's instructions,
The secret of the mind, without relying upon effort
And such things as the qualities of the senses,
With ease, without needing to be convinced.

Elaboration and analysis, the extension of misconception,
Seeking and practice, the cause of exhausting oneself,
Observation and meditation, the trap of further bondage,
May the elaborations of torment be severed from within.

Tsong kha pa's text is known by heart by many. In one of the more famous passages, he writes:

What need is there to speak of your many teachings?
Even conviction in just the general idea
Of a mere point of one portion
Bestows supreme happiness.

Alas! My mind has been destroyed by delusion.
I have long taken refuge
In the collection of such virtues,
Yet I have not gone in search of even a portion of [those] virtues.

Still, to have slight faith in you,
Until my life disappears
Into the jaws of the Lord of Death,
I consider this to be good fortune.

Among teachers, the teacher of dependent origination;
Among wisdoms, the wisdom of dependent origination.

These two are like chief of kings in the world.
No other knowledge is as perfect as yours.

After commenting on their beauty, he said, "The madman Gecho has already seen all the sights of the world. Now, I have heard talk of a famous land down below. If I went to have a look, I wonder what it would be like?" He died shortly after that, on October 14, 1951, at 4 p.m. He was forty-eight. His body was cremated three days later.

On December 1, 1951, the following obituary appeared on the front page, center column, of *Melong*.

Admonition to Remember the Uncertainty of Death

We have been saddened ever since hearing the most distressing news of the passing from this lifetime on the fifteenth day of the eighth month due to water sickness of the supreme being renowned as a spiritual friend skilled in the outer and inner sciences, Gendun Chopel. Earlier, he had gone to India, the Land of the Noble Ones, and although he only stayed there for twelve years, he carefully examined the various Tibetan treatises and histories concerning the holy places and cities of India, and while visiting the holy places along the way, he studied the Devanagari script of Sanskrit and the English script, and he translated various Sanskrit books into Tibetan. He performed many auspicious deeds to benefit others, such as composing a pilgrimage guide in order to assist those who go on pilgrimage. In the foreign year 1947, he went to Tibet via Bhutan. During that very year, the Tibetan government, for whatever reason, ordered his imprisonment. Last year, after being released from prison, he was writing a chronicle of Tibet on the orders of the government. Nowadays, if one needed to acquire the learning of the likes of this excellent spiritual friend, even if one spent several hundred thousand coins, it would be difficult for such a scholar to appear. Alas, such a loss, such a loss. I do not know whether or not anyone is publishing the book that he wrote about his long stay in India as well as whatever he had finished of his newly written chronicle of Tibet.

CHAPTER 5

The Buddhism of Gendun Chopel

GENDUN CHOPEL seemed always to be floating between worlds. He was born when the British invaded Tibet; he died when the Chinese invaded Tibet. He floated between Nyingma and Geluk, monk and layman, Tibet and India, Tibetan and Sanskrit, positivist historian and philosophical skeptic. Gendun Chopel's critics, of whom there were many, condemned him as a Communist, an atheist, a traitor, an apostate, even an enemy of Buddhism. To those who have read what he wrote, these charges are clearly false. He remained a Tibetan patriot and a devout Buddhist until his last days, requesting that prayers by Mi pham and Tsong kha pa be read to him on his deathbed. Yet, he was unlike other Buddhist masters. Although identified as a tulku, he never had a *labrang*, monastic disciples, or wealthy patrons. His collected writings are unlike those of the masters of previous generations, or even his own. As he writes in a poem:

> Not acting as a real cause of heaven or liberation,
> Not serving as a gateway for gathering gold and silver,
> These points that abide in the in between,
> Cast aside by everyone, these I have analyzed in detail.[117]

Some have sought to see him as a mahāsiddha, his sometimes unconventional behavior proof that he was a practitioner of "crazy wisdom." Yet to see him in that way is to simplify him. This was a man who blew cigarette smoke on a statue of Tārā, but recited her prayer a hundred thousand times when he was in prison; who asked a friend who was filling the morning offering bowls with water why he didn't fill them with shit instead but wrote heartfelt prayers to the Buddha; who put out a cigarette in the forehead of a statue of the Buddha then defeated monks in debate on the question of whether the Buddha feels physical pain; who mocked his compatriots for their credulity but reported that a statue of Avalokiteśvara spoke to him in a dream. This was a man who developed a sophisticated scholarly method for the writing of accurate histories yet wrote a long poem with the refrain, "I am uncomfortable about positing conventional validity."

That Gendun Chopel was a Buddhist is beyond question. Exactly what his Buddhism was is a more complicated question. One way to eventually arrive at its answer is to begin by looking at what he had to say about other religions. In *Grains of Gold*, he writes extensively about Hinduism and Islam, to a lesser extent about Christianity, finding fault with each. Let us begin with Hinduism.

Like the "Hīnayāna" discussed in chapter 3, Gendun Chopel's encounter with Hinduism prior to his arrival in India would have been entirely textual. Apart from the occasional merchant, there were few Hindus in Tibet. In the standard study of doxography in the Tibetan Buddhist academy, there was usually a brief section on the Hindu philosophical schools, especially Sāṃkhyā, Mīmāṃsā, and Vedānta, all referred to as *chirol mutegpa*[118] in Tibetan, "outsider tīrthika," using the Sanskrit word that refers in Buddhist and Jain contexts to someone who does not belong to one's own religious system. The Hindu schools would be seen only as opponents to be defeated, the classic examples of those who have fallen to the extreme of permanence in their belief in a permanent self, the eternal Veda, and a creator God, all concepts

A sketch of the Buddha by Gendun Chopel, July 7, 1938

refuted at length in the works of the great Indian masters like Bhāviveka, Dharmakīrti, and Śāntarakṣita. The other literary context in which Hinduism would be encountered was in the tantras, where various Hindu gods, notably Śiva (called Maheśvara in Buddhist texts), would be defeated and humiliated by various buddhas and bodhisattvas.

Arriving in India, Gendun Chopel would come to worship the works of the great Hindu poets, marvel at the great Hindu temples, and praise the beauty of Hindu women. But his admiration did not extend to the Brahmins, the traditional rivals of the Buddhists. Following in a long line of Indian Buddhist thinkers, including Dharmakīrti, whose critique of caste would have been well known to him, Gendun Chopel has nothing good to say about Brahmins:

> They place rice and flowers in front of them, and with their pigtail thrown around their neck, they think, "We are the objects of the world's offerings," and they chant in Sanskrit. Sometimes, this kind of feeling about Hindu [Brahmins] arises in us [Buddhists] as well. It is not only non-Buddhists; even Buddhist [texts] say, "A thousand people of the common caste / Are equal to one pure Brahmin." With the phrase *śramaṇabrāhmaṇa* they are treated with importance [in Buddhist texts]. However, the Brahmins are of bad character, ill intentioned, and crave wealth much more than others. They view all others as unclean and they always turn up their nose in scorn. Apart from being worthy of prostrations with folded palms, they are not worthy of being treated kindly or being a friend. They say that if a non-Brahmin reads the Vedas or learns Sanskrit, he will go to the lowest hell. However, since we live in the degenerate age these days, this [rule] too has come to be gradually violated.[119]

His contempt for the caste system in general and for the arrogance of Brahmins in particular did not stop him, however, from occasionally assuming their identity, at least for the sake of appearances. He writes:

> Although this caste law is so strict, one interesting thing is that when a new person is asked what caste he is from, the answer he gives is taken to be true without any investigation at all. Because I wanted to see things, I could not resist smearing white dirt on my forehead and covering my head in cloth, thus disguising myself as a Brahmin. I went into all the Hindu temples that others are not allowed to enter. Then, my arrogance grew and I told some that I was a Brahmin from Mount Kailash, which made them respect me even more. Otherwise, there is no means to even place your foot inside the walls of an Indian temple. The low caste groups who seek refuge in Śiva and Brahmā never have the fortune in their entire life to enter the temples of their own gods. This is what the so-called religion of the heartless Brahmins is like.[120]

Prior to his arrival in India, Gendun Chopel was unaware of the great Bengali saint Sri Ramakrishna (1836–1896). However, in Darjeeling, he visited the Ramakrishna ashram and later collaborated with one its teachers, Swami Prabuddhananda, in translating several chapters of the *Bhagavad Gītā* from Sanskrit into Tibetan; as noted earlier, one of the chapters was published by the Ramakrishna Vedanta Ashram in Darjeeling. Ramakrishna had famously declared, based on his own mystical experience, that all religions lead to the same ultimate reality, that all water is the same, it is simply known by different names. Gendun Chopel was clearly intrigued by this ecumenical view, providing a lengthy description of Ramakrishna and his disciples, before offering his own scathing judgment. "Because he did not offend any of the religions, today is a period in which his teachings are flourishing like the lambs of a rich man. In general, when there are many scholars upholding different religious traditions, they regard each other as enemies, even on subtle philosophical points. Once these scholars are no more, and after their subtle and refined reasoning has disappeared, all boundaries will become mixed into a single flavor, giving rise to something that is easy for anyone to follow. This seems to be the unsurpassed quality of fools."[121]

Gendun Chopel was not a pedant or a polemicist, and he was too sophisticated a thinker to be attracted to the claim that "all religions are one," seeing in it an unreasoned abandonment of philosophical subtlety. That his view derives not from some Buddhist partisanship but from a deeper commitment to the analysis and critique of doctrine, whatever its source, is found in a lengthy discussion of the difference between Madhyamaka and Advaita Vedānta. Arriving in India, he was exposed to Sanskrit texts and Hindu paṇḍitas that were unknown in Tibet, finding there a more nuanced view of Vedānta than the rather two-dimensional presentation available in Tibet. In the passage below, after noting that the Madhyamaka view is so irresistible that it has crept into modern Vedānta thought, he wonders aloud whether the difference between the two might be much smaller than Buddhists would like to believe:

> In general, with respect to the view of the mode of being taught by the father Nāgārjuna and his son [Āryadeva], there is no intelligent person whose mind would not be captivated by it. Therefore, later, when even the Hindu masters teach, they mix it into their final positions in whatever way they can. In a way, it seems that when the vase containing

the teaching of the Buddha was broken, its contents were absorbed by the very ground [it broke on], leaving a swirl of oil that somehow cannot be sucked up or licked up. And so it still remains.... For today's Hindus, however, "emptiness," "lack of true existence," "non-dependence," and so forth are well-known philosophical terms. They speak of the entire [world of] appearance and existence as being the play of the "I" or the self, and say that this "I" is the great emptiness, *mahāśūnyaṃ*, beyond the eight extremes of existence and nonexistence. There is not one who says that this ordinary conception of "I" is an unmistaken awareness or that a golden-colored self exists inside us. They assert that the conception of self is the root of all faults, just as we do....

Of course, for those learned ones [in Tibet] who have difficulty even counting the Jonang and *dzokchen* [views] among Buddhists, faulting them with having the conception of self, how could these [Hindu views] be confused with Buddhist views? However, for those like me with cruder intelligence, sometimes we have to stand with our mouth agape. Yet, if they were to meet a Hindu who belongs to the Advaita school, I wonder what those [Tibetan] scholars might say. Would they say, "This is not your view, it is a copy of ours." Or would they say, "This is excellent; continue to meditate on it." Or would they say, "You are not allowed to [practice] my religion." ...Thus, [regarding the modern Hindu view], when it comes to something like this, other than resolving disputes [peacefully] in the spirit of dharma, what other suitable option remains? Alternatively, just as latter day Tibetans insist that it is not correct to make a difference of superiority and inferiority between Mahāyāna and Hīnayāna and between sūtra and tantra in terms of the view [of no-self], I wonder if someone might not say that

> Buddhists and Hindus are not differentiated in terms of their view but are differentiated in terms of their conduct. As for me, since I haven't given any weight to the dispute, the statement, "If one denigrates the tīrthikas, / Vairocana will remain distant from you" seems to be true. Having simply cited this statement, I remain content at heart.[122]

Gendun Chopel is far less forgiving when it comes to what he calls "the religions of the foreigners," that is, Christianity and Islam. He often speaks of them together, with thinly veiled contempt, in passages like this:

> Regarding other stories of origin of the human race, there is one told both by the followers of Moses and by those who practice the religion of Muhammad. They say that Adam was the first human and so on. The Hindus are of the type that loves immensity. Therefore, when they set forth history, they say things like, "King so and so ruled for a hundred thousand years. He had eight hundred million queens." In contrast, the non-Buddhists who tell the story of Moses pride themselves in specificity and detail. Therefore, they tell great lies in the guise of accuracy, saying things like, "[Moses] reached that land on this day of such and such month. On the first day he became ill, and the next day at noon he died." Between these two [approaches], it is the latter alone that can easily deceive people's minds. Thus, their followers include those who have such strong and irreversible convictions. Even when they speak of heaven, which is the fruit of one's virtuous deeds, they describe it in such terms as, "The pillars in the divine mansions are this many spans high and this many finger-widths wide, and there are seventy-three angels as brides," and so on, as if they had gone

> there yesterday and are giving you the figures. Thus, they are capable of making people drunk on faith.[123]

Gendun Chopel fills many pages of *Grains of Gold* describing the rulers of India who preceded the British, presenting the tenets of Islam, a biography of Muhammad, and the history of India under Muslim rule. It is not a dispassionate history. Drawing a connection between the tenets of the Christianity and Islam and their manifestation in the conquest of India, he does not hesitate to express his disdain:

> In the scriptures of the Muslims it is definitively stated that if someone mercilessly kills people who will not enter the Muslim faith, *kafirs*, that is, someone like us, the killer will attain a rank higher than that of anyone else and will be given many exceptional goddesses by Allah. Therefore, for Muslims, the roots of compassion for people of other religions are severed. There is not even an iota of a reason that can be shown for how benefit could come from such killing. But they say, "Bring me the book adorned with gold from atop the high altar." Opening it, the end of the third line of the tenth page shows what bliss is attained as a reward for killing *kafirs*. If they do not believe in what has been spoken from the mouth of Allah himself, [then they assert that] they should be burned alive. This is the approach of those who believe only in scripture.[124]

This leads him to conclude, "Thus, the religion of the Muslims was brought by armies wielding weapons. Making pools of blood, it spread through the world. In the same way, the Christians sent out great forces in the name of 'just wars' and expanded their religion just as [the Muslims] had in the past. However, the teaching of our compassionate elder was carried by monks who would not even kill an insect, across the great oceans in the east and west. One should understand this difference in the history of these religions."[125]

Gendun Chopel, who had spent most of his life to that point as a Buddhist monk in the great Geluk monasteries of Tibet, recoils at the bloodshed wrought by Muslims and Christians; he ascribes this violence above all to what he regards as blind faith in their sacred scripture. His implied point, which he makes more explicitly in another passage, is that whereas the Abrahamic religions have only scripture, *āgama*, Buddhism has both scripture and reasoning, *yukti*, and it is the combination of these two that accounts for Buddhism's more sophisticated ways of interpreting its scriptures. Furthermore, it is the Buddhist approach to scripture that has prevented the excesses he sees in Christianity and Islam from being committed in the name of Buddhism. Yet, there is something else, something less reasoned, something more emotional, behind Gendun Chopel's criticism of Islam.

Among all the Buddhist monasteries in India, none was more famous in Tibet than Nālandā, the great monastic university in the modern state of Bihar. According to Tibetan histories, many of the most significant figures in the history of Indian Mahāyāna, including Asaṅga and Vasubandhu, Dignāga and Dharmakīrti, Candrakīrti and Śāntideva, were monks at Nālandā. Each of these figures is of towering importance for Tibetan Buddhism. Indeed, in recent years the current Dalai Lama has described Tibetan Buddhism as the Nālandā tradition of Buddhism. In *Grains of Gold*, Gendun Chopel describes the monastery in almost rhapsodic terms, drawing on the work of what he calls "the Chinese monk," that is, Xuanzang, who spent at least two years studying at Nālandā, probably beginning in 637. After describing the monastery as it was in its glory during the visits of Xuanzang and Yijing, he mentions the visit of the Tibetan pilgrim Chak Lotsāwa, who studied there in 1235 and 1236. He then goes on to provide his own eyewitness description of the state of the monastery when he visited the site in the 1930s. Referring to the thirteenth century, Gendun Chopel writes:

> By that time, in our country, many chapters of history had been completed: the establishment of the teaching of the Buddha, its dissemination, destruction, and its restoration. During this period, although so many great scholars and adepts of the new translation schools had gone at earlier and later points to this monastery and to Vikramaśīla, when it is divided into periods of time, almost all of these [Tibetans] visited during one generation. It appears to be quite close to the time when the [Buddha's] teaching was in its final stage of survival in India. Shortly after the time of the mendicant, the great Kashmiri paṇḍita [Śākyaśrībhadra], both monasteries were completely destroyed by Muslim armies. In our country, it has been long known from former times that Nālandā was destroyed. Yet due to intense affection for this monastery, and the fact that no one wants bad news, [people] trusted the lies of some Indian wanderers who came seeking musk, and wrote many falsehoods about the *vihāra* of Nālandā still existing, thus consoling themselves. In fact, it has been around seven hundred and thirty years since the Muslim Qutb-ud-din destroyed it in 1205. Over this period, even the ruins of the walls gradually crumbled almost down to the level of the ground and a forest of mango trees grew over them. Then, in recent years, the Indian government spent immeasurable funds and excavated most of the site over a period of two years. Thus far, two stories of the monks' quarters have emerged from under the ground. Today if someone were to look at it without knowing its history, one might think that it has been only about fifty

years since it was destroyed. In the past, there were four stories; the top two have crumbled.

Thus, first, there was the Nālandā of the monk Xuanzang, adorned with the dharma and with wealth rivaling Tuṣita, the abode of gods. Then, there was the Nālandā of Chak Lotsāwa, fraught with danger from the Turkic army. Then, there is the Nālandā of humans whose merit has been depleted, a naked ruin of crumbled walls. These can be called the fulfillment of its three periods of rise, decline, and emptiness.[126]

It is clear from all of this that Gendun Chopel does not like Islam. But, as noted above, he also does not like Christianity. Although Chinese Muslim armies repeatedly sacked Tibetan monasteries in Amdo during his youth, his particular antipathy for Islam seems to derive from an earlier moment in history, or at least from how he understands that history.

Nostalgia, despite its Greek sound, is a term of relatively recent coinage, first occurring in 1688. It literally means, "aching to return home." Gendun Chopel was a Tibetan and from a region of Tibet far away from India. And in *Grains of Gold*, and especially in his poetry, he longs to return to the mountains of Tibet, to his home, to his friends, to his family. But nostalgia is not always geographical; it can also be chronological. And though very few Tibetans, and almost no Tibetan scholars, had traveled to India during the previous seven centuries before the time Gendun Chopel arrived in 1934, for them India, what they called *phagyul*, the Land of the Noble Ones, was home, not just because it was the birthplace of the Buddha, not just because it was a place of pilgrimage, but because the works that Tibetan monks had memorized and debated for centuries had all come from India. And so many of these works had come from Nālandā.

In a sense, then, Gendun Chopel had left his homeland to return home. Like so many Tibetan scholars, he had an idea of what India must be like and he somehow expected to find it. Yet when he arrived, it was very different. Thus, his antipathy for Islam does not stem from the fact that, in his view, it is charitable only to its own; he says the same thing about Christianity. Furthermore, it is clear from *Grains of Gold* that Gendun Chopel had read Xuanzang's account of India carefully, and there he must have seen that even in the first half of the seventh century, Buddhism was in decline, often serious decline, in many regions of South Asia. So it is not so much that Buddhism vanished from India, but that the place that Tibetan scholars revered most, even more than Bodh Gayā, the vihāra that their own massive monasteries took as their model, had been destroyed. Gendun Chopel arrived in India to find Nālandā in ruins and its library in ashes. And he blamed the destruction on Islam. This, for him, was an unforgivable sin.

One key to Gendun Chopel's Buddhism, then, is that in his discussions of Hinduism, of Christianity, and of Islam, he measures each against Buddhism and finds them lacking. In each case, and for specific reasons, Buddhism is the superior religion. We gain further insight into Gendun Chopel's Buddhism when we examine his attitude toward his fellow Buddhists.

As we saw in chapter 3, he had an ambivalent attitude toward the Theravāda monks of Sri Lanka, deeply admiring their strict adherence to the vinaya but disappointed by what he saw as their narrow-minded dismissal of the Mahāyāna. He writes:

> In general, all these Siṅghala monks tend to hold only their own system to be supreme. With respect to the systems of others, regardless of how good or bad it may be, they tend to reject it completely without making distinctions. However, there are many who have some interest in the philosophical

> aspects of Mahāyāna; there were a few who have even memorized the verses of Nāgārjuna's *Madhyamakakārikā*. Regarding the other presentations [of the Mahāyāna] related to the aspect of the vast practice, such as the *sambhogakāya* (enjoyment body), they say that these are explanations copied from the Great Brahman [concept] of the Hindus. On the question of the cessation of the continuum of matter and consciousness in the nirvāṇa without residue, their understanding of it has something that is both profound and confused. They assert that the statement that a bodhisattva is superior to an arhat is the talk of Hindu kṣatriyas.[127]

As we noted, Gendun Chopel suggests that Tibetans and Sinhalese should celebrate their kinship as co-religionists, but that those celebrations should take place in separate locations, specifically Tibetans in Tibet and Sinhalese in Sri Lanka.

Thus, by a certain process of elimination, we can say with certainty what Gendun Chopel was not: he was not a Hindu, Muslim, Christian, or a Theravāda Buddhist. In his discussion of Buddhism and science (included in part 2), he criticizes those whose devotion to science causes them to renounce Buddhism. Thus, he also was not an atheist. Knowing with some certainty what he was not, we must turn now to the question of what he was.

We can say with certainty that he was a Buddhist, and a devout Buddhist. This is clear from his writings—both prose and poetry—and from the many reminiscences of those who knew him. His was not a modernist Buddhism that focused only on philosophy and ignored the magical. We have alluded to his recitation of the Tārā prayer one hundred thousand times while he was in prison. He was often heard loudly singing the "Praise of the Twenty-One Tārās." Tārā is renowned for her power to free those who call upon her from the "eight fears": lions, elephants, fire, snakes, bandits, prison, water, and demons. Gendun Chopel would credit her with his release from prison. He also composed his own prayer to her:

> Your form, the deeds of all the victors of the three times;
> Friend to the host of beings seeking liberation;
> Mother who loves all miserable migrators.
> I pray at the feet of lady Tārā.
>
> Your beautiful body, the color of turquoise, restores health;
> Your sweet speech dispels the longing for existence and peace;
> Your compassionate mind purifies the stains of the two obstructions.
> I pray at the feet of lady Tārā.
>
> You serve as a guide, showing me the path in an unknown land;
> You serve as an escort, protecting me on a frightening precipice;
> You grant the resources I need when I'm impoverished.
> I pray at the feet of lady Tārā.[128]

After he was released from prison, he continued to ponder the reason for his arrest, considering possibilities beyond the mundane machinations of British colonial officers and Tibetan aristocrats. In a conversation with a friend, he recalled the famous story of Sakya Paṇḍita's debate with the Hindu scholar Harinanda. Around 1240, Harinanda and five other Hindu masters made their way to Kyirong in western Tibet to debate with Sakya Paṇḍita on logic. With assistance from Mañjuśrī, Sakya Paṇḍita defeated them and converted them to Buddhism. Gendun Chopel explains that after the debate, Sakya Paṇḍita instructed the twelve *denma* goddesses—fierce local deities converted to protectors of Buddhism by Padmasambhava—

to thereafter punish anyone who brought a single page of a non-Buddhist scripture into Tibet. Gendun Chopel said, "I translated a portion of the *Bhagavad Gītā* from Sanskrit and brought it to Tibet. I must have been punished by the twelve *denma* goddesses for that."[129]

The question, then, is not whether Gendun Chopel was a Buddhist. The question is: What was the Buddhism of Gendun Chopel? Although the Madhyamaka doctrine of the two truths—conventional truths and ultimate truths—has been used in modern writings about Buddhism to the point of cliché, it provides a useful structure here. Gendun Chopel himself explored the categories and their boundaries in his *Adornment for Nāgārjuna's Thought*. Before turning to that, however, we can begin with what we might call his historical method, which he lays out clearly in *Grains of Gold*.

As we saw in chapter 3, Gendun Chopel does not dismiss the storied supernormal powers of Buddhist masters. He spent two weeks during his time in Sri Lanka looking for an Indian yogin who would have been nine hundred years old. Yet with his encyclopedic knowledge of Tibetan Buddhist texts, Gendun Chopel was skeptical of the knowledge that could be derived from them for the writing of history. Therefore, in order to write history—both of ancient India and of ancient Tibet—he developed a historical method that was not previously known in Tibet. In chapter 6 of *Grains of Gold* (p. 153), he describes his method for writing a history of ancient India:

> What I shall explain in the following is based on compiling these sources: [*a*] The fragments of histories that have been discovered, written by some of the scholars who were contemporaneous to particular kings and so on, [*b*] the important events of their lives and legal systems inscribed on some of the kings' own rock edicts and copper plates that survive to the present day, [*c*] the clear identification of the years

from the few *kārṣāpaṇa* coins discovered from individual reigns, [*d*] what was written by envoys from other kingdoms during that time, describing what they saw in India, compared with what was translated from the languages of different countries, and [*e*] comparing as much as possible the events in the ancient histories with what can be reconstructed from the remains and ruins of towns, palaces, monasteries, and stūpas mentioned in the histories.

Here, Gendun Chopel describes what might be called a critical historiography, even a scientific method, one that makes extensive use of archives and of archaeology, relying whenever possible on material culture—inscriptions, coins, and ruins. When texts are consulted, he seeks contemporaneous sources and is always skeptical of mythologized accounts. In his *Guide to the Sacred Sites of India*, he had discussed a similar method for accurately locating the events in the life of the Buddha, making use of modern geography.[130]

It is therefore fascinating to see Gendun Chopel express a profound skepticism for conventional knowledge in his more overtly Buddhist works, especially in *Adornment for Nāgārjuna's Thought*. We should note, however, that Gendun Chopel's position on the standard topics of the Tibetan Buddhist tradition is often difficult to discern. There are a number of reasons for this. First, his collected works are unlike any other, delving into topics that few Tibetan scholars have explored. Second, many of his more overtly religious works appear to be lost; in addition to the book on emptiness that he wrote in English with George Roerich, we find references to such titles as *A Presentation of Cittamātra Tenets*,[131] *Difficult Points in Madhyamaka and Pramāṇa*,[132] and *The Very Difficult Path of Reasoning*,[133] none of which have yet been located.[134] Third, Gendun Chopel was exceedingly well read, even by the high standards of the day, not only in his natal Nyingma tradition and the Geluk tradition of his monastic life, but in the other sects as well. People remarked on his chameleon-like quality of seeming to be a Kagyu when speaking to a Kagyu and a Sakya while speaking to a Sakya. We can ascribe this to his remarkable mind and memory, but also to the place and time of his birth, in Amdo at the turn of the century, away from the often rabid sectarianism that would plague Kham and Lhasa, a sectarianism that would lead many to condemn him after his death. In the biography of the great Sakya lama Dezhung Rinpoche (1906–1987), we learn that he wanted to meet with Gendun Chopel in Lhasa but was warned against doing so:

> Gendun Chöphel had traveled widely and had lived for years in India and Ceylon. He was famed for his excellent knowledge of Sanskrit, which made Dezhung Rinpoche want to meet him all the more.
>
> But already at Sakya, Dezhung Rinpoche's Minyak friend and student Trulku Kunzang (himself an accomplished scholar of Sanskrit grammar by Tibetan standards) had discouraged him from contacting Gendun Chöphel, saying, "Yes, the Amdo scholar is learned. But he is living a dissolute life, drinking spirits, smoking cigarettes, and so on." An acquaintance in Lhasa had also warned Dezhung Rinpoche not to contact him, as the Amdo renegade was under suspicion for political reasons, so in the end he decided not to attempt to see him. Dezhung Rinpoche was disappointed by this turn of events, for he considered Gendun Chöphel to be a "realized master" (*rtogs ldan*) and had also heard about his unusual Madhyamaka views.[135]

In 1955, those Madhyamaka views prompted a young Geluk tulku to publish a refutation of Gendun Chopel entitled *The Magical Wheel of Slashing Swords Mincing to Dust the Evil Adversary with*

Words to Delight Mañjuśrī, where he writes, "Those who are enemies of the teachings of the Buddha are not to escape arrest by the government."[136]

The work that led to that condemnation was the *Adornment for Nāgārjuna's Thought*. The full title of his text might be translated literally as *Eloquent Explanation That Combines the Profound Key Points of the Middle Way into Their Essence, An Adornment for Nāgārjuna's Thought*.[137] There, he offers a scathing critique of the Geluk presentation of the two truths. In discussing the category of the conventional, he offers example after example of the inability of benighted beings to make statements that are even conventionally true, seeing the conventional instead simply as opinion, with the beliefs of the majority, no matter how parochial, being elevated to the level of truth. He tells the story of an Indian king who is able to save himself from a poison rain; drinking its waters leads to madness. Eventually, everyone else in his kingdom drinks the water and goes mad. When the people declare that they are sane and the king is insane, he decides to drink the poison water and lives happily ever after as their ruler. This section of the text ends with a long poem with the refrain, ""I am uncomfortable about positing conventional validity."

Thus, despite his strong commitment to what might be called the historical method and his mockery of Tibetans who gullibly believe, and worship, all manner of factual mistakes, when he considers the status of the conventional from a philosophical perspective, he sees it merely as the majority view of the ignorant, with no ontological basis whatsoever. He extends his critique into the realm of the sacred, noting that the descriptions of the enlightened are simply the fantasies of the unenlightened. Furthermore, they are not universal; they are culturally specific. The accounts of the pure lands clearly reflect an Indian sensibility. As he writes, "For example, if the Buddha had been born in China, it would certainly be the case that the saṃbhogakāya of Akaniṣṭha would have a long shiny beard and would wear a golden dragon robe. Similarly, if he had been born in Tibet, there is no doubt that in Akaniṣṭha there would be fresh butter from wish-granting cows in a golden tea churn five hundred *yojanas* high, and there would be tea made from the leaves of the wish-granting tree. Therefore, all of this is merely the way that we common beings think." He explains that the buddhas appear to us in this way out of their compassion for sentient beings; "they are merely set forth with skillful methods so that the qualities of the buddha level, which in reality cannot appear to our mind, can appear to our mind in order to create admiration and delight within us."[138]

To declare that the qualities of the Buddha cannot appear to our minds seems a radical statement, but it is central to Gendun Chopel's middle way. Again and again in his writings—and not simply in his philosophical works—we encounter the term "inconceivable" (literally, "not encompassed by thought").[139] For example, in what was likely one of his earliest essays, the opening chapter of *Grains of Gold*, he describes his visit with Rahul Sankrityayan to the famous monastery of Radreng, founded by Atiśa's disciple Dromton (1005–1064) in 1057. Gendun Chopel writes, "The caretakers of Radreng monastery gave explanations of the sacred images. Pointing to two juniper trees on the circumambulation path, they said, 'This is a white sandalwood tree and that is a red sandalwood tree.' The paṇḍita [Rahul] laughed derisively and said, 'Sandalwood requires very warm soil. They do not exist even in central India, only in the south. How could they grow here?' However, because those like the paṇḍita have little familiarity with the inconceivable—things that do not need to depend on our [ordinary conceptions] of place, time, causes, and conditions—he made such a statement."[140] Gendun Chopel considers the question of the status of the two truths at length in his *Adornment for Nāgārjuna's Thought*, especially in the first section of the text (presented in its entirety in part 2). There he mocks those who seek to domesticate reality (*dharmatā*) by seeing it as somehow accessible to reason, and who dilute the potency of such statements by the Buddha as, "Kāśyapa, 'existence' is one extreme; 'nonexistence' is the second extreme. That which is in the center of those two is the inexpressible and inconceivable middle path." As he writes:

> When many hundreds of thousands of common beings to whose minds [things] appear similarly gather together, then the thing that they decide upon becomes firmly grounded and unchangeable, and those who speak in disagreement are proclaimed to be denigrators, nihilists, and so on. Therefore, our statements about what does and does not exist are in fact classifications of what appears before our mind. Our statements that something does not exist or is impossible are classifications of what cannot appear before our mind. The reality (*dharmatā*) that is neither existent nor nonexistent does not belong to the former class, it belongs to the latter.[141]

Knowledge of conventional truths, what can be known by what he calls "the fiction-making mind" cannot in itself bring knowledge of the ultimate. The purpose of the Buddhist path is to create an understanding of what the mind has never previously known. When we concede that all of our thoughts are fabrications that have no objective foundation, with no basis whatsoever, we feel great fear. Gendun Chopel calls this the fear of emptiness and regards it as the essential first step toward the ultimate. Reality must be feared before it can be comprehended.

Gendun Chopel wants to radically discredit any conventional knowledge that may be claimed about the state of enlightenment, while constantly recalling those wondrous abilities ascribed to the Buddha that are logically impossible. He lampoons the monks who are willing to sacrifice the rhetorical and philosophical impact of such miracles on the altar of dogmatic consistency. He sees in their obsession with consistency a domestication of the rhetoric of enlightenment, until the sūtras serve no other purpose than to validate their plodding logic and the operations of ignorance. This is suggested, however subtly, in the famous poem that opens the *Adornment*, where one must note not only that he praises the Buddha, but how he does so:

> To the sharp weapons of the demons, you offered delicate flowers in return.
> When the enraged Devadatta pushed down a boulder, you practiced silence.
> Son of the Śākyas, incapable of casting even an angry glance at your enemy,
> What intelligent person would honor you as a friend for protection from the great enemy, fearful saṃsāra?

The first line refers to the story of the Buddha's enlightenment when Māra and his minions attacked the Buddha with a hail of weapons. The Buddha transformed their hail of spears and arrows into a gentle rain of flowers. The second line refers to the Buddha's evil cousin, Devadatta, who tried to assassinate the Buddha by pushing a boulder down Vulture Peak to crush him. The Buddha did not retaliate. The third line says, "Son of the Śākyas, incapable of casting even an angry glance at your enemy, what intelligent person would honor you as protector from fearful saṃsāra?" When reading this line, one wonders if it is right. One would expect a Buddhist prayer to say, "what intelligent person would not honor you as protector from fearful saṃsāra?" Yet Gendun Chopel meant what he wrote: if this is how the Buddha responded to attacks on his own person, what intelligent person—the Tibetan word is *loden*,[142] perhaps better translated as "what person in their right mind"—would look to the Buddha, who would not even protect himself, for protection from the sufferings of saṃsāra? Gendun Chopel's suggestion is that the purpose of the Buddhist path is to overturn the ordinary; his implication is that being in one's right mind has been the problem all along. As he writes,

> Thus, in general, in the Mahāyāna and also, especially, in all of the Vajrayāna, from the point when it is suitable to view the lama as a buddha through to meditating on yourself as Vajradhara and believing that you have a fully established body *maṇḍala*—these are only for the purpose of turning upside down this present valid knowledge. All of this, such as offering the five meats [beef, elephant flesh, horse flesh, dog flesh, human flesh] and the five ambrosias [feces, urine, semen, blood, brains] to the Buddha, are set forth for the purpose of smashing to dust the conceptions of the ordinary together with the reasoning of logicians.[143]

Gendun Chopel thus exalts the ultimate, praising it as inconceivable, impossible to be encompassed by the thoughts of the unenlightened and their fallacious canons of reason. Beyond this exaltation, however, he says little about how to reach the inconceivable. He does suggest that it is reached by the tantric path, explaining that "one should know that the union which non-dualistically mixes as one such things as object and subject, desire and hatred, hot and cold, pure and polluted, is the body of great wisdom or the body of union, the mixture of body and mind in one entity."[144] Yet, he offers few hints of how this is achieved in *Adornment*. Hints, and only hints, are found in an unlikely place, in his *Treatise on*

Passion, where the power of pleasure is depicted as leading to the bliss of union:

> In this saṃsāra, thick with the mirages of appearance,
> Which [even] the Tathāgata's hand cannot stop,
> The mind is placed in the nature of emptiness of all things.
> Who can let go of belief in existence and nonexistence?
>
> The child of awareness swoons in the sphere of passion;
> The fickle intellect falls into a wormhole,
> Being dragged down by lustful thoughts;
> Behold, O being, the true nature of pleasure.
>
> This wave of illusion, where the non-two appears as two,
> Dividing into subject and object,
> Wishing to merge the ground of being with the ocean of bliss,
> Do you not feel the motion and rising of the desire for sex?
>
> Why would this reality, unsupported by magic, move about?
> Where does this mind, with nothing pursuing it, run away to?
> Because, abandoning their true nature, they are unable to
> stand still,
> This couple, appearance and mind, move in the direction of
> bliss.[145]

In my first book about Gendun Chopel, *The Madman's Middle Way*, I described him as "a philosopher, a poet, an essayist, an artist, a linguist, a translator, a geographer, an historian, a social critic, a sexologist, a botanist, a journalist, an ethnographer, and a sometime tantric yogin." But was this man—who described himself as a "discerning beggar" and a "cosmopolitan traveler"—also a Buddhist master, deserving of a volume in this series?

He had many of the conventional qualities: he was a tulku and a monk, he had profound knowledge of a vast array of texts, he was endowed with a prodigious memory and a powerful intellect. He was a consummate stylist of Tibetan poetry and prose, as is evident across the pages of this volume. He excelled at each of three traditional activities of the Tibetan scholar: explication, disputation, and composition. Yet there have been many such figures in Tibetan history. Is this enough to make Gendun Chopel a *khedrup*, a *paṇḍita-siddha*, a scholar-adept, a master?

Like the greatest of those masters, he was a denizen of multiple worlds, both real and imaginary, visible and invisible, worlds that he described in a voice that is unmistakably his. He moved dexterously through a maze of concepts yet was devoted to the inconceivable, seeing the apparently unbridgeable divide between ignorance and enlightenment not as a cause for skepticism but as an inspiration for deep faith in the Buddha. That he maintained this faith under the harsh light of modernity, even as he was destroyed by the country that he loved so much, would seem to be enough to merit our admiration.

The Writings

CHAPTER 6

Reasons for Writing, from *Grains of Gold*

Grains of Gold: Tales of a Cosmopolitan Traveler *is a large collection of essays composed by Gendun Chopel during his time in India and Sri Lanka. He considered it to be his most important work, although it would not be published in its entirety until long after his death. The opening pages are provided here, which include his fateful meeting with Rahul Sankrityayan.*[146]

THIS IS ENTITLED *Grains of Gold: Tales of a Cosmopolitan Traveler.* I pay homage with body, speech, and mind and go for refuge with great reverence at the lotus feet of the Blessed One, the perfectly awakened Buddha.

You destroy the world of darkness with wisdom's wheel of light,
profound and clear.
You step down upon the peak of existence with the feet of the
samādhi of liberation and peace.
You are endowed with the mind of stainless space unsullied by
clouds of elaboration.
May the sun, the glory of all beings, rain down goodness upon you.

Whatever expressions of civility are seen
To come from the fine past traditions in the Snowy Land,

Remain like a picture casting a reflection
Of the three doors of conduct of the people of the Noble Land.

Thus, for those who enjoy the flavors of meaning
From the learned treatises of ancient times,
To speak in detail about the conditions of this land [India]
Might help them complete the branches of learning.

However many things there might be, both subtle and coarse,
That cannot be known through investigation at home in bed
Without becoming objects of the senses of sight and hearing
I shall explain here using the clearest examples.

Here in our country, due to the example set by the bodhisattva kings and ministers, everyone—the eminent, the lowly, and those in between—has immeasurable faith, affection, and respect for India, this Land of the Noble Ones, the special land from which the teachings of the Conqueror came to Tibet. Because of this, everything we do with our body, our speech, and our mind—the manner in which our scholars express their analysis, our style of composition, our clothing, our religious rituals—all of these are permeated by Indian influence as a sesame seed is permeated by its oil, so much so that when it is necessary to provide a metaphor in a poem, only the names of Indian rivers, mountains, and flowers are deemed suitable. For example, if one composes the following: "Your body is majestic like the Vindhya Range, / Your speech pure and stainless like the flowing Ganges," the stanza would be worthy of being counted as a well-composed verse. If one composes the following: "Your body is majestic like Mount Machen Pomra, / Your speech flows ceaselessly like the Machu River," although this composition is not inelegant—the first two syllables of the two lines are identical—it would cause laughter.

Because this type of discourse has always been abundant [in Tibet], there have been occasions when numerous amusing yet meaningless things were written due to failing to recognize what are essentially everyday objects in India. In general, most of these things can only be determined by seeing them with one's own eyes and hearing them with one's own ears. It is not the case that knowing about them makes you a scholar and not knowing about them makes you a fool. Still, there is no need to say that if one speaks about them pretentiously one does become a liar. Furthermore, in some cases, some very important points have been [mistakenly] inferred and errors have often been made due to confusion. Thus, if something can be understood exactly as it is, it is absolutely certain that this can serve a great purpose. Therefore, I have gathered here in one place whatever insights I have gained about various fields of knowledge that I have seen and heard about during my wanderings in many places and regions of India and Tibet. As for drawing conclusions on the basis of guesses, writing the most astonishing tales that have no authoritative sources in order to please many people, making clear distinctions between what is and is not in order to protect one's own sack of *tsampa* [roasted barley] but lacking the courage even to tell true stories out of excessive concern for the opinions of others, all these things, I have set aside with abandon. Giving up such things as hope for a good reputation, I wish to write a volume, from time to time inserting—in the style of ordinary conversation—whatever I have found, only for the sake of those few intelligent people who remain open-minded.

If one remains very timid, afraid of contradicting the accounts of others, then the understanding that is capable of enhancing wisdom cannot grow. But if one were to take an honest approach, saying, "This is an error," "That too is an error," and so on, this can trample on the hearts of many, great and small, and can do much damage to such things as one's means of livelihood. As a Tibetan,

I am very familiar with my own country, so I know all this very well. Still, I shall write without giving this any thought. Thus I beseech the feeble-minded a hundred times not to bear malice against me.

Empty talk that makes fools amazed,
Fawning words piled up to flatter great men,
Stories that make the faithful sigh,
Leaving these far behind, I set out upon the straight path.
This is the intention with which I begin.

So it was in the Male Wood Dog Year of the sixteenth sixty-year cycle [1934], when I had reached age thirty-two, that I set off for India. That year was the two thousand four hundred and seventy-sixth year following the Buddha's passage into nirvāṇa according to the Sthavira sect of Sri Lanka. This system of calculation also seems to be respected as authoritative these days in other countries where the Buddha's teaching has recently spread, and there is a need for such things as looking up dates easily. Therefore, in what follows, in whatever context, such as the royal lineages [of Tibet], I will use this [system] for years counted after the Teacher's passing. The great Sakya Paṇḍita's statement that the śrāvaka schools are unreliable because they calculated their year of the Teacher's birth by confusing the construction of the Buddha's image at Bodh Gayā with the birth of the Buddha is highly offensive talk.

From the time I was a child I have wondered again and again whether I would be able to go to India just once. Having been at Drepung monastery for about seven years after arriving in central Tibet, I met a paṇḍita by the name of Rāhula [Sankrityayan] who had come to Tibet. He encouraged me to go [with him]. This was a wish come true, and we set out. First, the paṇḍita and I went on a pilgrimage to places such as the Phenpo region and Radreng. In our spare time I began to study a little Sanskrit with the paṇḍita. He had a lot of money and knew about as much Tibetan as a seven-year-old child. He was under the protection of some Lhasa aristocrats, so we were able to examine closely the sacred objects of the various monasteries, such as Radreng.

CHAPTER 7

The Wonders of India, from *Grains of Gold*

As is clear from the previous selection, one of Gendun Chopel's motivations in writing Grains of Gold *was to describe India, both its past and its present, to a Tibetan audience after many centuries of limited cultural contact between Tibet and India. This excerpt from the beginning of chapter 2 is his lyrical description of what India is like.*[147]

THE PLACE is the great land called India. Homage to the Blessed Buddha.

Regarding the general formation [of this land], it is the source of different races, of different regions, and of a variety of different religions and modes of human behavior. From the very tall mountains with peaks reaching to the sky, all the way down to plains as flat as the surface of a mirror, it has ruling classes with the complexion of a lotus who are attractive and happy and lower classes with the color of charcoal who are hungry and destitute. It has the teaching of the compassionate, who avoid harming any living beings, even an ant, and the religion of those who seek salvation through sacrifice with blood from killing the three creatures: humans, horses, and cattle. It has desolate landscapes with mountains and plains that resemble the back of a camel, verdant islands that look like the neck of a peacock, and a variety of things that reside at the limits of good and bad, as checkered as the canvas of an astrological chart.

Now, the general shape of this land is a triangle, the shape of the shoulder blade, with Vajrāsana [Bodh Gayā] roughly at the center. The long corner of the shoulder blade points in the direction of the south. Located near its tip and separated by a sea of just a few yojanas lies the island of Siṅghala [Sri Lanka]. It is triangular with its tip pointed toward Jambudvīpa [India], like the handle of the shoulder blade. The statement in works such as the *Tang Annals* that the formation [of India] is like this appears to be most accurate.

The base of the Himalayas is at the northern edge of the triangle. The range of the Himalayas or "snow mountains" can be seen without a break, like a curtain of white silk. It stretches from Yunnan in China in the east to Persia in the west, coming down as far as Magadha. Thus, it extends to the regions of India and Tibet, and the lower parts at the center of the northern edge are in our country. Then, to the south, there is a series of many thousands of snow mountains, like pillars of crystal, which form the outer rim of our country. When you cross the snow mountains, there are many mountains and valleys with juniper forests and then, farther on, pine forests like banks of black clouds. As you descend, there are deep green bamboo forests, and when you go farther down, there are forests of *sāla*, *nyagrodha* [banyan], *aśvattha*, and plantain. There is not a hill or valley that is not filled with glittering flowers. Huge flat leaves glistening with dew, like parasols and platters, grow densely on both the right and left sides of the roads. Various little birds that one has never heard before call out. On mountainsides adorned with clusters of forests, the peaks visible through openings in dense white clouds, villages of two or three dwellings are connected. They have a roof of straw and a canopy supported by four bamboo pillars, covered with various flowering vines. At dawn, as I looked up from one such spot, the peaks of the tall snow mountains appeared bathed in early morning light; they shone like refined gold. In the breaks in the massed waves of white clouds that extend for many yojanas, forests and the peaks of great mountains appear like islands. This is renowned everywhere as the "cloud ocean of the Himalayas," and people come especially to see this sight.

In the lowlands, the great rivers twist back and forth, making thundering sounds. At the fording places, in all directions there are fields and vast expanses of various crops, such as rice, wheat, and lentils, ornamented with many large and small towns and villages with open markets. Most of these are occupied by people who have the fair complexion with a reddish tinge of those from lands where cool and warm weather are well balanced. Just by climbing down or up for a single day, if you wish to be cool, you arrive at a cold land of mountain peaks. If you wish to be warm, you come to the hot flatlands. In other countries, it is not possible for the terrain to change that much from the top to the bottom of a single mountain pass. But in the mountains of India, if you descend just a little from a very cold mountain peak even in the winter, when you have made a half-day's journey, the temperature changes. All the kinds of trees and flowers that grow there [in the lower part] are completely absent on the mountain summits. Even the birds are different. Then, going down [farther] just the length of time before stopping for tea, everything from before changes; in that single day you feel that you are in a dream. In later times, supervised by the English, iron bridges have been built across the rivers and the roads have been paved with stones. On the slopes of the hills and in the valleys, with all sorts of things like gardens and beautiful mansions, many wondrous things have been created. However, these things are not appropriate to discuss here. In any case, because of the way they have been formed over aeons, this realm of snowy mountains became what is certainly a heaven or a dreamland. It is said that nowhere else does such a beautiful and pleasant region exist, and in fact that is true.

In the months of spring, it is not too cold or too hot. The sky is brilliant, like the color of *vaiḍūrya* [lapis lazuli], and fragrant winds fill the forests. Around the fourth lunar month, the rain clouds rise from the Arabian Sea and move toward the north, where the snow mountains block them like pillars in the sky. Not venturing too far into the land of Tibet, they bring down great floods of rain continuously for many weeks onto the forested lands to the south. The mountain peaks are encircled in mist; even the houses remain invisible to each other.

Then, when the end of the summer arrives, the master Kālidāsa says, "When the sixth month ends, the clouds lie down at the peak and foot of the mountain. / My mind wonders if these are graceful elephants at play." As he says, pieces of scattered clouds lie hovering and rise over the riverbanks and at the foot of the hills. Slowly ascending higher and higher, they rest in masses on the turquoise-like mountain peaks. During the three periods of the day the birds exchange their songs with many melodies. Some types of insects make noises that sound like bells. Around sunset, the sun departs into the western mountains, shaped in different forms like the mouth of a lion or the hump of a camel, displaying all sorts of hues. Then, when dusk, the seventh part of the day, arrives, rising from a dark green meadow in an empty plain, the amber moon, like a great drum made of white copper, emerges. From the immaculate hills and valleys, permeated by a white light, flow pearl-like rivers; such marvels are beyond expression.

In winter, on the higher peaks of the hills, a little snow falls as well. Although the wind is not very strong, its sharp coolness can bring shivers, making you wish that you were wearing wool-lined leather clothes. At the foot of the mountains, apart from the changing of the leaves on the trees, the barrenness of the appearance of winter never occurs. In any case, even the mere sight of these pleasing hills and trees of India gives rise to a variety of experiences in your mind. Thus, it is said that in this land an unbroken line of great poets appeared, their throats adorned with an elegance endowed with a hundred flavors.

Starting from the snowy mountains in the north, continuing to the forested hills, reaching down to the southern plains, the group of hills and valleys in general is known as the Himavat or "snowy region." Because this term has been sometimes translated as "land of snow mountains" and sometimes as "snowy region," "snowy mountains," etc., [some people] take this to mean that the lions, birds, and the many medicinal herbs found in the forests live on pure white snow mountains. This seems to be like someone having heard, "This man comes from Sakya [white earth]," takes it to mean that the person emerged from a pit of white earth. The *Lalitavistara* also speaks of "the snowy regions with a vast variety of peaks." In the composition inviting the elder of Bhakṣaskandha as well, the growth of pine trees, floating clouds, and stones broken by yaks' hooves are described as features of the snowy mountains. Furthermore, look at the Indian poems that refer to the snowy region—forests, wild rice, fields of flowers, and so forth are always mentioned. In the story of the physician Jīvaka [in the *Divyāvadāna*] as well, it is said that various medicinal herbs grow in the snowy mountains, and in the *Kāśyapa Chapter* (*Kāśyapaparivarta*), there are extensive statements, such as, "whatever medicinal herbs that grow in the mountains of the snowy region, the king of mountains." The *Sūtra on the Establishment of Mindfulness* (*Smṛtyupasthāna Sūtra*) also says, "Beyond that lie various mountain peaks called 'the snowy region,' a thousand yojanas long, filled with juniper, lotuses, sāla, *tāla*, and *tamāla*," and "Beyond that is the white Kailash."

Thus, just as in many regions, there seems to be a tradition of giving a single generic name to a great mountain range, so "Himalaya" is the name of a mountain range, and in this range alone are located the Kongpo region of Tibet, Sikkim, Nepal, Kinnar

[Kinnaur], Kāmarūpa [Assam], Kuluta, and Kashmir. However, since "Kailash" is taken to refer simply to the Tisé range, those who say that "Kailash" is the Sanskrit word for "snowy mountain" are wrong. This kind of confusion occurs when one thinks simply on the basis of the meaning of the words "snowy mountain." This is like the story of the son of the Muslim emperor Shah Jahan, who, upon hearing the name "Crystal Mountain of Yarlung," sent someone to Tibet to ask for some crystal.

CHAPTER 8

A Description of Bodh Gayā, from *Guide to the Sacred Sites of India*

Gendun Chopel's famous guidebook to the Buddhist holy places in India was published by the Maha Bodhi Society in 1939. Throughout his time in India he kept a close association with the society, publishing essays and poems in its journal, The Maha-Bodhi. *His trip to Sri Lanka was likely made with the assistance of the society. It is therefore not surprising that at two places in the guidebook he discusses Anagārika Dharmapāla, the founder of the Maha Bodhi Society. Gendun Chopel was especially inspired by Dharmapāla's efforts to reclaim and restore Bodh Gayā and Sarnath. Two passages from the guidebook are provided here, one describing Bodh Gayā and Dharmapāla's efforts there, the second his efforts to restore Sarnath.*

THE SMALL STŪPA at the top of the central *gaṇḍoli* was erected by Nāgārjuna and has one measure of relics of the Teacher inside. Our own Jowo statue in Lhasa is known to have resided in the upper of the two temples in the past. These stone railings around the circumambulation path [of the Mahābodhi Temple] were erected by Nāgārjuna. It is said that one attains various siddhis if one can see the faces of all of the eight protectors and the eight Tārās on the tops of those pillars. They are the ones that look like human faces in the middle of the lotuses.

To the side of the stūpa that is in front of the Bodhi tree is a statue [of the Buddha] smiling upon the Bodhi tree. This is where the Teacher sat in the first week after becoming enlightened. There are footprints in the place where he first stood up in the second week. Then there are five pairs of left and right footprints in the place where he strode. There were footprints on seven stones at the place where he stood up, but these days there are only three—one pair and a single footprint. There are twelve garlands of lotuses on top of a long platform on the northern circumambulation route in the place where the footprints were made.

On the northern side, outside of the stone railing, there are small stūpas with holes in them containing the remains of many arhats. It is explained that if one leaves such things as one's hair and fingernails there, it closes the door to rebirth in the lower realms. At the side of the enclosure to the east of the [main] stūpa, there is a large stūpa shaped like the central stūpa. This is the place where the Teacher stood when he first arrived. Rays of light emanated from his face and incinerated the trees that were not the real Bodhi tree. It is called the Gaṇḍoli of the Stream of Light. A Bodhi tree called Agaru Bodhi grew from the pile of ashes of the burned trees. Today it is the one beyond the circumambulation path on the north side. At the foot of that tree is the Rasakula spring. The Teacher magically turned its water into quicksilver. It is said to [cure] stomach illness if one drinks from it. Although the spring has not been dug out, the outline is clearly there. Some years ago, a clay facing was made that is still holding. To the south of the central stūpa, there is a very wide platform of earth. It is there that the Teacher cast the grass he sat upon. In the past there was a large structure there that was like the central stūpa.

༄༅། རྒྱ་གར་གྱི་གནས་ཆེན་ཁག་ལ་བགྲོད་པའི་ལམ་ཡིག །

GUIDE TO BUDDHIST SACRED PLACES
IN INDIA

མཛེས་རྒྱས་རྒྱ་ཅན་ལས་འདས་ནས་ལོ་ཉིས་སྟོང་བཞི་
བརྒྱ་བརྒྱད་ཅུ་གཅིས་པ་ལ།

བོད་སྐྱེད་པ་དགེ་འདུན་ཆོས་འཕེལ་གྱིས་བྲིས་ཤིང༌།

ཕ་ཆ

ག་ཡི་གད་ ༈ ཨེ—ཀྱི་ཇི་མཁེར །
མ་ཧ་བོ་དྷིའི་སོ་ས་ཡི་ཏེ་ནས་དཔར་དུ
བསྐྲུན་པ་ནོ༎

Published by Maha Bodhi Society
4A, College Square, Calcutta

2483 B.E.
1939 C.E.

Price As. 6.   རིན་ཨ་ ༦

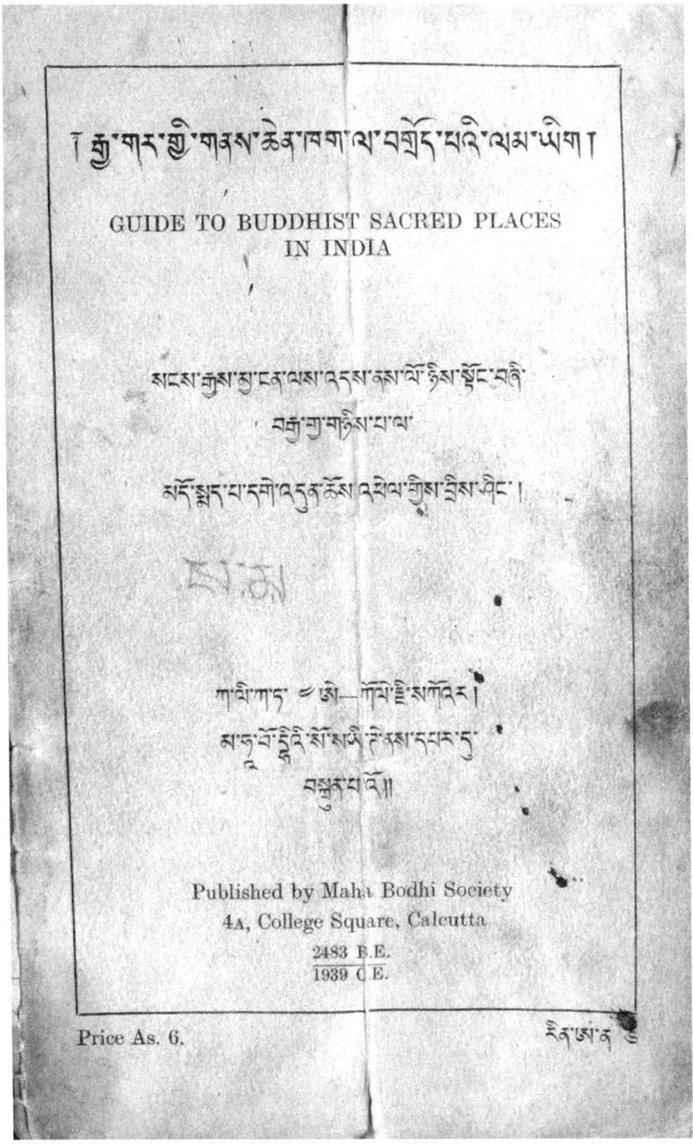

The cover of Gendun Chopel's *Guide to the Sacred Sites of India*

There is a maṇḍala inside the charnel ground near the eastern fence. Several of our histories say, "The master Buddhajñāna used his mind to erect the stone Kālacakra maṇḍala that exists in Vajrāsana." I wonder if that is it. Because this connects well with statements by such authors as Chaklo and Jomden Rikrel, it is something that can be believed. It is difficult to say that about many other things.

Furthermore, the period when Chak Choje Pel (1197–1264) came [to Bodh Gayā] was a period when the temple was flourishing. He says that there were continually about three hundred monks there serving as caretakers.

Then, because of the degenerate age, the place [Bodh Gayā] and its sacred relics fell into the hands of tīrthika yogins. They did many unseemly things such as building a non-Buddhist temple in the midst of the stūpas, erecting a statue of Śiva in the temple, and performing blood sacrifices. The lay disciple Dharmapāla was not able to bear this. He died while constantly making great efforts to bring lawsuits and so forth in order that the Buddhists could once again gain possession [of Bodh Gayā]. Still, although that earlier effort continues, up to now the pure outcome [of his efforts] has not come to fruition. Therefore, Buddhists from all of our governments, uniting our deeds and aspirations, must make all possible effort so that this special place of blessings, which is like the heart inside us, will come into the hands of the Buddhists who are its rightful owners.[148]

~

From about the time that the omniscient Butön (1290–1364) lived in our country, the teaching has been destroyed in Madhyadeśa, without anything remaining. It has been that many years. During that time, in general in India, apart from Bodh Gayā, even the names of where the other places are were not known. Specifically, in this area [Sarnath], around sixty years ago there was nothing else other than a temple of the naked tīrthikas [Jains], and the present ruins of the monastery were used to raise pigs. In the end, when it was difficult even to know that this was the place where [the Buddha first] turned the wheel of the dharma, a courageous person arrived from the island of Siṅghala in the south, the great being known as the layman Dharmapāla. Undergoing hundreds of hardships without concern for his body, his life, or his property, he established a temple and the Maha Bodhi Society here in the Deer Park of Ṛṣivadana. From the island of Siṅghala he invited a saṃgha that had all three sections of the vinaya. In Magadha, the Middle Country, those who wore the banner, the robes of the monks of Śākya, were seen again. In the same way, in Bodh Gayā, Calcutta, and foreign capitals such as London, he established temples and saṃgha groups. The latter dissemination of the teaching in India had begun. That great being completed those deeds, which he had taken upon himself and, at the end of that time, he went forth from the home to the homeless life and lived in this very temple [in Sarnath]. Striving at the deeds of the two wheels, he completed his life; it has been five years since this present Fire Ox Year.[149]

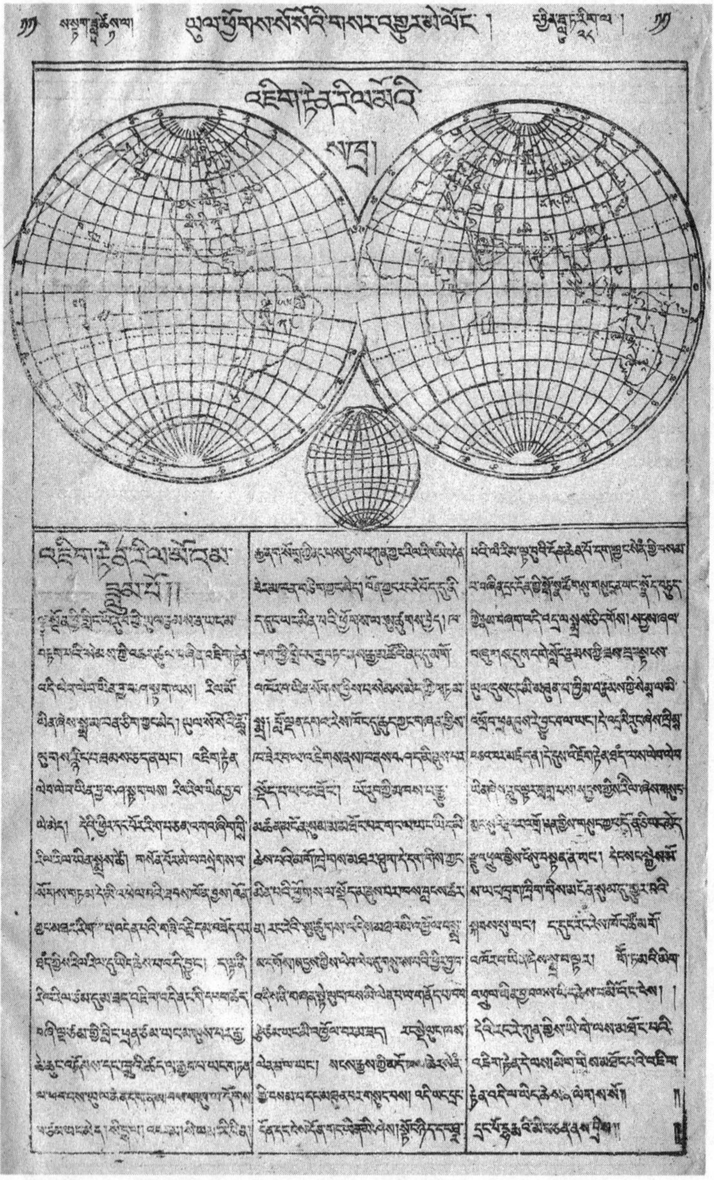

Gendun Chopel's article and map in the June 28, 1938, issue of *Melong*

CHAPTER 9

The World Is Round, from *Melong*

Gendun Chopel contributed both poetry and essays to Melong *("Mirror"), the Tibetan-language newspaper published in Kalimpong by the Tibetan Christian from Khunnu, Dorje Tharchin, also known as Tharchin Babu. Its full title in Tibetan was* Mirror of the News from Various Regions. *In the June 28, 1938, issue, Gendun Chopel published an essay entitled "The World Is Round or Spherical" under the pseudonym Honest Dharma (Drangpo Dharma). Above the essay was a map of the world drawn by Gendun Chopel, showing latitude and longitude, with the names of the continents written in Tibetan cursive script. There are two circles, with North America and South America in one, and Africa, Europe, Asia, and Australia in the other. Below is a single globe, perhaps meant to show that the earth is not two globes but one. Above the maps one reads in Tibetan "Map of the Round World."*[150]

The World Is Round or Spherical

In the past, in the lands of the continent of Europe it was only said that this world is flat, just as it appears to the non-analytical mind; there was not a single person who said that it was round. All thc ancient religions in the various lands said only that the world is flat; there was not one that said that it was round. Thus, when some intelligent people first said that it is round, the only method to keep it from spreading was to order that they be burned alive. However, in the end, unable to withstand the light of true knowledge, everyone came to believe that it is round. Today, not only has the fact that it is round been determined, but also the size of all the islands in the world just four or five yojanas long have been measured down to spans and cubits. Therefore, in the great lands there is not a single scholar who has even a doubt.

Among all of the Buddhists in Siṅghala, Burma, Ceylon [presumably Siam], Japan, and so forth, there is not one who says that it is not true that it is round. Yet we in Tibet still hold stubbornly to the position that it is not. Some say mindless foolish things, like the foreigners' sending ships into the ocean is a deception. I have also seen some intelligent persons who understand [that it is round] but, fearing slander by others, remain unable to say so. When even the most obstinate European scholars who do not believe in anything without seeing the reason directly were not able to maintain the position that it is not round and accepted it completely, then there is no need to talk about this stubbornness of ours coming to an end.

[Saying that the world is not round] because the Buddha stated that it is flat is not accepted as authoritative in other [non-Buddhist] schools and thus does not do a pinprick of damage [to their assertion that it is round]. Even with regard to the scriptures of our own [Buddhist] school, which does accept [the Buddha's statement] as authoritative, because the majority of the sūtras were set forth by the Buddha in accordance with the thoughts of sentient beings, even in this case, we do not know what is provisional and what is definitive. If he set forth even matters of great importance such as emptiness and the stages of the path to liberation in various types of provisional meaning in accordance with the thoughts of sentient beings, what need is there to discuss these presentations of environments and their inhabitants? During the lifetime of the

Buddha, when it occasionally happened that the way that the monks ate their food did not accord with [the customs] of the time and place, causing slight concern among the laity, he would make a rule that it was unsuitable. At that time, throughout all the world, the words "[the world] is flat" were as famous as the wind. Thus, even if the Buddha had said, "It is round," whose ear would it have entered? Even if he had said so emphatically, it would have had no purpose, even if he had demonstrated it with his miraculous powers. Nowadays, at a time when [the fact that the world is round] has become evident to billions of beings, there are still those of us who say, "This is your deception." In the same way, I am certain that they would not have believed it, saying, "This is the magic trick of Gautama." If all of us would believe in this world that we see with our eyes rather than that world that we see through letters, it would be good.

CHAPTER 10

Selected Poetry

Among the Tibetans, a people who revere poetry, Gendun Chopel is famous as a poet; he is considered one of the greatest Tibetan poets of the twentieth century, renowned both for his mastery of the various forms of poetry as well as for his ability to compose verse spontaneously. His poems are admired especially for their immediacy and ease. He was also a student of poetry, both in Sanskrit and in his native Tibetan. He studied Daṇḍin's Mirror of Poetry *in his youth and is said to have made his own translation from the Sanskrit when he was in India. During his time there, his poetry was strongly influenced by his study of the great Sanskrit poets; he admired Kālidāsa above all others. Gendun Chopel wrote poems throughout his life, from his childhood to his last days. A selection of his poems is offered here.*

Unknown here by anyone in any way
This long cord of the changeless god
Ties the boundless sphere of reality to the sphere of awareness,
Ties the awareness of the child to the interior of the body,
Ties the stone heap of the body to food and drink,
Ties food and drink to external causes.
Thus the cord is tied, one to the other.
There are no points where it can be cut but these:

The first place is desired by none;
It is death, where the cord of body and mind is cut.
The other place is known by none;
It is where the cord decays, merging sphere and mind.

This mind is a goddess, beyond all bounds.
The homeland of this goddess is not this world,
Yet the little toe of the goddess of the mind
Is tied tightly to this body by a thread.

Then, until this thread is cut
Whatever the body feels seems to be felt by the mind.
Whatever help or harm is done to this little toe
The goddess feels as pleasure and pain.

If the cord is cut, all is well.
Yet the whole world fears the cord's cutting.
In striving to keep the cord connected,
The ends of the cord become wrapped in thorns.

To extract the point of each thorn,
We study each category of culture;
We stay busy with this taxing toil,
Extracting thorns until we die.

This unfinished busyness, never abandoned,
Seems an entrance; its purpose the rebirth of beings.
When just one part of this mind, equal to space,
Sinks into the mire of deeds of flesh and blood,
Then come terrors of hot and cold, hunger and thirst,
hope and fear.
I wonder if this suffering ever ends.

Yet this body, fashioned by the glory of culture,
Achieved through a hundred endeavors,
In keeping with the truth of the queen of heaven's prophecy
Must remain on this earth a few more years.

I sang this song.[151]

~

Compassionate power of the three jewels,
Reliable refuge that never deceives,
Calming all illusions of meaningless saṃsāra
Bless our minds to turn to the dharma.

Whatever we ponder, the affairs of the world
Have no more essence than a sesame seed.
Transform our minds in this short life;
Starting now, reveal the essential sacred dharma.

The time of youth is but a summer flower
The luster of beauty but a winter rainbow.
Since human life does not last long
Practice the essential sacred dharma now.

In times of sorrow, we hope for joy.
In times of joy, we fear the coming sorrow.
There is no time free from the straits of hope and fear.
Practice the essential sacred dharma now.

Cherished and protected, base of sickness and disease,
Made elegant with ornaments, its nature is impurity.
The impermanent body has no essence.
Practice the essential sacred dharma now.

The rich complain from the place of the rich.
The poor weep from the place of the poor.
Each human mind has its own burden of suffering.
There is no happy time in saṃsāra.

In general, all joys and sorrows that seem outside
Are magical creations of one's mind alone;
Reflections from inside that appear outside,
Not things outside that have come near.

Knowing this well, when analysis
Severs the root of the basic mind,
You will abide in the true sky of reality
Beyond this fog of appearance.

This so-called existence is a fiction.
This so-called nonexistence is a fiction.
Untainted by all such fictions,
The nature of the mind is perfect buddhahood.

Thoughts of "is" and "is not" are like ripples in water;
They follow one after the other.
Dissolving easily into the aimless state,
They arrive at the ocean of the primordial sphere of reality.

Appearances are the magical display of the mind.
The mind is empty, without base, without foundation.
By holding baseless phenomena to be the self
You and I wander in the realm of saṃsāra.

Without pursuing perceptions,
When you look directly at the perceiver itself,

You will see your own inexpressible face;
The path to achieve buddhahood is not far.

Through the blessings of the divine three foundations,
May you quickly find the emptiness of your own mind,
And from the kingdom of the ever-pure great perfection,
Bring about the great aims of boundless beings.[152]

~

If the unchanging nature of the mind is not seen,
Though it has been with you always without beginning,
How can you see wondrous visions
Newly created through forceful meditation?[153]

~

The mirage of a lake of clear water with patterns of waves
Is recognized to be a plain of dry sand.
Unwanted things that come to be true
Are but portions of the suffering gathered in saṃsāra.[154]

~

Leading worldly beings from the path of worldly conventions
To the sphere beyond the world,
Lord of the dharma, guide for beings of the three worlds,
I bow down to the leader of existence and peace, the Holder of
the Diamond Throne.

Objects of veneration are the paṇḍitas and translators of the past
Who gathered well into a treasury ringed by snowy mountains
The jewels of knowledge of all vast realms
To safeguard them even to the end of four ages.[155]

~

Shabkarwa, sole lord of the dharma
Inseparable from Padmapāṇi, embodiment of compassion,
Whose life story is Brahmā's drum,
Summoning countless migrators with the richness of his merits.

Abiding at a lofty stage, all treatises on logic
Were perfected long ago in wondrous ways,
Appearing without obstruction
In the mirror of your clear mind.

Yet with words easy to understand, suited to the minds
Of beings beset by a hundred sufferings,
He who teaches even the most profound doctrines with ease
Among virtuous friends of the degenerate age is but you.

The crystal realm of your pure intellect is
A divine abode of spontaneously created qualities
Shimmering with reflections of texts of a hundred colors.
You are the dharma friend, ever active.[156]

~

Who would reproach the shining of the full moon?
Who would not bow at the feet of Śuddhodana's son?
What peacock does not rejoice at the thunderclap?
Why would my mind be unsatisfied with the ambrosia of true
dharma?[157]

~

Like a bee circling again and again
Around a gently swaying lotus,
In the vast and splendid temple,
I am moved by devotion again and again.[158]

~

The naked truth, terrifying to behold,
Is not to be covered with robes of self-deception.
This is the first vow of the scholar.
Please keep it though it costs you your life.[159]

~

As they draw near to the nature of things,
The words of the learned become mute.
All phenomena, subtle by their very nature,
Are said to be beyond expression in words or thoughts.

The mind is placed in the nature of the emptiness of all things.
In this saṃsāra, thick with the mirages of appearance
That even the Tathāgata's hand cannot stop,
Who can let go of belief in existence and nonexistence?[160]

~

The wisdom beyond existence and nonexistence
Is the essential point of the profound thought of Nāgārjuna,
father and son.
This eloquent explanation distills into one the Snowy Land's traditions
Of the true forefathers of the new and ancient schools.

When from the expanse of my lama's compassionate mind
The sun of knowledge shone in all directions,
Though it pained the heart of one blinded by wrong views,
It caused the calyx of the mind of one with sight to smile.

The essence of the minds of all the victors in space and time,
The refined, cut, and polished jewel of scripture, reasoning, and
instructions,

The gold of the inconceivable sphere of reality;
It is due to my past karma that I hold these in my heart.

Yet in all the water in the mouth of the lama Mañjunātha [Tsong kha pa],
The ocean of eloquence forming the wheel of the dharma,
If there is a part muddied by the swamp of my ignorance,
I confess it from my heart to the assembly of the impartial.

At the instant that the sun's rays of the eloquence I strove for here
Shine upon the lotus of the minds of scholars,
May sweet nectar, the honeydew of self-arisen wisdom,
Always ripen as the nature of peace.

May I be cared for in all my lives by the lama
And know without error and just as it is
The sphere of the profound nature of reality, free of elaboration,
And then proceed to the end of the path of purity.

Through the strong wind of a thousand virtuous deeds,
May the autumn clouds over the capital of mistaken appearances of the nonexistent
Become of one taste in the sky of the sphere of reality,
And the sun of the triple-bodied victor shine forth.[161]

~

Hey! After I had gone away,
Some nonsense-talking lamas
Said that Nechung, king of deeds,
Did not let me stay because I was too proud.
If he is a protector who purifies,
How could he permit those impure monks to stay,

Wandering all over, the known and unknown,
Selling tea, beer, and dried mutton?
Their lower robe hiked up, folded like palm leaves,
The worst carry weapons, knives, and clubs.
If they'd been expelled, it would be fine;
Between last year and this, there are more and more.
Because I lacked faith, pure as Venus,
Some say I was banished to far off lands.
Why weren't impure beings banished
Like cows, female yaks, birds, and bugs?
There is no purpose in four-fanged king Nechung
To banish to who knows where
Those who study and ponder the Victor's teachings
Braving hardships of heat, cold, and fatigue.
Destroyers of the good dharma with fine hats, robes, and boots
And destroyers of the dharma who eat simple food;
When we look at them, there is great difference.
But when the king above [Nechung] looks at them, there is no difference.
Rather than banishing to distant mountain passes, valleys, and towns
Those who take pride in studying the books of Ra and Se,
Would it not be better to banish to another place
Those proudly selling meat, beer, and tobacco?
Ha ha. Consider whether this is true.
Carefully ask the elder geshes too.
The speaker of these words is the sophist,
Sanghadharma, lion of reasoning.[162]

~

Son of Śuddhodana, friend to transmigrators unfamiliar,
Delighting in the festival that fulfills two vast aims,

Send down the seasonal rains of blessing, without limit or end,
From the pavilion of dense clouds filled with the water of
compassion.

The froth of clouds of smoke on a great endless plain,
An unfamiliar friend plays a thighbone trumpet,
The pattern of a huge land where five colors shine;
Whatever I see, I am melancholy.

The relatives and servants we meet are but guests on market day.
The rise of power, wealth, and arrogance are pleasures in a dream.
Happiness alternates with sorrow, summer changes to winter.
Thinking of this, a song spontaneously came to me.

When we lack it, fearing hunger, we seek food and drink.
When we have it, fearing loss, we arrange our gathered profits.
Slowly counting the beads of an old rosary, striving at such petty
affairs,
The thread of this short human lifespan comes to its end.

Worldly affairs, no matter what they are, never end.
At the end of doing deeds, there grows despair.
When all pleasures and wealth proudly gained are gathered,
They make up but one tenth this pile of pain.

Matching the games of lies and deception
With worldly schemes, pursued with great pains,
After waiting so long, it turned to nothing, just deceit.
Three years of miserable labor have worn me down.

When you are rich, they slink up close;
When you are poor, they scorn you from afar with pointing fingers.

The nature of bad friends who do not know kindness as
kindness;
I think of this; tears and laughter rise up in me.

The talents of a humble scholar seeking only knowledge
Are crushed by the tyranny of a fool, bent by the weight of his
wealth.
The proper order is upside down.
How sad, the lion made servant to the dog.

Endlessly busy with the work of the seasons, summer and winter,
Human life is wasted in pointless distraction.
Still, I indulge in the flamboyance of careless distraction.
How sad, this sense of being old in body, not old in mind.

On a flowery plain in the land of the mind's six objects,
A child of uncertain knowledge wandered afar.
The way I used to think about meaningful things
Is now lost without a trace. I see this and it makes me sad.

Wandering like a deer from the realm of six ranges
To arrive in a distant kingdom of unfamiliar humans,
There I lost my heart to a glamorous fickle woman.
A wretched son who has forgotten his kind parents, I am sad.

Following the dance steps of the demoness of ignorant thoughts,
These false confusing phenomena move to and fro.
Material things seen today are forgotten tomorrow.
Being in this aimless state is sad.

When looked at, the marvels of the world seem pleasing.
When attained, each has its own suffering.

After moments of brief happiness become but a dream,
There is always something that makes me sad.

Curdles of suffering, misconceptions beneath our hopes and fears,
Mix with the milk of the experience of spontaneous delight.
Although the comforts of food, drink, and possessions are all arranged,
The experience of inner happiness, content and carefree, is missing.

The basis of my ambition for greatness is consumed in fire;
The unwanted tax of the monk's robe is left in ashes;
If only I had the utter freedom to wander from one land to another
With a madman's behavior, chasing whatever comes to mind.

The castle of the threefold reason is utterly destroyed;
The knots of claims about the eight extreme views are severed at their very site.
If only I had the joy of the deepest awareness,
Knowing that whatever appears is without foundation, has no basis.

Into the sphere of clear light, empty, without edge or center,
The nature of the mind, grasping nothing, dissolves as one taste.
If only I had the good fortune to practice this day and night,
Knowing for myself unspoken untainted bliss.

A sad song recalling fleeting appearances, my mother's changing frowns and smiles,
And my own experiences, sometimes happy, sometimes painful,

Was sung by the gullible wanderer Gendun Chopel,
In the land of Bengal, unfamiliar realm beyond the mountain range.[163]

~

The wealth of the world is mist on the mountain pass.
My closest friends but guests on market day.
Uncertain joys and sorrows are last night's dream.
I think and think; they have no essence.

Led by the unknown envoy of Yama,
My friend wanders the long and narrow path to the next life.
Sublime refuge, three divine foundations,
Please be his compassionate guide.

Being born then dying is the nature of saṃsāra;
Its manifestation, the illusion that nothing changes.
The royal decree of relentless Yama
Has befallen my helpless friend.

When the drizzle of past prayers and deeds is falling
The afternoon rainbow appears, seeming so real.
When the sun of yearning begins to shine,
It vanishes in the realm of invisible sky.

Dear childhood friend, radiant half of my heart,
When the flower of youth blossomed,
The streams of our minds mixed.
Where in the six realms could you be now?

At the end of three days of bountiful friendship,
In the narrow riverbed of Gyishö Lhasa,

We promised to meet before too long.
The time has come to meet within a dream.

All beings, old, young, those in between,
See what unpredictable death looks like.
Yet there is no means to end the inner grief
Of those left behind by childhood friends.

To feel remorse at someone's death is foolish;
It only ruins the body and mind.
Yet I cannot overcome the accustomed,
This habit of mind so long familiar.

As your body lay dying, a skeleton's image appeared;
Hoping only to remain alive,
You stared with death's eyes.
If what they say is true, it devours my heart.

In the way things appear to the ordinary mind,
You are still with me; you seem so real.
When the bow of memory is bent,
It only causes an empty heart.

Pondering how love and friendship endure,
I dispatch to my friend in the land beyond
The few good things I've done
In the field of the infallible three jewels.[164]

~

When they see you in happiness, they bow down before you.
When they see you in sadness, they turn away and hide.

This nature of all ordinary beings
I have known from long ago.

When they see your prospering, they gather before you.
When they see you in decline, they turn away and hide.
This nature of all ordinary beings
I have known from long ago.

For people whose behavior is untamed and coarse,
If a law is not made to behead them,
What other way is there to compassionately change their ways
Than to teach them the sufferings of hell?

In the presence of the officials of the lord of humans
The marginal human Gendun Chopel says,
"I won't drink, I won't drink, I won't drink liquor."
I offer this promise to the assembled common people.[165]

~

Today the vagabond has arrived
At Bodhiviṣa in the eastern land,
The place to encounter Vajravārāhī,
Consort of Ghantapa, lord of adepts.

The wind horse, the so-called deeds of former lives,
Has no direction on the road.
I, a child of Tibet, born in Tibet,
Have spent a portion of my life in the land of India.

Completing the whole cycle of twelve years
Without seeing my delightful homeland and

Most of all, not meeting my kind old mother;
When I think about this, I feel pangs of separation.

The long northern path
And the great ocean in the south,
These are roads for those endowed with courage,
The one route that leads to weariness.

At the monastery of the glorious and incomparable Narthang
I met the omniscient supreme incarnation.
Not regarding me as an inferior person,
He generously engaged in pleasing conversation.

The commentaries on the *Bodhicaryāvatāra*,
Of Chumigpa, Yangonpa, and so forth
Fell into my hands, I, a seasoned lover of words.
If they arrived, they would be the monastery's centerpiece.

The heat of the plain of India is hard to imagine
For those who have only heard of it.
Unless they have gone there and felt it,
You may ponder it, but it does not appear to the mind.

Even when the breeze blows, it is like a tongue of flame.
Even when you drink cool water, it is like black tea.
Although this is so, thus far it has been my fortune
Not to have suffered from heatstroke.

In an unfamiliar region of a foreign land,
I am like a human deer, without companions.
There are no signs on the roads as to where they lead,
There is no way to know where to stay in this land.

In the early part of my life, I gathered bundles of books;
In the later part of my life, I carried the burden of harsh words.
I have led my life in sorrow;
I wonder if this will serve the teaching of terminology.

But now there is no purpose in speaking words
That have the sharp edge of a rock.
This painful interior, filled with conflict,
Spontaneously emerged to my familiar friends.

My longtime pundit friends
Set out to act for the welfare of all beings.
To the writing of this unrequested book
They may respond with criticism and derision.

More than that, there is a sense of loss;
Although I have gone on pilgrimage to India and Tibet
I have not felt my obstructions being purified,
Though my wisdom has clearly increased.

With two-thirds of my life now gone,
I have the teaching on achievement but not the teaching on
conduct.
Because I am a person from a faraway land,
My affection for my homeland is stronger than before.
What is it that will show me the love of my friends?
I yearn to return quickly to my own land.[166]

~

Calcutta, Nepal, Beijing,
The city of Lhasa in the Snowy Realm,
When I look at people wherever they are,

I see they have the same nature.
Even those who don't like chatter and hubbub,
And are restrained in their ways,
When they see butter, tea, silk, or money,
Are no different from an old fisherman.
Officials and nobility like flattering talk.
Common people like cunning and deceit.
Today most like cigarettes and beer.
The young like to be pretty and flirtatious.
They keep to their father and mother's side
And hate anyone who is different.
The natural state of mind in humans and cattle
Is seen to be the same.
They go on the Tsari pilgrimage for the sake of their name.
They practice asceticism of heat and cold for the sake of food.
They read the scriptures of the Victor for the sake of offerings.
If we consider it calmly, it's all for the sake of wealth.
Ceremonial hats, monks' robes, banners, canopies,
Ritual offerings of food and drink,
Whatever we do,
I see nothing more than a wondrous spectacle.
Like arriving at a goat shed or a dog house,
In all mountain passes and valleys, there is no happiness.
Yet until this illusory body of flesh and blood perishes,
We have no choice but to remain on this earth.
A statement like this, so honest,
Alas, may irritate others.[167]

~

The meat-eating wolf, the grass-eating rabbit,
Instead of discussing the nature of food,

It is best if they kept to their own ways for a while
Within the circle of their own kind.

Making nomads eat pork,
Making villagers drink melted butter.
If they don't like it, there's no point in insisting;
If they do, there's no point in stopping them.

The blind ant runs about for the sake of happiness.
The legless worm crawls about for the sake of happiness.
In brief, all the world is racing with each other,
Running toward happiness, one faster than the next.

Sometimes, seeing a goddess is revolting.
Sometimes, seeing an old woman creates lust.
Thinking, "This is it," something else comes along.
How can the deceptions of the mind be counted?

Our attitudes change so much
From childhood to when we are old and decrepit.
Analyze your own experience and you know this.
How can you have confidence in today's thoughts?

Due to the mind's insanity, we do not recognize our own face,
Yet we constantly measure the secular and sacred, heaven and
earth.
Courageous are we who seek lasting refuge
In this series of mistaken appearances.

If we get used to something long enough,
Nothing in this life does not make us sad.

True divine dharma, solace of this sadness,
At least once, is certain to come to mind.[168]

~

In this world of the human land, pleasing yet painful,
All beings, with a hope that looks to the future,
Naturally seek to leave behind
Some trace of themselves.

Some leave a son or a disciple who bears their lineage.
Others leave behind their eloquence, wealth, or fame.
Some pass away after establishing a monastery or images of holy beings.
The trace of others is the wealth they gathered and their beautiful homes.

As for the imprint of the beggar, lacking both dharma and wealth,
There are none of these things mentioned above.
So to pay for the free meals I ate for far too long,
I leave this small book in a stranger's land.

Through the hectic writing of this unrequested book
That slowly consumed thirteen years of my life,
Although it is uncertain whether it will be praised or blamed by others,
I see that it is certain to be of some small benefit to others.[169]

CHAPTER 11

Erotic Instruction, from the *Treatise on Passion*

Perhaps Gendun Chopel's most famous work, certainly his most scandalous, is his Treatise on Passion, *composed during his first years in India. It is based both on his extensive study of Sanskrit erotic literature as well as on his own experiences with a variety of lovers. The selections presented here derive from the latter.*[170]

82. To deny that the amazing is amazing,
Sakya Lama said this is the sign of a fool.
Of course, these days I am a madman.
Those who are not mad can go ahead and laugh at me.

83. The experience of bliss is no small matter.
The creation of families is also no small matter.
If the path of passion can be sustained within bliss and
emptiness,
How could that be a small matter?

235. Like a timid thief eating a meal in hiding,
To churn in and out and then ejaculate
Silently and quietly in a darkened bed,
This is not a true celebration of sexual passion.

236. Thus one should know passion's sixty-four arts,
Which offer various flavors of pleasure
To the passionate man and woman,
Like the flavors of molasses, milk, and honey.

264. First kiss the arms and then under the arms,
Then slowly kiss the belly.
Becoming more intoxicated, kiss the thighs and *bhaga*.
In this way draw the streams of rivers into the sea.

334. Both hearts pounding with passion,
They gaze at each other, their faces flushed and fearless.
Leading the jewel of the organ with her hand,
She places it inside her bhaga.

335. Putting in just the tip, she takes it out again.
Putting it halfway in, she takes it out again.
Finally, pushed down to its root,
It points upward for a long time.

336. Bending her legs back,
She strikes his buttocks.
Her knees touching his armpits,
Her thighs and calves bind him, rubbing down.

337. Whenever the *liṅga* comes out,
She holds it in her hand, stroking it,
Then lets go, sending it slowly inside again,
One, two, three finger breadths deep.

338. When it has disappeared inside
She gently caresses the testicles.

Squeezing the liṅga's base with two fingers,
She stirs it inside her bhaga.

339. After two or three strokes,
She wipes the tip with soft silk,
Making it very thick and hard.
She also wipes the opening of her bhaga.

340. Always keeping the base moist,
She wipes the tip and shaft again and again.
Women who seek the power of pleasure
Should learn this secret instruction.

341. Then, with the longing for sex burning bright,
Their arms entwined, he goes below.
From one end to the other of their broad bed,
They roll back and forth, making love.

342. As they long, they weep.
As they remember, they speak.
When they have scaled all the walls of shame,
Their pleasure has great power.

343. Performing in every way
Their favorite postures of passion,
They come to know all the pleasures
Set forth in the treatises.

344. Close, trusting, free of worry,
When both are drunk with deep desire,
What would they not do when making love?
They do everything; they leave nothing.

345. Not right for a third person to see,
Not right for a fifth ear to hear,
Those who share such special secrets
Become best heart-friends in the world.

558. To excellent beings, you display the true nature of reality.
To benighted children, you play tricks.
Indefinable, you have defining characters.
I bow down to you, the god of self-arisen pleasure.

559. You appear to non-meditators and to the mind of a fool.
You befriend all and all are your friend.
Seen by all, understood by none,
I bow down to you, god of self-arisen pleasure.

560. Sky dancer, unclothed by convention,
Magical forms, all without color or shape,
Casting the meteor of awareness, glimpsed but not grasped,
I bow down to you, god of self-arisen pleasure.

561. Where the rainbows of diverse elaborations dissolve,
Where the ocean of illusion is free from waves,
Where even the wavering mind does not waver,
I bow down to you, great self-arisen bliss.

562. The eyes of the Buddha see it without blinking.
The learned ones know it by ceasing to speak.
The ungrasping mind encounters it without concepts.
I bow down to you, the sphere of self-arisen bliss.

578. As for me, I have little shame and great faith in women.
I am the kind who chooses the bad and discards the good.

Although I have not had the vows in my head for some time,
The guts of pretense were destroyed only recently.

579. The skills of fish are impressive in the water.
One is most familiar with what one has experienced.
With this in mind, it was my lot
To write this treatise with great effort.

580. If monks condemn it, that's not untoward.
If *tāntrikas* praise it, that's not unfitting.
To old Lugyal Bum, its benefit is small.
To young Sonam Thar, its benefit is great.

581. The author is Gendun Chopel.
The place of composition is the city of Mathurā.
The difficult parts of the text were explained by an old Brahmin.
The practical lessons were given by a Muslim girl.

582. The explanation is rooted in the Indian treatises.
The verses are arranged in Tibetan style, easy to understand.
Thus, from the convergence of causes complete,
I feel that a marvelous fruit is certain to appear.

583. The monk Mi pham wrote from reading.
The wanton Chopel wrote from experience.
The difference in their power to grant blessings,
A passionate man and woman will know through practice.

584. Yet if there are faults of excess or deficiency here,
Being too much for those without desire,
Being too little for the passionate,
I apologize from my heart, concealing and hiding nothing.

585. Do not blame a lowly person [like me],
Whatever faults might befall you:
A monastic friend undoing his way of life,
A narrow-minded poser losing his façade.

586. Through this virtue [of writing], may all like-minded friends
Cross the dark road of misty desires
And see the sky of the true nature of reality
From the summit of the sixteen peaks of pleasure.

587. Yudön, Gangā, Asali, and the others,
The women who joined with my body,
May they persist on the path, from bliss to bliss,
To arrive at great bliss, the place of dharmakāya.

588. May all humble people who live on this broad earth
Be delivered from the pit of merciless laws
And be able to indulge, with freedom,
In common enjoyments, so needed and right.

CHAPTER 12

On Islam, from *Grains of Gold*

Part of Gendun Chopel's purpose in writing Grains of Gold *was to bring Tibetans up to date on what had occurred in India since the last Tibetan pilgrims studied there in the thirteenth century, a period that coincided with Muslim raids into northeast India. Much of the subcontinent would eventually come under Muslim rule during the long Mughal Dynasty. To explain this period, Gendun Chopel made a study of Islam, producing the longest description of the religion to appear in Tibetan.*[171]

Now, I will write about the origins and histories of the Muslims who ruled India for a long period in the later times, exactly as they appear in the chronicles, without slipping into even the least criticism stemming from my own personal [feelings]. Now, with respect to them, the Indians call them *mleccha*, which means "barbarian" or "bandit," a derogatory name. Their actual name is Musulman and their religion is Islam; some of their later kings who ruled India are called the Mughal kings. The religion of those called Jew or Yehuda, which appeared prior to Jesus, and the system of the Musulmans have the same root. Thus the religions of Jesus and Islam also have the same original source. When slightly modified, it is possible even to combine them with the fundamental views of the Indian Hindus. Thus, latter-day Indian teachers such as Nanak and Ramakrishna combined the three religions [Hinduism, Christianity, and Islam] into one, founding new religions.

All three—Christians, Jews, and Musulmans—say that there is one principal God who is the creator of the entire world of appearance and existence, who controls all happiness and suffering, and that he alone must be held as the object of refuge. The Hindus of India understand Brahman in the same way. However, influenced by Buddhism, they sometimes describe Brahman as something like the expanse of reality (*dharmadhātu*), thus making it an object of much meditation and analysis for the wise. Given this, if we refer to the God who is their object of refuge with the term "creator," it is a more convenient description for us, so I will do so. However, the Jews and Christians call him Yahova or Jahova; the Musulmans call him Allah. The nature or idea [of God among them] is the same [despite these different names].

The religion of the Jews is accepted as valid by the Muslims. For example, in the *Kālacakra*, in the chapter on the elements, a Muslim teacher named Mouse [Mūṣa or "mouse" in Sanskrit] appears before the name of Madhumati [Muhammad]. I think this is the translation of Nabī Mūsā, which is what Muslims call Moses, the first teacher of the Jews. There [in that chapter], when the earlier Muslim teachers are cited, the names *ā dra a no gha*, "possessor of pigs," and so on appear [in the Tibetan translation]. These are undoubtedly what appears in the Indian text as Adam, Nogha, Varāhī, and so on; confusing the division between the former and latter names, the word "Nogha" was translated as *labden* ("river"). In general, it seems that one of our [i.e., Tibetans'] great mistakes is to think that any name that happens to appear in an Indian text is Sanskrit. These seem to be the names Adam, Noah, and Abraham (= A bar haṃ bār hm); these are the famous teachers who appeared before Muhammad. Thus, I think an error was made in the break in the last word and Varāhī was translated as "possessor of pigs" (*phagden*).

The first teacher of the Muslims is Muhammad; Mamathar is clearly a corruption of this. In [the Tibetan translation of] the *Kālacakra*, the name appears as Drangtsi Lodro (Madhumati or "mind of honey"). In the *Kālacakrottaratantra*, the line "the savior of the Muslims Madhumati" explicitly occurs, and there is no doubt that this [name] was translated thinking it was Sanskrit. There, some of the names of Arab Muslim cities are written as if they were Indian words and translated accordingly, such as Vāgdā [for Baghdad], which is translated as "giver of speech" (*ngag chin*), and so on. Similarly, although [the text] says that Makka [Mecca] is in India, from the perspective of today's borders, it lies even beyond Persia, at about the distance from Amdo to India. In actual fact, "Muhammad" is an Arabic word and both names, Madhumati and Mamathar, are just corruptions of this.

Regarding the history of their teacher, [in our sources] it is written that he was a disciple of Nāgārjuna who violated the rules and created a false religion and so on; I think that most of this is prejudiced talk. Similarly, it is said that a monk who was expelled from the monastery volunteered to leave with the drum being beaten. When no one listened, he became resentful and created a barbarian religion. In an old Tibetan commentary on the *Kālacakra*, it is written that when the precepts of the abbot of Sanchi monastery degenerated, out of resentment he authored a false religion and called on the king to disseminate it. This story is told in connection with how Islam first spread to Khotan. It says that when the Islamic religion had existed for about six hundred years, it declined, and was then revived. I think this could be true.

Muhammad was born in the city of Makka or Mecca in the land of Arabia. He was born into a noble family that had become poor and was the son of Abdullah, his father, and Aminah, his mother. While he was still in the womb, his father died. Shortly after he was born, his mother also died. Left as an orphan, he was then cared for by his grandfather. When he also died, his maternal uncle cared for him and he grew up. He worked as a servant of a wealthy widow named Khadijah and, leading camels, he went to do trade in Syria, Persia, Egypt, and so on. Eventually, he and the widow became husband and wife. At that time, it is said that Muhammad was twenty-five and she was forty years old. Not long after that, he began hearing someone calling him by name, Muhammad. Each time he heard that voice he would faint, tormented by suffering. Unable to remain at home, he fled to a cave called Hira. Remaining in a kind of meditation, he stayed there for a long time. However, it is said that when he was about forty-two he actually became the *paigambhar* or "messenger of the word."

Because he said, "There is only one object of refuge in this world, it is Allah, and I, Muhammad, am his messenger," most people took him to be insane. But after a while, his wife came to believe in him and she became his first disciple. Because at that time the religion of the Arabs involved the worship of fire, the sun, and various images, the people of the land inflicted much suffering on him, such as arresting him and putting him in prison. Then, not being able to remain there in peace, he fled to the city of Yathrib [Iatribu], called Medina today. The year of his flight is called Hijarah or "moving the abode." It is the basis of the Muslim calendar. This is the one thousand one hundred and sixty-sixth year after the passing of our Teacher [622 CE, which is correct]; up to now one thousand three hundred twenty-four years have elapsed [in the Muslim calendar]. The residents of Medina quickly converted to the new religion. Then, they all formed an army and, led by Muhammad, forcibly brought all corners of Arabia under his control by the time of his death.

Because it is stated that both those who kill and are killed for the sake of the religion attain the supreme state in heaven, they go into battle without concern for their own life or the least compassion for the enemy. Thus, people say there has never been an army more powerful than this. The teacher's own grandson, Hussein, was asked why on the eve of battle he bathed and anointed himself with perfumes. He said, "I do so because there is nothing between us and the black-eyed divine maidens." They believe that if you die in battle you are born in heaven. It is known that because Muhammad loved his wife, he respected her feelings and did not take other wives until she died. When she had died, he took about seven very young women, in the earlier and later stages [of his life]. Saying, "I have permission from Allah," he enjoyed the wives of others and even his own daughters-in-law, and said, "Apart from me, no one else has permission to do so." He said, "I went to the seventh heaven and met Allah. He said that his followers must worship him fifty times a day." Muhammad said that this was too much, so in the end, it was decided that they would worship five times each day; this is exactly what they do. He said, "For me, in this world, there is nothing more pleasing than three things: sweet fragrance, maidens, and worship." He died in the one thousand one hundred and seventy-sixth year after the passing [of the Buddha; 632 CE, which is correct]. Since he was said to be sixty-two years old at that time, he was born in the one thousand one hundred and fourteenth year after the passing [of the Buddha or 570 CE, which is correct].

If we take their Hijarah to be the beginning of the spread of the Muslim religion in the land of Mecca, given that here we are using the Sinhalese tradition of the year of the Buddha's nirvāṇa [544 CE], an incompatibility [of dates] arises on the question of in what year after the Buddha's passing the Muslims began. However, the beginning of the Muslims according to [the Kālacakra calendar], where the sixty-year cycles of the nirvāṇa year are integrated with its "fire, space, and ocean" years, seems to fit [with the Hijarah year] except for a discrepancy of about two years. It is said that when [Princess] Wencheng was dispatched to Tibet, it had been three years since this teacher of the Muslims had died. Thus, it was during the lifetime of Songtsen [Gampo]. Although it is said that Songtsen took [Wencheng] as his wife when he was sixteen years old, when one compares the various chronicles, it appears that he did so when he was very old. This should be researched.

The words that the Creator is said to have spoken to Muhammad were written on walls, on stone, in books, on bones, and so on in the land of Arabia. All of these were later compiled by Abu Bakr in a rough way and in their entirety by Caliph Uthman. This is the root scripture of the Musulmans known as the Koran. It has one hundred and fourteen chapters. The Koran is not only a root text; a commentary on it also exists with it. It primarily teaches the practice of the religion and the system of laws. It sets forth many things that are like reasonings. For example, [it states that] it is incorrect to say that Jesus is the son of the Creator and that he is an object of worship; it is a lie to say that he rose again after his death, and so on. However, it is written that Jesus must be recognized as a chosen prophet of the Creator. This Koran is written only in the Arabic language, and they vow not to permit its translation into another language. However, in recent times a powerful man named Pasha translated it into his own Turkish language. It has similarly been translated into English, and I have read it carefully.

The followers of Islam who spread to other countries separated into the two groups of Sunni and Shia. The majority that spread to other countries are Sunni. It is said that in India and Persia, there is also the Shia group. The primary holy place for all Muslims, however, is Mecca. At its very heart is a great black stone called the Kaaba, a stone said to have fallen there from the sky. All the Muslims in the world bow down to it. It is said that Muhammad himself went on pilgrimage to it seven times. Even Muslims in such places as China bow down toward the west, the direction of that stone.

After the death of Muhammad, his disciples led a great army, as they had done before, to Egypt and so forth in North Africa, to

Syria, to Persia, and crossing the ocean to distant western countries such as Spain. Within a single decade they controlled these [lands] and placed them under their religion. Within a cycle of sixty years they had even reached the western part of India, such as Oḍḍiyāna and Sindhu. At that time, the Muslim kingdom stretched from Arabia to Sindhu, and the caliph Umar held the throne as the regent of Muhammad. What was under his sway was known as the kingdom of the caliph. Prior to this period, although they had raided many parts of western India, there was not much impact. The period when all the lands of Sindhu were firmly under their control was around the one thousand two hundred and fifty-sixth year after the passing of our Teacher. Some parts of Arabia had been raided by the Sindhus.

When a minister from the eastern province of the caliphate named Hussein sent an envoy to the Sindhu king Dāhir, saying that his people and goods must be returned, [the king] would not listen, causing a war. The Musulmans sent an army twice and defeated the Indians. Then Muhammad bin Qasim was made general and sent. The Buddhists in Sindhu, who had been suffering under the hands of the Hindus before that, sought refuge with the Muslims out of desperation. Eventually, Dāhir's ministers together with other leaders went over to the enemy. Dāhir himself acted as general and fought near the iron-walled city of Arore. But in the end, the king died in battle. The queen barricaded the doors and attempted to defend the castle but failed, and so threw herself into the fire and died. The army destroyed the cities. Not long after that, the capital of Alor also fell. Thus Sindhu came under their control. However, the minister of Dāhir, who had become a friend of Muhammad, appealed to the king and was granted permission for the Hindus to practice their own religion for the time being. The damaged temples were restored as well. However, because the Buddhists had no protector whatsoever, [their temples] remained in ruins. Muhammad bin Qasim acquired limitless wealth from looting; from the destruction of one single temple he obtained gold weighing thirteen thousand *mon*. The fame of India as a land of riches spread to other regions. Thus, for a rather long period, the Musulmans of Arabia and the Indians who lived in Sindhu practiced their own religions and lived in harmony without doing great harm to one another.

The first [Muslims] to control the land of India were the Turks. Alp Tigin, a young Turkish slave of the Samanid king, over time became the king's favorite. Establishing a small kingdom in the land of Ghazni, he remained there as a vassal king. That was the one thousand two hundred and sixth year after the passing of the Teacher. Then, about fifteen years later, Sabuktagin, the dearest slave of Alp Tigin, who would later become his son-in-law, gained the throne after his master's death. Leading armies several times to the northwestern edge of India, he captured some fortresses.

Now, the Turks and the Arabs both have the same religion of *mleccha* or Islam. Because the Turks were especially devoted to that religion, they referred to Indians and others as "idol worshippers" and considered them to be in the category of those who hold the most evil views. Forsaking even the smallest compassion for those who belonged to religions other than theirs, they did whatever they could to persecute them, including torture. They have irreversible faith in their scriptures, including the certainty that one needs no greater virtue than being able to kill a few idol worshippers who do not seek refuge in Allah. Thus, their courage was greater than that of a demon. Each time they led an army, they killed innocent men, women, and children beyond number. Thinking, "They have abandoned Allah and follow other teachers," they killed them without mercy, as if they had caught the murderers of their father red-handed. Eventually, they came to control all of India. Muhammad himself is said to have cut off the limbs of six hundred Jews in one day; plucking out their eyes, he cast them into the desert and made a law that no one was allowed to give them water. For the merciless deeds of the kings who will be described below, one must understand that they rely on such scriptures.

In that scripture, whatever is clearly visible is not falsified by direct perception. It does not say anything concerning slightly concealed facts [known by reasoning]. Thus [what is not visible] only [falls into the category of the] very concealed. In that [text], one should understand that there is no fault at all of contradiction between earlier and later words. Furthermore, whatever discussions there are of compassion, charity, decency, and so forth in the Christian and Muslim scriptures, it is taught that they are only to be directed to those known to be brothers who belong to their own religion. They do not teach anywhere that there is even the slightest sin in committing such acts as killing, beating, and deceiving other people who belong to different religions.

CHAPTER 13

The Monks of Sri Lanka, from *Grains of Gold*

Gendun Chopel spent almost sixteen months in Sri Lanka in 1940–1941. Despite the extensive knowledge of "Hīnayāna" doctrine that he had gained in Tibet through studying works like the Abhidharmakośa, *his time in Sri Lanka was his first encounter with a Buddhist tradition that rejected the Mahāyāna sūtras and the tantras. He found himself in the comfortable position of living and interacting with fellow Buddhists but the uncomfortable position of finding little sympathy for the form of Buddhism he himself practiced. His fascinating description of the Theravāda tradition of Sri Lanka appears here, written in a style reminiscent of participant-observation ethnography.*[172]

It is said that altogether there are a little more than twenty thousand monks in the entire island. For all of them, there is not even the slightest need to be concerned about alms and shelter. Even in what are considered to be large monasteries, not more than twenty monks reside there. The beds and the provisions for all of them are almost suitable for a king. Furthermore, when a rich person dies, it is a custom to offer his everyday possessions, such as his bed, to the temple. Thus, the monks receive only the best of everyday possessions. However, all of this must be considered as belonging to the saṃgha; as for personal possessions, nothing is allowed other than the necessities and other minor things. For those monks who stay in the temples, the villagers take turns bringing alms. Although the people very much like [the monks] coming for alms, apart from those who live in hermitages, the wandering monks, and the newly ordained monks, the majority do not perform it. Some make a vow to beg for alms for a short time and count this as a form of virtuous practice. This is similar to our attending the regular tea offerings at the great assembly. Because all the old people are familiar with the details of the inappropriate activities, such as cutting down a plant, touching precious material, and eating what is not offered, there is no opportunity [for monks] to do whatever they please.

Some monks have quite large amounts of money that supposedly belongs to the saṃgha, but since they cannot touch any of it, this can lead to laughter. For example, when they count their money, a boy spreads it in front of the monk. The monk holds a long stick in his hand and uses it to turn over [the notes and the coins] and counts the money; whenever the boy makes a mistake in counting, he gets hit on the head with that same stick. Thus, apart from being humorous, this is not something that inspires admiration. However, it is undeniable that this does represent a vinaya regulation. When midday has passed, it is considered a sin to offer food to an image of the Buddha, not to mention to the monks. The afternoon offerings include drinks and butter lamps and so on. Because the Teacher was a fully ordained monk, there are many customs, such as novices not sleeping in his presence, not being touched by women, and so on, which although connected to the dharma in essence, seem somewhat amusing in practice. I cannot write about all of these here.

From time to time, alms would be offered to the saṃgha. A procession of monks, in order of seniority and carrying a stūpa and a palm-leaf book, would proceed. They are received from up to a yojana away, [the laity] spreading a large white cotton cloth under their feet, which is moved [as the monks proceed]. When the monks reach the door of a house, a layman brings a copper container and water and washes the feet of each of the monks. Another person wipes their feet with a cloth. Then they sit on the cushions and the most senior monk makes all the family members repeat after him the refuge formula and the five root precepts. Then the food is brought and all the donors melodiously chant three times, *imaṃ bhikkhaṃ bhikkhu saṅghassa dema*, "I offer this food to the saṃgha of monks." Then, while reciting these words, they offer cooked rice and distribute cooked vegetables, then yogurt, sweets, and fruits; finally betel leaf is offered. After the meal is over, the male and female donor together hold a single vase and repeat several times, "By this merit, may all of our relatives enjoy happiness." Repeating this several times, they would dedicate the merit to a relative who had died. Then, the elder monk, holding a white fan in his hand, would explain [the benefit of] the offering, saying such things as, "This giving, even if not done with deliberate intention for it, is certain to bring about the happiness of gods and humans. However, if it has been dedicated with deliberate intention, it is conceivable that [this act] will become a cause for the attainments and the unsurpassed bliss of nirvāṇa." He would then read a long list of names of the benefactors of the Buddha himself, such as Nanda, Upananda, Yaśodharā, and Anāthapiṇḍada, apportioning their roots of virtue to everyone. In general, when someone sees these practices for the first time, there is no Buddhist whose mind is not impressed.

When the monks eat food inside the temple, they each sit kneeling on a small stool arranged in rows and then eat [their meal]. This is not very pleasing to our eyes, but in the travel journal of the monk Yijing, who traveled in ancient times, he describes even the monks at Nālandā eating in this manner. The [Chinese] monk states that although in general it is not clear in the vinaya, it is certain that this is the intention of the Blessed One; in the vinaya, it states such things as, "if food falls near your feet." But if the monks were seated comfortably on the ground there would be no way for it to fall near their feet. Also, there is a statement about monks washing their feet after finishing their meal; if one sits cross-legged on a cushion, what need would there be to wash one's feet? He presents these two arguments. So great is the monk Yijing's reverence for the Buddha that he is insistent about even this fine point of religious behavior. Again, the monk says that in the past, we in China also ate sitting on a stool, but later, during the time of the Tang emperor there arose the evil custom of everyone sitting on the ground. In any case, by the time of the Republic of China this good custom of the past had again become widespread; this is something we can see for ourselves. This Yijing is said to be a contemporary of Dharmakīrti, and this story about him came up as an aside.

On the nights such as a full moon, new moon, or eclipse, all the laypeople gather at the monastery and a monk teaches the dharma throughout the night. He is offered the three religious robes and the like as a gift. In brief, all of the things that we have heard from the vinaya scriptures with our ears can be each seen with our eyes in real life when we reach Siṅghala. Once a good monk was walking through the middle of a field, and with an attitude of faith, I bought some fruit and offered it to him. He saw that there were still two *pana* [coins] in my hand and said, "You can still buy more." Having bought them, he made me carry them and we went on a little way. He received chickpeas from the farmers and obtained a large amount. Then, as we went, he saw coconut bark and said, "This is good for sweeping." He made me carry a big bundle on my back, and we returned to the temple. I thought that all these monks live by the same dharma and the same path of [disciplinary] actions, yet when it comes to the way they display their greed, they are similar to that "group of six" in ancient times. Reflecting on this, I felt like laughing while feeling a tinge of sadness.

At each monastery there is a temple where the image of the Teacher resides, one stūpa, one Bodhi tree, one guesthouse used for visitors, a place for teaching the dharma called *dharmaśālā*, and a large structure called the *sīmā* or "boundary hall," with stone markers set in all directions establishing a single boundary. This is where all the vinaya rites, such as the confession and recitation of sūtras, are performed. Laypeople are not allowed to enter, and like our protector temples, this is strictly enforced. The monks have a custom of not bowing to any god or human other than the Buddha and one's elders; this seems to be exactly what our Chak Lotsāwa saw in Bodh Gayā. No matter how important a layperson may be who is paying his respects [to the monk], there is no custom of even bowing one's head in response. In the temples, there are three types of images of the Teacher—sitting, standing, and lying down—which represent the four activities. They have a tradition of making Śāriputra white and Maudgalyāyana dark. There are also many images of Dīpaṃkara and so forth, renowned as the twenty[-four] buddhas of the past who were the teachers of the bodhisattva, and also those displaying the postures of the Buddha in the forty-nine [days after his enlightenment]. Perhaps because it is easier to sculpt, in each monastery there is a huge image of the Teacher passing into nirvāṇa. This nirvāṇa image is also very widespread in other countries such as China; it is astonishing that it is never seen in Tibet. It seems that in the depths of our hearts we think the death of the Buddha is a bad omen. The members of the śrāvaka sect have an excellent understanding of the dharma, and because they assert that when one passes into nirvāṇa, one achieves the ultimate state, they take this to be the principal representation [of the Buddha].

The group of sixteen sthaviras (elders) is not known to them. However, among what are known as the eighty principal members of the Buddha's retinue, the sixteen are included. Among these, in the stories in the sūtras of monks who receive prophecies, one sees such monks as Udāyin, who engenders faith in the laypeople, and Vasumallaputra, who assigns shelters and beds. There is also no custom of drawing the wheel of life [the wheel of rebirth] in the vestibules [of the monastery]; similarly they do not have the monk's *khakkhara* staff. They say that there is no sūtra source whatsoever for these two. In some monasteries, there are four protector temples that have Samantabhadra, Avalokiteśvara, Viṣṇu, and Ṣaṇmukha [Skanda]. They call Avalokiteśvara, Nātha, or "protector," and this is precisely his rank. All four of them are considered to be bodhisattvas and are objects of worship by laypeople and are oath-bound protectors of the monks. However, some five hundred years ago, there were many monks who took Avalokiteśvara to be their meditation deity and there are beautiful hymns of praise to him composed by these monks. There is also a rock carving of Avalokiteśvara at a place known as Wäligama. Adorning the doors of some temples are images of Mṛgāramātā and Anathapiṇḍada; these two are similar to dharma protectors. In particular, Mṛgāramātā, or Viśākhā, is considered to be like a goddess of wealth and a goddess of sons. They make protection amulets from charts inscribed with the Teacher's birthday, age, astrological sign, and so forth and wear it around their necks.

With regard to the everyday conduct of the monks, they rise early in the morning and, while chewing on a neem stick, they sweep the enclosures around the stūpa and the Bodhi tree with a long-handled broom so they don't have to bend down. Then, washing their hands and feet, they make prostrations to the Buddha and the stūpa, reciting the relevant stanzas. Then, having bowed down to the abbot and the elders, when they arrive at the kitchen they prepare the morning offering of alms. After they have eaten, they perform their regular chores. When a bell is rung, everyone goes to the well, where they wash their entire body and change their wet clothes. The young ones go to the seashore every day where the laypeople cannot see them and go swimming, run around naked, and so forth, maintaining the lifestyle of the "group of seventeen noble ones." They return and eat their noon meal. When they have finished eating they return to their beds and take a nap for a little while. This is the custom found in all the hot countries. When noon has passed, they drink a cup of boiled black tea without milk. Even in the winter, they drink tea and those who are hungry eat something that is like molasses.

At dusk, everyone gathers in the temple and recites stanzas. The younger ones confess their violations to the elders. Then, sitting down according to their rank, they remain, or pretend to remain, in *samādhi* [meditation] for a rather long time. While everyone is absorbed in a state of actual concentration with their eyes closed, the elder begins reciting a sūtra, saying, "Thus did I hear." At that moment, the others suddenly open their eyes and recite together. They chant in turn the *Recollection of the Three Jewels Sūtra* (*Ratana Sutta*), the *Dependent Origination Sūtra* (*Paticcasamuppādavibhaṅga Sutta*), the *Loving Kindness Sūtra* (*Mettā Sutta*), and so on.

Walking before the stūpa and the Bodhi tree, they also recite a stanza for each. Then, bowing to the elders, they return to their beds. There they remain reading or talking until almost midnight. Then, they wash their feet and go to bed wearing their yellow robes [as a blanket]. During the night, the older monks sometimes wake up with a sense of terror and repeatedly shout in their confusion, "All conditioned things are impermanent, impermanent, impermanent" (*sabbe saṅkhārā aniccā aniccā aniccā*) or "Caused by ignorance, volitional actions arise," and so on, disturbing the sleep of everyone around them. Thus, this must be something that can be either inspiring or annoying. Some monks carry rosaries and recite what sound like mantras, but when you listen, they are reciting the above phrases. Some [recite], "The Blessed One, Tathāgata . . . teacher of gods and humans," while others repeat the first syllables of these words in their original Indian language. They refer to this as practicing meditation; they do not use the expression "mantra repetition" for this. Even when they see someone holding a rosary, they say that he is performing *bhāvanā*, practicing meditation. Because there are references [in the texts] to "counting meditation" and "enumerating meditation," it seems appropriate to use such expressions.

The early rains retreat begins from the sixteenth day of our sixth month and the late [rains retreat] begins from the sixteenth day of the seventh month, thus they remain [in retreat] for three full months. During the early rains retreat there are many benefactors who offer fresh food; there is even a saying about monks getting fat [during this period]. When the ceremony for ending the early rains retreat is concluded, all the people from the surrounding villages gather for *kaṭhinadāna*, an offering of cloth for robes, and the festival of saffron. For this, all the villagers—men, women, and children—rise around midnight and form a procession, carrying large oil lamps. Above their heads they each carry a container with long bolts of white cotton for making robes, patches of cloth, and rolls of cloth, in accordance with whatever they can afford. With the sound of *sādhu* and various kinds of music, they circumambulate all the stūpas in the area.

Finally, they come to the temple and make offerings to each of the monks. At the break of dawn, they spread a great bolt of cloth on a large table decorated with flowers and anointed with fragrances. Four monks bring small knives, cords, needles, and so on. Then, a long cord soaked in saffron is held at one end by a monk and at the other end by a donor, with children crowding behind to hold the end of the string, creating a scene similar to a boat being pulled by a rope at the mouth of the Machu River [in Tibet]. Then, as lines are drawn [with the cord], all the laypeople outside say, in unison, "*sādhu sādhu*" and beat big drums. They play music, sing, and dance, with shouts of "the doctrine of the Teacher endures" and "the ocean of ethical discipline remains undamaged." Everyone, such as the seminary monks, can recite many mantras from the vinaya. [This ceremony] is more extensive even than the self-empowerment ceremony of the *Sarvavid Vairocana* [*Tantra*]. In brief, the obtaining of the robes seems to be the largest ritual of the year for śrāvaka monks. Then, up until noon, everyone takes turns sewing one yellow robe and even dyes it. They offer it to the saṃgha and give it to a monk who needs it. I found this ritual to be most fascinating, so I have written about it in some detail here.

The festival of saffron is in our ninth month, and this month is also called the "month of saffron." During this month very heavy rains come to this island; it is said that this is due to the power of the positive gods being pleased. The upper robe is about the length of half a roll [of cloth] while the third robe has only five lines of patches. However, saying that there is no contradiction in having up to twenty-five line patches, some wear a ceremonial robe filled with small square patches. The way they wear their robes is quite surprising. Aligning two corners of the robe, they roll these together. The end of the rolled part is then wrapped behind the right shoulder [in fact, the left shoulder] and one end is held by the hand and pulled from under the armpit. By doing so, they have a marvelous way of covering everything from the throat to the end of the lower garment. When you get accustomed to it a little, it is quite pleasing to the eye. In all the ancient Indian sculptures as well as the Chinese style sandalwood buddhas, the monks' robes are like this. Even the holding of one corner [of the robes] in one hand is found in all of these [sculptures]. I think that this is exactly the posture being referred to in the context of the making of prophecy about the disciples at the conclusion of an empowerment ceremony, where it states that in his right hand Śākyamuni holds the corners of his robes in the shape of the ears of a deer. However, this manner of wearing robes is possible for their robes because they are five cubits in width; because our monks' robes are too small, this is not possible.

Now, all the monks of this island are exclusively Sthavira Nikāya. Within that, stemming from different ordination lineages, there are three main divisions: the Siyam Nikāya or the "order of the dark blue ones," the Amarapura Nikāya or the "order of the immortal city," and the Rāmañña Nikāya or the "order of the joyful." Although it is mentioned [in some sources] that the Sthaviras have second names like *ākara* or *varma*, there does not appear to be any certainty about these names here. As for the name *varma*, it seems almost nonexistent here. There are many with the name Vanaratna. Among the three, the Siyam Nikāya is the wealthiest and most powerful. They are also the proprietors of the canine tooth of the Teacher and of the Bodhi tree. They only ordain people of high caste. In the past, people of lower castes were also ordained [in this order], but when the king, ministers, and others bowed down to them, they could not bear this and rose from their seats. Thus from that point on it is said that they were prohibited from being ordained [in this lineage]. Like us, they wear the upper robe over one shoulder. They even shave their eyebrows. This is the tradition that takes the rule in the vinaya that one should shave the hair around the mouth to mean to shave the hair on one's face. The Amarapura wear their upper robe over both shoulders. They have a great many monasteries.

The Rāmañña have the strictest practice of the vinaya. For example, when they perform the ordination ceremony, to [clearly maintain] the boundaries, it must be performed in a boat in the middle of the water. They say that because the ordination lineage of the other two groups is not pure, their ordination is not authentic. They will not recite sūtras or eat food with [the other two orders]. Because of this the other two groups dislike them. However, the laypeople admire them over everyone else. Only those of the lower caste take ordination [in this group]. Since they do not think it proper even to carry an umbrella of cloth, they carry an umbrella made of palm leaves, shaped like an oyster shell. It is they who are supreme in abiding in the ascetic virtues. Among them, the group Kalyāṇavaṃsa, "bone of virtue," has the strictest practice of all.

In general, all these Siṅghala monks tend to hold only their own system to be supreme. With respect to the systems of others, regardless of how good or bad it may be, they tend to reject it completely without making distinctions. However, there are many who have some interest in the philosophical aspects of Mahāyāna; there were a few who have even memorized the verses of Nāgārjuna's *Madhyamakakārikā*. Regarding the other presentations [of the Mahāyāna] related to the aspect of the vast practice, such as the *sambhogakāya* (enjoyment body), they say that these are explanations copied from the Great Brahman [concept] of the Hindus. On the question of the cessation of the continuum of matter and consciousness in the nirvāṇa without residue, their understanding has something that is both profound and confused. They assert that the statement that a bodhisattva is superior to an arhat is the talk of the Hindu kṣatriyas. Furthermore, there is a lengthy list [they cite] that states that the Mahāsāṃghikas composed the *Pile of Jewels Sūtra* (*Ratnakūṭa*) and that the followers of Vajriputra composed the *Web of Illusion Tantra* (*Māyājāla*), and so on. Because I do not wish to be forced to antagonize you [my fellow Tibetans], I will not list them here. At the conclusion of that list, the following is written: "Be that as it may, the bare essence of the Sugata's teaching remains undamaged in the midst of all of these [texts]. In particular, the Tripiṭaka recited by the Haimavata sect, both in terms of word and meaning, is very similar to that spoken from the Buddha's own mouth."

The master Bhāvaviveka states that the Haimavata sect split off from the Sthavira Nikāya. Thus, it is certain that their sūtras and the sūtras of the Sthaviras were similar, and this similarity seems to consist of this fact [of shared origin]. Apart from referring to them as the Śrāvaka Nikāya or the Theravāda, that is, Sthaviravāda, if one calls them Hīnayāna (inferior vehicle), they explode, asking, "Who gave that name? In that case you should call the Buddha the inferior teacher." In particular, they consider the Vajrayāna to be a deplorable thing and condemn it as *pañcamakāra*, or the "five *m*'s." When I tell them that even ordained monks like Butön and Tsong kha pa admired the Mantra[yāna], they will not hear about it. There was a monk who heard the story of Milarepa and felt that he must have been a wonderful lay practitioner and felt strong admiration for him, but when I told him that he too was a practitioner of secret mantra, he got up and left without even listening to the rest of the story. Regarding the explanation that summarizes [tantric practices] into the "five *m*'s," I have not seen such an account in our own [Buddhist] tantras, but it certainly appears in the Hindu tantras. For example, in the *Kālīvilāsa Tantra* one reads, *madyaṃ māsaṃ tathā matsyaṃ mudrāṃ maithunameva ca / pañcatattvavihīnaṃ pūjāṃ na phalodbhavaḥ*:

> Beer, meat, and likewise fish,
> Mudrā and sexual union;
> Offerings inferior in these five principles,
> They shall bear no fruits.

In the Indian language there are five *m*'s [at the beginning of these words].

Similarly, there are not even stories of the Mahāyāna masters who came to this land in the past, such as Āryadeva, Śāntipa [Ratnākaraśānti], and so on. Hoping to find the direct disciple of Śāntipa whom Buddhaguptanātha said that he met in Kandy in Sri Lanka, I wandered around in that region for more than a fortnight, but no one had even heard of him. At that time, he was said to have been about seven hundred years old; now he would be more than nine hundred years old. Or he must have passed away. Otherwise, I wondered why he would not grant an audience to the one Mahāyāna person who had come from Tibet. Similarly, no one seems to know the place where the sthavira Vajriputra resides, so if someone happens to travel here in the future, please look for him in the region of Mount Masdenatala [?]. As for the lineages of *nada* [?] and so on, how can they even know about these? Nevertheless, everyone is familiar with the fact that in the past the Mahāyāna did spread here; this is even described at length in their annals. There is also a history of the Bodhi tree composed in the past by a layman named Guruḷugōmī who was a follower of the Mahāyāna. He is also said to have composed some commentaries on Mahāyāna sūtras. I wonder whether this is the same as the commentary on the *Karuṇāpuṇḍarīka* composed by a Sinhalese layman, one Pṛthivībandhu, included in Butön's Tengyur catalog; there is no doubt that the name of this layman is definitely Guruḷugōmī as well.

Now, the three Mahāvihāra or the "great monastery," Jetavana or "conquering grove," and Abhayagiri or "fearless mountain" were in the past chief among all the religious sites of this island. They were built by the kings Tissa, Mahāsena, and Abhaya, respectively. At the sites of all three, there is a stūpa that resembles a mountain, ruins of the ancient monastery as far as the eye can see, and a small monastery for the caretaker. There is no doubt that these are the principal sites of the three sects, Jetavana, Abhayagiri, and Mahāvihāra, which are counted among the eighteen sects. That all these three were Sthavira is clearly stated by both Padmasambhava and Vinītadeva. The disagreements of these sects with each other and how they engaged in debates are described at length in Sinhalese royal chronicles, and, in particular, it is reputed that the Mahāyāna views and practices of the Abhayagiri were disapproved, as many as three times. In sources such as the *Blaze of Reasoning* (*Tarkajvālā*) there are many ways of enumerating [the eighteen sects], yet there is no mention whatsoever of these three. However, I believe that this is due to the fact that those three only came to be known in later times. Furthermore, it is said that among the Sarvāstivāda and so on, there emerged many Mahāyāna paṇḍitas who were well versed in logic. At that time the Sthaviras lacked the confidence to debate with them and were at the same time reluctant to discard the stainless scriptures of the Blessed One. Thus, they abandoned the central land and gathered in the land of Laṅkā. The travel guide of the Chinese monk also mentions, "These days the Sthaviras have departed from the central land."

With respect to the three piṭakas of the Sthaviras, if one were to measure the volumes, they are about a bit more than one-third of the Tibetan Kangyur [translations of the word of the Buddha]. Within the Tripiṭaka, in the Vinaya, there are the "five sections": the defeats (*pārājika*), the downfalls (*pācittiya*), the large division (*mahāvagga*), the small division (*cūlavagga*), and what is referred to as the "surrounding path" (*parivāra*), as well as the *prātimokṣa* [vows] of nuns. In the Sūtra Piṭaka, there are five: the *Long Discourses* (*Dīgha Nikāya*), the *Middle-Length Discourses* (*Majjhima Nikāya*), the *Connected Discourses* (*Saṃyutta Nikāya*), the *Gradual Discourses* (*Aṅguttara Nikāya*), and the *Minor Discourses* (*Khuddaka Nikāya*). In the *Long Discourses*, there are thirty-four sūtras, such as the *Sutta of Brahmā's Net* (*Brahmajāla Sutta*). Among them [in the *Gradual Discourses*], there is the *Wood Pile Sutta* (*Dārukkhandha Sutta*), which is referred to in the *Blaze of Reasoning*. In this sūtra, the Teacher sees a burning tree and describes the faults of immorality. As a result, sixty monks violently vomit thick blood and die, sixty more return their precepts, while another sixty attain fruition. There exist [in this sūtra] references to numerous sets of sixty. In the *Middle-Length Discourses* there are one hundred and five short sūtras [in fact, one hundred fifty-two], and it is considered to be principal among all the sūtras. In the *Gradual Discourses*, there are 2,308 sūtras. Among the fifteen subdivisions of the *Minor Discourses*, there is a text that resembles the *Udānavarga*, and it also contains the *Jātakas* and so forth.

In the Abhidharma, from among the seven books, there is the *Collection of Dharmas* (*Dhammasaṅgaṇi*), the *Analysis* (*Vibhaṅga*), the *Points of Discussion* (*Kathāvatthu*), the *Analysis of the Person* (*Puggalapaññatti*), the *Discourse on the Elements* (*Dhātukathā*), the *Divisible Pairs* (*Yamaka*), and the *Thorough Engagement* (*Paṭṭhāna*). Now, the seven books of the Kashmiri Vaibhāṣikas are the *Entry into Wisdom* (*Jñānaprasthāna*), the *Enumeration of Transmigrators* (*Saṅgītiparyāya*), and so on. Thus, they have different names; whether the actual texts are the same or not I do not know. The seven books of the Kashmiris are said to be extant in Chinese translation. They assert that these seven books are the words of the Teacher and that they were spoken to an audience of celestial beings. They also make these the primary focus of their study. It is said that in the past their study flourished particularly in the country of Burma. They divide the sūtras into two parts, a section spoken from the mouth of the Teacher himself and another section understood to be the speech of the compilers, called *aṭṭhakathā*, thus making a very clear distinction. In our sūtras, these two parts remain undifferentiated. In texts like the vinaya, if a comprehensive comparison was to be made of the stories in theirs and those in ours—such as [determining] what is unclear in one and clear in the other, where they converge or where they completely diverge—there might be many surprises. For example, in the context of the infraction pertaining to handling wool it is clearly stated in our vinaya that the group of six went to Nepal. In their scripture, however, it only states that they went to a country in the north. Similarly, [their scripture] speaks of two Udāyī: red Udāyī who engaged in deeds that lead to inferior states and black Udāyī [Kāludāyī] who later attain arhatship. This is not evident in our scripture, and there is a discrepancy.

[Their scripture] states that Virūḍhaka held a grudge against Mahānāma for washing his house after his visit so he killed the Śākyas, and, dragged away by the waves of the ocean, he [Virūḍhaka] went to hell. This [story] is also a little different. Similarly, they say that [the Buddha] thought that if Nanda took Sundarī as his wife, his good fortune [for nirvāṇa] would come to an end, so he had him ordained on the very day of the wedding. This is not found in our [version]. The story, passed from one hand to another, is applied to places where people gather. I don't think that the story of Yaśodharā being ordained and becoming an arhat exists in our account either. I think that in the *Lotus Sūtra* (*Saddharmapuṇḍarīka Sūtra*) there might be some mention of Yaśodharā being a fully ordained nun. Please look.

There is also a very sad story of how Ānanda was banished. It is said that when he went to Jetavana, the monks who were staying there would not speak to him or recite sūtras with him. So he went off to one end [of the monastery] and set up a place to sit and sleep. Staying there, every morning he would go to the Teacher's empty perfumed chamber and prepare the water, tooth stick, and so forth, as he had done when [the Buddha] was alive. Taking a branch from the Bodhi tree, he planted it at the door of the perfumed chamber. Later, this became the tree called Ānandabodhi, to which the wandering monks would come to pay homage. Such accounts are mentioned. The monk Xuanzang states that he saw this tree.

There is a story of how the parents of Śyāmakā, fearing the plague, broke through the wall and escaped and died on the road, and how, as Śyāmakā was wandering, she was adopted as a daughter of Himavat. [Also] there is the story that Udayana and Vāsavadattā[173] were separated by a curtain. She called him a repulsive name, and when she made a mistake while he was teaching her [the charm] to tame [elephants], Udayana called her "big mouth." Angry, she ripped open the curtain, and then lived in a bird's nest.

There is also a story of how Anupamā verbally attacked the Teacher using ten harsh names, such as "donkey monk." [These stories] are not found in our [scriptures]. In the *Sūtra of the Wise and the Foolish* (*Damamūkanidāna Sūtra*), there is the story of the sufferings experienced by Utpalavarṇā, but they connect it to the haggard Gautamī. Because it is found in the same manner in our own *Bhikṣuṇīvibhaṅga*, it seems that in some cases, such as this one, the names are exchanged. There is the story of how haggard Gautamī, carrying the corpse of her dead child, urgently implored the Buddha, "Gautama, since your power is great, please bring him back to life," and how, the Teacher, knowing that the time was appropriate, replied, "Bring me a handful of white mustard seeds from a house where no one has died." Although she went all around Śrāvastī, she did not find one. Thus, saying that death is certain for all, she attained the fruition [of enlightenment].

Abhaya took ordination and became known as Vimalakīrti. His mother, Āmrapālī,[174] heard him reciting the sūtras and she also became ordained. Because of her beauty, the monks became distracted. Ānanda taught them the dharma. [This story] as well as a verse uttered by Āmrapālī is in the *Therīgāthā*. I do not think these [stories] are familiar to us either.

There is also a story of the birth of a second prince Abhaya, from the union of a prostitute named Padmāvatī in Ujjayinī[175] and Bimbisāra. [There is also the following story.] The people of Rājagṛha were jealous of Āmrapālī's beauty and put a beautiful woman named Sālavatī to replace her. She gave birth to a boy named Jīvaka Kumāra and a girl named Śrīmā,[176] and everyone was captivated by Sālavatī. When she died, the Buddha said that her body should be left alone. After a few days, seeing it decomposing and infested with worms, many attained the fruition. I think there is a similar story in our *Pile of Jewels* [*Sūtra*]. It is said that the people of Rājagṛha respected Kāśyapa greatly. Thus, a woman first offered alms to the Teacher by mistake, then snatched it back from the Teacher's hands and offered it to Kāśyapa. Because of that, Kāśyapa always stayed behind in the monastery and did not go into town.

In general, because all the stories in the Hīnayāna [scriptures] are narrated in an ordinary way, when the deeds of the Buddha are recounted, they are always quite moving. The majority of what appears in the Mahāyāna sūtras is excessively elaborate. Thus, apart from the extremely wise and the extremely stupid, it is difficult for them to appeal to the minds of all common people. I will not write about the disparities in the life of the Teacher [between the Pāli and the Mahāyāna sūtras]. Similarly, their sūtras use so many amazing analogies that it can be very confusing. For example, there was once a man who, having heard that Gautama did not react to either praise or blame, went before the Teacher and spoke abusively until he was exhausted. Then, the Teacher asked, "If a recipient does not take possession of a gift, then whose property does that gift become?" The person thought about this and replied, "It then becomes the property of the person who gave it." "In that case," the Buddha responded, "I have not taken possession of the harsh words you just uttered, thus they are yours now."

Similarly, once someone called Mālunkyaputta posed [to the Buddha] such undetermined questions as whether saṃsāra has a beginning and end, saying that if these were not decided he would return to being a layman. The Teacher responded, "If a person were struck without warning by a poisonous arrow from somewhere in a great forest, he must immediately extract the arrow and tend to the wound. Instead, if he analyzes, wondering 'who shot the arrow; what is it made from?' and so forth, he will die. In the same way, with respect to conditioned suffering and the method to overcome it, if you do not cultivate introspective awareness, but analyze whether [saṃsāra] has a beginning and end, this would be a waste of one's life." There are many accounts like this. I don't know whether or not you want to listen to them. It would be quite difficult to ask you to do so, so I shall stop here.

You might wonder what kind of language all these scriptures, such as the Sthavira sūtras, are in. They are in Prakrit, an ancient language of Magadha. They call it Pāli, which means "established everyday use." The Pāli language is a form of Sanskrit, but because the sounds have become softer, most of the *r* sounds are lost. Also, letters that are difficult to pronounce like *kṣa* are read as *kha* and so on. A very clear example of this language is found in the first section of the great commentary *Stainless Light* (*Vimalaprabhā*), where one reads, "Now, stated in the Magadha language of the Tripiṭaka of the śrāvakas, it is thus: *iti pi so bhagavā arahaṃ sammāsaṃbuddho vijjā-caraṇasampanno sugato lokavidū anuttaro* [*purisadammasārathī satthā devamanussānaṃ buddho bhagavāti*]. It is thus: 'He is the Blessed One, the completely and perfectly awakened one, reasoned, reverent, the Sugata, the knower of the world, and unsurpassed.'" Please look at this [passage] there. The Sthaviras maintain that this was the common language of all the people of Magadha in the central land when the Buddha was alive.

Regarding how long the teaching will remain, they maintain that it will be for five thousand years. Now, up to this Wood Monkey Year of the sixteenth *rabjung* cycle [1944], it has been two thousand four hundred and eighty-six years since the Teacher passed away. The year of the nirvāṇa is the Fire Snake Year according to the Chinese calendar. In general, that it had been over two thousand three hundred years since the Buddha's passing is well established by statements in the travel account of the Yavana [Greek] minister Megasthenes, who arrived in central India during the period of King Aśoka's [grand]father, Candragupta, where he wrote about seeing ordained Buddhist monks. That it is not more than two thousand five hundred years can be discerned from the fact that in many scriptures, such as the *White Lotus of Compassion* (*Karuṇāpuṇḍarīka*), [the Buddha] says, "One hundred years after my passing, Aśoka will appear." Even at the latest, it is certain that Aśoka appeared within three hundred years after the Teacher's passing. This chronology, therefore, has great significance. In general, the śrāvaka sects of the past were renowned for counting each month and each day since the Teacher's passing. However, on this issue, some great Tibetan scholars of the past disparaged them, asserting that the alms-begging śrāvaka monks confused the date of the birth of the Buddha and the creation of the Mahābodhi image at Bodh Gayā and calculated the year of the Buddha's birth on that erroneous basis. In their own system, these Tibetans add around a thousand more years.

CHAPTER 14

Gendun Chopel's India, from *Grains of Gold*

Grains of Gold *consists of seventeen chapters, with much of it devoted to history. There are chapters on the Gupta Dynasty, the Pāla Dynasty, and a chapter called "From 1,600 Years after the Passing of the Buddha to the Present." The final chapter, entitled simply "Conclusion," is devoted to the political and religious landscape of India during his years there. It includes discussions on a range of topics, including his extended thoughts on the question of "Buddhism and Science." The chapter is presented here in its entirety.*[177]

About one thousand nine hundred fifty-nine years after the Teacher passed away [1415], the Europeans began crossing the oceans, demarcating great distances. In particular, the people of Portugal, a small country located in a remote corner of the western foreign lands, became emboldened. By crossing the distant ocean, they discovered many lands, such as Africa. Before long they even controlled the maritime routes of India, and in the one thousand nine hundred forty-third year after the passing of the Buddha [or 1399; in fact, 1498 CE], a ship captain named Waliko [Vasco da Gama] arrived at the coast called Calicut.

Generally, the intelligence of the Europeans in every kind of worldly pursuit is superior to ours in a thousand ways. Because they were accomplished in the ability to easily spin the heads of those peoples of the East and the South, who, honest but naive, had no knowledge of anything other than their own lands, they came to many countries, large and small, together with their armies. Their hearts filled only with self-interest, in their sexual behavior their lust was even greater than that of a donkey. They were sponsored by kings and ministers for whom the happiness of others counted less than a turnip trampled on the ground; it was they who sent out great armies of bandits, calling them "traders." The weak peoples who earned their livelihood in the forests of the small countries, who became terrified when hearing even the braying of donkeys, were caught like sheep and taken to the [Westerners'] own countries. With feet and hands shackled in irons and given only enough food to wet their mouths, they were made to perform hard and terrible labor until they died. It is said that due to this severe hardship, even the young ones were unable to last more than five years. Young women were captured and, to arouse the lust of the gathered customers, were displayed naked in the middle of the marketplace and sold. Thus, they treated the bodies of humans like cattle. If thoughtful people were to hear what they did, their hearts would bleed. It is in this way that the foundations were laid for all the wonders of the world, such as railroads stretching from coast to coast and multistoried buildings whose peaks cannot be seen from below. From Africa alone the people thus captured [for slavery] were more than one million; they filled great boats with the incapable ones and abandoned them at sea. The things the Europeans did like this cannot be counted.

During the reign of the Mughal king Shah Jahan, Hindu and Muslim orphans were captured and taken into slavery by the Portuguese. Because two servants of his queen [Mum] Taz were also captured, the king became angry. He destroyed the cities that had been built by them and took three thousand people prisoner. In addition, he went to the small Portuguese villages with his armies;

those who refused to change their religion immediately were fed alive to the crocodiles.

The religion of Jesus is strict in the way that it carries out everything that its scriptures say about the appropriate way to punish those who believe in false religions. They have laws prohibiting the birth of any new children. If someone has the great courage to give birth to a child, they forcibly seize the people from the Hindu and Muslim temples and perform their own baptism ritual and so forth. They did such things as place children inside a brass vessel and make people count the beads. They told them that, once they had renounced their old faith and joined theirs, they must destroy the lineage of those who believe in false religions. Thus, they alienated everyone wherever they went. Still, these others, forsaking shame, traveled to distant places and talked about how their kingdom would be filled with compassion because of the Christian religion. How pathetic. Some scholars from Christian countries say that nothing has spread sexual perversion, killing, lies, and malicious speech like the religion of Jesus. In my opinion, when it comes to putting the empty [words of their] scriptures into practice, the Dutch and especially the English are not like that at all. They go abroad with deceit, and as long as the power and money they need for themselves is not interfered with, whatever religion someone chooses to practice is fine with them. They are unbothered by thinking about anything. Indeed, because they are certain to punish those who forcibly convert people to the religion of Jesus, in most places the people began helping them.

The kings Shah Jahan and Jahangir very much liked the Dutch. The English first established the East India Trading Company in the region of Madras. The city of Calcutta was newly built by Job Charnock, two thousand two hundred thirty-seven years after the Teacher passed away [1693; in fact, 1690], about two hundred fifty years before now. A young Muslim king named Daulah was enthroned in Bengal about sixty years later. He did not think about anything other than drinking and fornicating. Due to a minor disagreement, he plundered the factories of the foreigners who lived there. He captured all the women and children who were there. In each place, he gathered one hundred forty-six people and forced them into a dungeon less than three arm spans [across], where they remained for an entire day in the terrible heat of the summer. At sunrise all but a few had suffocated and died. Hearing about that, the English army captain named Clive arrived with an army of three thousand and waged a battle on the banks of the Bhāgīrathī River, defeating the Indian side. They caught the fleeing Daulah and beheaded him. After the death of that king, they installed the Muslim king Mir Jafar. However, all the authority of the new king, apart from his title, was taken away by the foreigners. Every year they had to gather 264,000 gold coins. Then, from that point on, when the Hindu and Muslim kings, such as the kings of Mahārāṣṭra and Malayalam, fought with each other, the foreigners would ally themselves on the side of whatever income would be greater [for them] in the future. In each region they acquired, they would establish a nominal ruler. Their extraordinary desire, arrogance, and so forth remained utterly unaffected. In fact, they held authority over all the income of the entire region.

At the time of Paṇchen Lobzang Yeshé [1738–1780], a messenger of the foreigners named Bogle arrived in Tsang from Bhutan and stayed for a long time. He received great gifts from the supreme Paṇchen. It seems that there is an extensive account of how he met this Paṇchen. Because this Paṇchen's mother was a close relative of the king of Ladakh, the Paṇchen knew the Indian language very well and took great delight in Indian culture. At that time, at Shigatsé around one hundred sādhus and thirty Muslim priests were paid salaries from his monastic household and permanently resided there. It is said that he would come out on the balcony of his private quarters and converse with them each day. Two or three of the *sādhus* were even lay officials [in the Paṇchen's establishment]. The foreigners, in order to please the Tibetans, erected a Buddhist temple on the banks of the Ganges River and provided land, which remains like a mission to this day. In order to cause a permanent rift between the Chinese and the Tibetans, the foreigners wrote a history about this Paṇchen that strongly denigrated the Qianlong emperor, but I shall not go into this here.

Because it is extremely difficult for a single kingdom to be ruled by two kings, finally, during the reign of the English queen Victoria, she was proclaimed the empress of India. It has been eighty-one years up to this present Rabbit Year [1939] that the entire authority was held by the foreigners. She reigned for a period of sixty years. Some credulous Tibetans say things like this [Victoria] is an emanation of Tārā. I think that it would be amazing if she was even familiar with the name of Tārā. Then, the throne was held by her son Edward VII for only ten years, and then there was George V. He even came to India once and was crowned the emperor in the capital of Delhi. He died during the spring of this past Rat Year [1936]. Now there is a new king called George VI in their capital, and it appears that this is a period when his land is suffering from a great war. A governor was sent to India as a viceroy, and they made it the custom for each to remain for five or six years.

They introduced the new aspects of modern times, such as railroads, schools, and factories. Their law is only good for the educated and for wealthy families. If one has money and education, anything is permitted. As for the lowly, their small livelihoods that provide the necessities for life are sucked like blood from all their orifices. Such a bountiful land as India today appears to be filled with poor people who resemble hungry ghosts.

During the time of Governor Bentinck [governor-general from 1828 to 1835], because they [the British] forcibly prohibited the religious practice of wives being burned with the corpse of their husband, they ruled with great kindness. It is said that before, in Bengal alone, each year almost seven hundred women were killed [in that way]. As for the numbers in the rest of India, there is no need to say anything. However, [Hindus] say that in the end it was the women who were harmed because their great path, going to heaven like a soaring arrow, was blocked. This cannot be true.

Unalterable and unchanging,
The mistaken crowd is diamond-hard.
Who can possibly argue
With iron-faced fools?

One amazing thing is that, even during this recent period when the foreigners' traditions were becoming established in India, there emerged a new religion. Its teacher, named Ramakrishna, was born in the two thousand three hundred eightieth year after the Buddha's passing [1836] in a place called Kamala in Bengal, as the son of a mother named Candradevī. Since his youth he saw saṃsāra as without essence. When he was twenty-four years old, in accordance with local custom, he married a five-year-old girl named Śāntadevī. Later she also became a renunciant, becoming a wondrous yoginī. Having respected all women as if they were his mother since his youth, Ramakrishna took Mahākālī as his tutelary deity. He went to the temple of Kālī known as Dakṣiṇeśvar, near Calcutta, and lived there his entire life in the manner of a true renunciant. He had no possessions, not even a sack of sesame seeds. He went before the image of Kālī and sat every day, crying out, "Mother! Why don't you appear to me?" Eventually, he thought, "If I don't see her face, I will kill myself." And just as he held a sword to his heart, he saw Kālī's body filling the sky. From then on there arose in him a great uncontrived compassion for all beings. Having been cared for by a yoginī name Bhairavīsūryā [Bhairavī Brāhmaṇī], he trained without exception in the sixty-four tantras of secret mantra. That woman became his first master. Then he heard instructions on Vedānta from a Brahmin called Totāpurī and experienced direct realization of the truth of Brahman. Once, when he heard a Buddhist tantra from an ascetic woman, he had a vision of the Buddha, who dissolved into him. When studying the Koran from a Muslim known as a Sufi, he actually saw Allah, who dissolved into his body. In general, he saw everything in a manner of bliss alone; a hymn composed by a disciple says, "Each and every man he saw as Nārāyaṇa; / Each and every woman he saw as Pārvatī."

Even in the way that Ramakrishna led students, with respect to the six-branched yoga that is difficult to achieve and the wisdom [ellipsis in text]. It occurred to his mind that at first glance all these religions seem to be in disagreement with each other; however, just as all rivers flow into the ocean or just as one enters a great city by a hundred [different] roads, so the final place where they all converge is one. The Brahmins know it as Brahman, the Muslims as Allah, and the Buddhists as the Buddha. The profound realization arose in him that "this object of refuge—known to the Brahmins as Brahman, to the Muslims as Allah, and to the Buddhists as the Buddha—is, in reality, the great expanse called the self, which pervades the inanimate and animate world; apart from this, nothing else exists." He taught this earnestly to others.

It was natural that the majority of people were pleased by this teaching; before long, countless followers gathered and [his community] evolved into a great separate religious order. Within a short time it pervaded the entire land of India. Even in the lands on the other side of the ocean like America, they have built monasteries of this tradition. All the principal disciples, numbering more than ten, such as Vivekananda and Abhedananda, became very famous throughout the land. Of all the students who personally knew that guru, Abhedananda was the latest. He died on the seventh day of the ninth month of this Rabbit Year [1939]. His students wear saffron robes and yellow hats and care for the sick and the orphans, and they earnestly seek to stop sectarianism among the different religions. They revere all—the Buddha, Rāma, Allah, and so on. Because they do not offend any of the religions, today is a period in which their teachings are flourishing like the lambs of a rich man. In general, when there are many scholars upholding different religious traditions, they regard each other as enemies, even on subtle philosophical points. Once these scholars are no more, and after their subtle and refined reasoning has disappeared, all boundaries will become mixed into a single taste, giving rise to something that is easy for anyone to follow. This seems to be an unsurpassed quality of fools.

Another new religious tradition similar to this one arose. Its founder was a Russian woman named Blavatsky [Helena Petrovna Blavatsky, founder of the Theosophical Society]. I think that she was some kind of incredible self-made yoginī. In any case, she was someone who had attained magical powers. When she was a child, she was blessed in a dream by two Tibetan lamas named Mura [Morya] and Gutumé [Khoot Hoomi]. Then she began experiencing a kind of vision, until in the end she actually met them, like one person talking to another. They instructed her in everything, matters both subtle and coarse. When I carefully read her extensive stories about them, sometimes it reminds me of Guhyapati [Vajrapāṇi] who appeared to Lekyi Dorje, and at times I think it resembles the demon king that appeared to the venerable Gö Lotsāwa. As to making an unequivocal judgment about this, I have no idea.

She continually wrote letters to these [Tibetan masters]. It is said that a great many people actually saw their letters of response fall in front of her out of empty space, and some say that sometimes these letters are in *lañca* and Tibetan script written on birch bark. However, I have not seen this myself. In any case, her miracles convinced all the foreigners. Some wondered whether they were magical tricks, but I think it would be a difficult task to deceive the Europeans, citizens of technologically advanced countries who are very familiar with everything. One of her distinguishing features is a large scar under one of her breasts, which no one knows how she got and from which blood sometimes drips when it is uncovered. She would summon things she needed just by looking at them; she could light a lamp or blow it out with thought alone; by looking at another person's body they would freeze; what sounded like the tune of a silver bell constantly rang in empty space.

When she needed to send something like a letter or clothing to another place, she would burn it in a fire in front of her, turning them into ashes, and it would arrive at the very place and could actually be received. Most of the things she needed, she would take out of a tree, water, or thin air, [people say]. Among all those things, people say that what are most amazing are her replication of thoughts, sending of letters, and hearing the responses. When she came to India, the foreigners did not like her and said all these things were just magic. They sent soldiers, but no matter how much they investigated, they could not expose her as a fraud. In any case, that there are today truth seekers in all the Western countries who admire the Buddha, lining up one after another like the stars in the sky, is due primarily to the new system of this woman. Even among the Sinhalese monks, whose minds are narrower than the eye of a needle, today there are many who praise her. [Anagārika] Dharmapāla, the restorer of the holy site of Ṛṣipatana [Sarnath], is also said to have initially become interested in the Buddha through her. Because she expounded her religion in conjunction with the views of modern science, it captivated the minds of all the Westerners. In particular, she not only demonstrated miraculous powers to Europeans who do not believe in supernatural miracles, but she related the transformation of matter through miraculous powers to scientific principles. That mode of explanation seemed to impress everyone. However, if it were explained to us [Tibetans], who are not familiar with the assertions of science, it would only confuse us. To explain something easy to understand, for example, the way in which present consciousness takes rebirth, those who are angry [take birth as] a snake [ellipsis in text].

Now I shall offer a sincere discussion for those honest and far-sighted dharma friends who are members of my religion. The system of the new reasoning "science" is spreading and increasing in all directions. In the great countries, after baseless accusations by so many, both learned and foolish, who say, "It is not true," they all have become exhausted and had to keep silent. In the end, even the Indian Brahmins, who value the defense of their scriptures more than their lives, have had to powerlessly accept it.

These assertions of the new reasoning are not established just through one person arguing with another. For example, a telescope constructed by new machines sees something thousands of miles away as if it were in the palm of one's hand, and similarly, a glass instrument that perceives what is close by makes even the smallest particles appear the size of a mountain; it is like being able to analyze its many parts, actually seeing everything. Thus, apart from closing their eyes, they [the opponents of science] have found no other way to persist. At first, even those who adhered to the Christian religion in the European lands joined forces with the king, casting out the proponents of the new reasoning [science], using whatever means to stop them, imprisoning them, burning them alive, and so forth. In the end, when the light of the sun could not be concealed with their hands, they were forced to place their religion within the new system, even though it did not fit, and had to admit that it was utterly false. As the glorious Dharmakīrti said,

"Those who are mistaken about the truth cannot be changed, no matter how one tries, because their minds are prejudiced."[178] The rejection of reason is a most despicable act.

Even so, when we Tibetans hear the mere mention of the new system, we look wide-eyed and say, "Oh! He is a heretic!" Acting in this way, some, like those Mongolians from the Urga region [i.e., Communists], eventually come to impulsively believe in the new reasoning and lose all faith in the Buddha, becoming non-Buddhists. Thus, whether one either stubbornly says, "No!" to the new reasoning or believes in it and utterly rejects the teaching of Buddhism, both are prejudice; because it is simply recalcitrance, this will not take you far.

No matter what aspect is set forth in this religion taught by our Teacher [the Buddha], whether it be the nature of reality, how to progress on the path, or the good qualities of the fruition, there is absolutely no need to feel embarrassed in the face of the system of science. Furthermore, for any essential point [in Buddhism], science can serve as a foundation. Among the Westerners, many scholars of science have acquired a faith in the Buddha and become Buddhists; some have even become monks.

One of them said, "First, I followed the system of the ancient religion of Jesus. Later, I learned science well and a new understanding was born. Then I thought that all the religions in this world are just assertions rooted in a lie, requiring that one rely only on the letter. One day, I saw a stanza of the *Dhammapada* translated into a European language and thought, 'Oh! The only one who follows the path of reason is the Buddha. Not only did he climb the ladder of science, but having left that [ladder] behind, he traveled even further beyond,' and conviction was born."

These days, the famous monk Trailokajñāna [Nyanatiloka] who lives in Sri Lanka, said that in the future the religion of the Buddha will be the religion of science, that is, a religion of reason, and other religions will be religions of faith. Another Buddhist paṇḍita says, "Having mastered scientific reasoning, I came to especially respect the Buddha. The religion of my teacher works hand in hand with scientific reasoning; when one side tires, the other still is able to leap over [to assist]. If other religions join hands with science, they collapse, either immediately or after a few steps."

For example, the followers of the new reasoning [science] say that in the second moment immediately after any object comes into existence, it ceases or dissolves. These collections of disparate things disperse like lightning. Consequently, the first moment of a pot does not persist to the second moment, and even the perception of a shape does not exist objectively apart from unexpressed habit or the power of mind. Moreover, when examined as above, even colors are merely the ways a wave of the most subtle particles moves. For example, regarding waves of light, there is no difference of color whatsoever to be seen in the particles themselves that are the basis for that color; it is simply that eight hundred wavelengths in the blink of an eye appear as red and four hundred appear as yellow, and so on. Furthermore, they have invented another apparatus for seeing things that move too quickly to be seen, like drops of falling water. Something that lasts for one blink of an eye can be easily viewed over the duration of six blinks of an eye. More than ten years have passed since they made a viewing apparatus that is not obstructed [in seeing] things behind a wall or inside of a body. All of this is certain. They have also made a machine by which what is said in India can be heard in China in the following moment. Because they are able to show in China a film of something that exists in India, all people can be convinced. The final proof that all things run on waves of electricity is seeing it with one's own eyes.

Many great scholars of science made limitless praises of the Buddha, saying that two thousand years ago, when there were no such machines, the Buddha explained that all compounded things disintegrate in each moment and he taught that things do not remain even for a brief instant, and now we have actually seen this using machines. The statement by Dharmakīrti that "continuity and collection do not exist ultimately" can be understood in various ways, but in the end one can put one's finger on the main point. Similarly, because white exists, black can appear to the eye; there is no single truly white thing that can exist separately in the world. Some people say that this was first understood fifty years ago. However, our Nāgārjuna and others understood precisely that in ancient times. They also say that all these external appearances are projections of the mind; they do not appear outside. Whatever we see, it is seeing merely those aspects or reflections that the senses can handle; it is impossible to see the thing nakedly. Because these things are not even mentioned in other [religions] like Christianity, scientific reasoning is considered to be something that did not exist previously. However, for us, these [ideas] are familiar from long ago. Furthermore, the formation of the body's channels and drops that is actually visible is amazingly similar to the explanations in the *yoganiruttara* tantras.

Yet, to be excessively proud and continually assert that even the smallest details of all the explanations in our scriptures are unmistaken seems attractive only temporarily; it is pointless stubbornness. Nothing will come from your being angry with me. If I could remain silent, I could control the peace of my own ears; other than that, there is no benefit. For example, the followers of the new reasoning assert that trees are alive. Furthermore, in ancient times the Jains claimed that trees are sentient because they fold their leaves at night. [The Buddhist] could say, "Well then, it must follow for you that a piece of leather is sentient because if it comes near a fire, it withers." However, there are flowers named sundew and venus [fly-traps] that, as soon as an insect lands on them, grab it, suck its blood, hollow out the body, and discard it on the ground. Every sundew kills more than two hundred insects every day, and the bodies just keep piling up. Similarly, in another continent, there are many trees that suck blood when they catch humans or animals. This is evident to everyone. Since these are easy to understand, I have explained them, but recently a Bengali scholar in India [Jagadish Chandra Bose] invented an electronic machine that actually recognizes the presence of life. If such a flower were brought before us, would we dare contest its existence? Would we say it is the nature of the plant? Even those who assert that insects and so forth are alive must at some point show various proofs for the existence of life. Would we describe the plant as a trifling hell? However, all types of those flowers are just like that. Look at the illustration I have drawn.[179] The Sinhalese scientists who are Buddhists say the Teacher had this in mind when he prohibited [monks from] cutting plants. But that explanation is [only] temporarily convincing.

Only fifty years ago a great debate took place between a Christian and a Buddhist in Sri Lanka. On that occasion a monk called Guṇaratna [in fact, Guṇānanda] annihilated the opponents and admitted many thousands who had converted to Christianity back to Buddhism. Even then, none of the [Sinhalese] could deny the new reasoning like we [Tibetans] do. Whenever very foolish people of the Tibetan race hear talk about science, they say that it is the religion of Christianity. In countries that have no familiarity [with Christianity], even the Christians themselves shamelessly pretend that this is true. What could be more annoying than this?

A great desire arose in me to write a separate book on the advantages of thinking about this new reasoning, but because of the great difficulty involved and because it would disillusion everyone, I decided it would be pointless and set the task aside. Please do not think that I am a dullard, believing immediately in whatever others say. I too am rather sharp-witted. In matters related to the

[Buddha's] teaching, neither have I found disciples to whom I can expound the dharma nor have conditions been suitable for me to establish a monastery; I am not capable of those great deeds. My concern for the dharma is not less than yours. For that reason, do not dismiss my statements with only the wish to attack me. If one does not want the tree trunk of the [Buddha's] teaching and these roots of our Buddhist knowledge to be completely uprooted, one must be farsighted.

Having become an open-minded person who sees what is central and what is marginal, you should strive to ensure the survival of the teaching [Buddhism] so that it remains together with the ways of the new reasoning. Otherwise, if, fearing complaints by others, one is simply intransigent, then one may temporarily gain great profit and many friends. As it says on the pillar of Emperor Xuande at Drotsang, "Like the light rays of the sun and moon in the vastness of space, may the teachings of the Buddha and my reign remain together for tens of thousands of years." Please pray that the two, this modern reasoning of science and the ancient teaching of the Buddha, may abide together for ten thousand years.

When one's happiness is small, one still wants more, and the mind is tormented. Yet, when there is more, there is too much, and [the mind] is tormented because it cannot bear it. This is the nature of all things. When too much water is poured, flowers wilt. When one has a strong itch, it feels good [to scratch] even to the point of cutting the flesh. If that is the extent of one's hopes, in many cases, one can feel happy for an instant and remain in that state for a little while without the mind engaged in any act. However, subject and object cannot remain in such a state of equilibrium for a long time. Although the strings of a bow may stay tight at first, if they are left alone the strings become loose. So for the strings of a bow to remain constantly tight they must be reset again and again whenever the strings become too lax. Similarly, the happiness of mind becomes afflicted by suffering, and one needs to regain the happiness that one had before. Now, feeling satisfied from eating is pleasurable, but for this one needs to have been hungry for a long while. The melody made by a stringed instrument does not last long. There needs to be a stable [basis for joy] that is devoid of strings, and for this, the mind must have no object.

It is said that, while being free from the stains of conceit, Gandhi had an inner courage that could drill even through Mount Meru. However, nothing about his having magical powers, talk that is widespread throughout central Tibet, can be heard in India, especially in Vardhana. He lived by *ahiṃsādharma*, the dharma of relinquishing violence, as the system of political governance. There are some even more famous than Gandhi, such as the one known as Pandit Nehru. They work for the sake of the Indian people without hypocrisy. Below them, there are not a few empty-headed leaders who have found some meaningless title and lead the people into darkness. In the legal systems of the foreign nations, not being in conflict with the aspirations of the general populace is valued, so everyone has genuine freedom to speak out and act on their own views, and no one fears being prosecuted and executed merely for saying that the government's actions are wrong. Thus, they have a great many opportunities to act in whatever way they wish. As a consequence, today, apart from the central government of India, each of the regional governments has been entrusted to Indians. In more than seven regions, a government of the people has already been set up and they maintain authority over the land.

By repeatedly drinking the fabled beer
Made from amazing molasses, the head becomes drunk.
I am weary of always giving away
Pure water, free of the salts of falsity.

Because of the power of our own prejudices, I was not keen to discuss the origins of the Muslims and their histories. However, after the gradual demise of the [Buddha's] teaching, we had no familiarity with what had happened in India [from then] up to the present. In particular, nothing of the history of India of the past seven hundred years seemed to have been heard in Tibet. Therefore, I strongly motivated myself and wrote about it. In any case, the histories and chronologies prepared [by the Muslims] have extremely reliable sources. In contrast, when it comes to the histories of the upholders of the Buddhist teachings, it is as if they have utterly vanished in India. The little that is known seems to have come from Tibet and China. For example, even the fact that [Atiśa] Dīpaṃkara Śrījñāna went to Tibet was heard [of in India] from the Tibetans. Because there are treatises by Śāntarakṣita, his existence is known, but knowledge of him is limited to his name alone. The fact that he went to Tibet was repeated by some Indian merchants [who had heard it] from Tibetans. Furthermore, the various fragmentary accounts of Nāgārjuna and others that exist do not differ, even in the slightest, from those known to us from earlier times. If they were to be written down, it would just be repetition, so I have left those aside. Therefore Buddhism, while living in the midst of its Hindu adversaries, also came to be destroyed by the Turks in every possible way. Even things concerning [Buddhist] tantra are, for the most part, mixed with Hindu systems. As for others, since they were practiced in extreme secrecy, it is difficult to actually discern what their specific religious affiliations and lineages were. Even today some great adepts are alive and, although they may be individuals who have attained wondrous special powers, if even their place of birth remains unknown, what need is there to speak of what their religious tradition might be and so forth?

Atiśa is said to have remarked, "When I came [to Tibet], in eastern India every day another adept would emerge." Not only were the practices of Buddhist tantra very widespread throughout Bengal and Kāmarūpa [Assam] in the past, even today there exist many [who engage in such practices]. One can see those who actually pour the five nectars into the five skulls and partake of them and those who walk around naked adorned with bones and so on. Yet who can determine whether they have realization or are all simply crazy? Similarly, I have heard that in Oḍiviśa [Orissa] among ordinary householders there are Buddhist māntrikas with practices like those of our system, such as the four empowerments. There are also māntrikas who practice the sexual path with *caṇḍālī* [low-caste] women in places such as central India; whether these are Buddhists or not, I do not know. Similarly, I have heard very clearly about those known as the Kāpālikas who celebrate ritual feasts[180] at midnight; the women pile their clothes in the center and dance naked. Then the yogis pick up one of the clothes and engage in sex with whomever it belonged to, without making any distinction about whether or not she is an appropriate sexual partner. Many people believe they are Buddhist māntrikas. It is said that they take Mahābhairava, the "great terrifier," as their tutelary deity, but I do not know whether this is Śiva or our own Vajrabhairava. There is even a story about how inside the wall of the Viṣṇu Sun temple in Kaliṅga there remains hidden a great stone image of the Buddha touching the earth; some people claim to have seen it. There are those who say that, in general, Jagannātha, the "protector of transmigrators," is, in fact, an epithet for the Buddha.

The teacher of the foremost Tāranātha, Buddhaguptanātha, described how he went to the region of Haribhaṅga in this very same area and met with teachers and adepts. Perhaps they were of the same [practice] lineage. In any case, it is not clear that there is a large group of Buddhists in Oḍiviśa up to the present time. There do not appear to be any [left today], as if Buddhism is hidden. They are known as the Mahimādharmin, the "followers of the religious tradition of supreme greatness." They revere the mahāsiddha Gorakṣa. The king of Kaliṅga named Mukundadeva, who appears in some of our historical works, was considered to be a patron of this religious tradition. It is said that all the people who live around the forest in the region of Mayurbhanj, "peacock land," adhere to this religion, and there seem to be smaller groups elsewhere as well. In terms of their outer appearance, they praise the twelve learned qualities,[181] such as eating at only one spot,[182] the names of which no longer exist today in other regions of India. They go for refuge to the Buddha and respect him just as we do. Stating that at the end of the Kaliyuga it is more profound for the followers of the Buddha to rely on disguise, they also practice the vows of the Vaiṣṇavites. This appears to be a consequence of their oppression by Hindu kings in the past. They have the two categories of [practitioners]—laypeople and renunciants—but not those of novices and fully ordained monks. They do not drool [with envy] when they hear about there being actual monastic members in other places. Some of their more prominent texts include the *Secret Songs* (*Chautisa*), the *Śatruñjasaṃhitā*, *Anaṅgisaṃhita*, *Nirguṇamāhātmya*, and so on. There also seem to be many "unwritten teachings" (*alekhadharma*). There appear to be numerous texts such as these.

To say a little more about them here, more than fifty human years ago, the venerable Buddha[guptanātha] himself actually came to the blue-sloped mountain of Oḍiviśa. He cared for Govinda and predicted that he would go to Kapilasa. They say he stayed there for twelve years, after which he disappeared. This much I have felt compelled to say. In addition to my disparagement, if you were also to disparage these dharma brothers and sisters, I fear that it would not be good. This is all I shall say [here].

One event that occurred not very long ago [in 1875] is this. Bhimabhoi, whose actual name was Guptadāsa, was born as a low-caste person in the town of Granadihs in this same region. He was born blind but by praying fervently to the Buddha, at the age of twenty-five, his eyes opened. Because he also acquired the ability to perform miracles, most of the common people of the more affluent towns became his disciples. He proclaimed, "There in the temple of Jagannātha is a Buddha image hidden in the form of Viṣṇu; now is the time to reveal it." And he led all of his disciples to it like an army. The king of Puri became fearful and said, "They are coming to burn the Jagannātha and establish a new religion," and called out his troops for battle. When his side was nearing victory, Guptadāsa said, "This is not good; for us to kill many people is contrary to the Buddhadharma. Now, let us be content with those who have already died for the sake of the dharma. It appears that the Buddha himself still wishes to remain in the image of Viṣṇu. Therefore, even if we were to liberate the temple again, it would be pointless." Saying this, he withdrew the army. It is said that the king captured many people and turned them over to the British, who executed them. This master was considered by them to be a very important leader. They say that in the not-too-distant future, at the end of the Kaliyuga, the Buddha himself will once again return to the region of Oḍiviśa Samyavakṛta [?] and they sing numerous prophecies with melancholy tunes.

In particular, in Nepal, for example, it is said that there are unbroken traditions of Guhyasamāja stemming from Phamthing-pa [brothers] and so on of the past, as well as of Vajrayoginī and Cakrasaṃvara and so forth from the tradition of Maitrīpa. It appears that from time to time a couple of hundred people will gather for an initiation, ritual feasts, and so forth. One also sees some Nepalese who wrap a cloth around their knobby knees who are called *vajrācāryas*. In one sense, even when Lang Darma caused the dharma to disappear in Tibet, the laypeople ensured that the secret mantra did not decline and survived. In the same manner, in India as well, there has been no cause for the complete destruction of the secret mantra teachings. Therefore it is certain that there is still the practice, inconspicuously, of the majority of the instructions of the earlier tantras. In the commentary on the *dohās* by Advayavajra, for example, he explains that in the east there are tīrthika Salitisas [?] whose system is similar to that of a Buddhist school. Furthermore, there are siddhas and mahāsiddhas. Similarly, the followers of the songs of Kaliṅga of the tīrthika mahāsiddha Mahādevadāsa use a religious vocabulary similar to that of the Buddhists, with such phrases as "empty person," "empty form," "empty body," and so forth. Because it is said that there are many tīrthikas who were followers of Dhombipa, it is possible that many of them are from that lineage. Also, in one of the recollections of his past lives, the venerable Tāranātha says there were many who held the lineage of Omkaranātha, the disciple of Gorakṣa, combining his tradition with that of the tīrthikas. This appears to be the great sect known as the Nāthas that still exists in central India. They wear large earrings made of glass and rhinoceros hide and sing the dohā of that mahāsiddha, singing such lines as, "Gorakṣa is the protector of cows. He protects the cowherds too." In Nirhida [?] there is an excellent temple without an image that is said to be the remnants of the abode of that mahāsiddha. The city is known as Gorakṣapur [Gorakhpur]. Among the lineage of his students, a mixture of Buddhists and non-Buddhists, was Mahendranātha, reputed even to be an emanation of Avalokiteśvara. They expound their view and meditation using such Buddhist vocabulary as "empty" (*śūnya*), "innate" (*sahaja*), "natural cloth" (*ekanija*), and "single taste" (*samarasa*). In the tīrthika tantras, there are many texts such as the *Kṛṣṇalīlā*, the *Purāṇas*, the *Tantrābhidhāna*, the *Royal Tantra of Daṇḍābhidhāna* [?], the *Mahānirvāṇa Tantra*, *Brahmasaṃhitā*, and the *Kulacūḍamāṇi Tantra*. In eastern Bengal there is still a little Buddhist region called

Caityagrāma, "town of the stūpas"; what is left today is known as Chittagong. It is said that in the forest known as Sunajhari, on the slope of the mountain there, there are siddhas as well.

Once, I was wandering one evening in the forest when I saw a naked woman with many different pieces of bone tied to her body. Following her, I arrived at a cave. Hiding myself, as I looked I saw male and female yogis sitting face to face and engaged in meditation, touching each other's thighs, kissing, embracing each other, and performing many rites. People say that sometimes they laugh so loud, "Ha ha," that you think the rocks in the cave might crack. They are said to be yogis who practice the path of desire. People say that they were Buddhists because in that region there actually was an unbroken tradition of instruction in Buddhist tantra. I saw this quite recently, actually this very year. Even among the monks of Chittagong, there are those who say that the disappearance of the Vajrayāna was not that long ago. More than fifty years earlier, some monks wore the red hat of a paṇḍita and, preparing a maṇḍala, would perform a fire sacrifice. There are people who now are old who used to hear about these things from some older people. There were many rites for the dead and the sick, such as ablution empowerments. Then, due to its proximity to Burma, the monks went there and received ordination and listened to the Sthavira Piṭaka. On their return, they said, "Our dharma is not pure," and it appears that they converted everyone to the śrāvaka tradition. The monk known as Buddhadāha, who died in the current Rabbit Year [1939], was famed for his great learning in tantra; as to whether he engaged in the practices or believed in them, I do not know.

The transmissions of texts and empowerments that survived in this region until later times include some cycles of teachings of Vajrayoginī and that of Saṃvara, and of Avalokiteśvara according to the mahāyoga system. The religious sect known as Sāhajiya is said to be followers of the mahāsiddhas Kṛṣṇācārya and Luipa. In some regions of Rāḍhā, there is the custom of worshipping at the beginning of the fourth month, during which there is the custom of offering a goat to Luipa. Some of the songs written by these two masters in Sanskrit and Bengali, as well as some of their instructions, survive to this day. Sāhajiya refers to those whose primary practices are the path of the *avadhūti* [central channel], the path of *caṇḍālī*, and the path of *ḍombī*. For those who have attained siddhis, such terms as "one who has found *ḍaumim* [?]" are used. There is also a sect called the Dharmayogi; it is said to be Buddhists who became Hindus. Those who spread secret mantra widely in Bengal in the later period are said to have been Brahmānanda, Tripurānanda, Pūrṇānanda, and Kṛṣṇānanda. People say that a little more than three hundred years have passed since they died.

If one were to meet a Hindu who belongs to the Advaita school these days, it is true that someone like me would be reluctant to differentiate between the non-Buddhist and Buddhist views. I wonder how my [fellow Tibetan] scholars would respond. Would they say, "This is not your view, it is a copy of ours." Or would they say, "Well then, because you are satisfied with just that, you should meditate on it." Or, "That is ours; it is not appropriate for you to meditate on it." Or would they say, "Those who meditate on the mere elimination of true existence, which is a nonaffirming negation, are Buddhist while meditation on the absence of conceptual elaboration is common to both Buddhists and non-Buddhists"? This would be consonant with the position of Jamyang Gawai Lodrö (1429–1503). Or just as the latter-day Tibetans insist that, in the case of the Mahāyāna and Hīnayāna in general and between sūtra and tantra in particular, there is no superiority and inferiority or difference with regard to the view [of no self], I wonder if they might not say that Buddhists and non-Buddhists are not differentiated in terms of their view but are differentiated in terms of their conduct. In this way, I would like to tease you.

Nevertheless, if you wish to serve an Indian master whom you can call "My lama, the great paṇḍita," even now, if you go to either eastern Bengal or Oḍiviśa, I guarantee that you will meet with one. However, due to the power of the great doubts stirred up by those present-day people who are cunning and deceitful, first there will be no small measure of tests for the student. Thus, unless you have one-fourth of the perseverance of the venerable Marpa, you will surely not receive the teaching. Then, on returning to Tibet, because it is certain that you will be slandered by being called a tīrthika, you will need one-fourth of the power of the great lama Ra Lotsāwa. If this seems too fraught with hardship, it is better to abandon it. But if your realizations are ready to burst out simply by eating soup, then if you go to what today have been identified without the slightest doubt to be one of the twenty-four places, such as Kaliṅga, Kāmarūpa, Oḍḍiyāna, Kulutā, or Sindhu, many field-born and mantra-born yoginīs will surely be there. Certainly, there would be something like soup that you can drink; nevertheless, other than the soup just going into your belly, it would be difficult for it to go into your mind. Here I say:

Walking with weary feet to the plains of the sandy south,
Traversing the boundary of a land surrounded by the pit of dark seas,
Pulling the thread of my life—precious and cherished—across a sword's sharp blade,
Consuming long years and months of hardship, I have somehow finished this book.

Although there is no one to beseech me
With mandates from on high or maṇḍalas of gold,
I have taken on the burden of hardship alone and written this,
Concerned that the treasury of knowledge will be lost.

Though terrified by the orange eye of envy
In the burning flame of those bloodthirsty for power,
Accustomed to the habit of gathering what I have learned,
My mind is attached to reasonable talk.

If it somehow enters the door of a wise person, intent on
learning,
Then the fruit of my labor will have been achieved.
For the smiles of the stupid and the approval of the rich,
I have never yearned even in my dreams.

When this ink-stained body's need for food and drink is finished,
When this collection of bones—its thread of hope for gain and
honor snapped—is scattered,
Then may the forms of these letters, a pile of much learning
amassed through hardship,
Reveal the path of vast benefit in the presence of my unseen
friends.

Herein is the formation of the land of India in general; how names are given to [countries]; the mountains of the north and some critical analysis concerning them; what the famous regions of the past were like; concerning men, women, food, drink, and possessions; identification of various species of trees and fruits and how to recognize them; examples of writings in Indian scripts in various regions from ancient times to the present, concerning the elimination of doubts about Indian texts, the method of reading, types of script, et cetera; a brief history from the Buddha to the present, concerning the pivotal events; concerning Sri Lanka; concerning the conditions and customs of Tibetans in ancient times; a very brief religious history of Burma and Siam. All together, this is a medium-sized book of a little more than four hundred pages. I have

[now] completed the actual book. With minor necessary modifications through omissions and additions, I shall send the revised version to you [an unidentified Nyingma lama] immediately. In the course of telling true stories, there are many instances where I take the opposite position of some excellent and undisputed scholars.

Therefore, it is very important to read this with an open mind. In any case, if you were to be a supporter of this book, there is no greater kindness you can grant me. The mind of a discerning master like you is not swayed by those who carry thorny sticks in their hands to protect ideas born of seeing only [what lies in] their own palms. So I earnestly beseech you to look at this [work] before [others do]. If you explain something difficult with ease to Tibetans, you lose the luster of a scholar. If, in contrast, you utter whatever incredible lies you are capable of and, at the same time, make a path through a deep dark cave so that the lies of other people can also come out, you are granted the title of scholar. I would love to be a learned scholar, but this time, I would rather be honest. In any case, I am entrusting this little book of mine to you, beseeching your kindness to be its lord of refuge in any way you can so that it does not die as soon as it is born. It is very important that any spelling errors be corrected as much as possible, that the words be corrected without damaging the meaning, and the like. I beseech you from my heart not to forget this.

All humans born in this world are given, through their past karma, a task that is suited for them. This [book] seems to be the humble task entrusted to me. Thus, wandering through the realms, I have expended my human life on learning. Its fruit has taken the form of a book. Apart from that, I think that it would be difficult for me to either hope or succeed in benefiting others in this life through such things as teaching the dharma. On your side, the tradition of the Buddhist teachings of the earlier translation remains [fragile] like butter on hot sand. Still, in some way, my heart feels warmed knowing that someone like you remains its glorious protector. Today I have completed the conclusion and am sending it to you with this. If any part of my work is lost, please attach this conclusion to whatever part you may receive so that my hardships can be brought to light. I ask that whatever spelling errors there might be in the body of the text be corrected. Since there is no contradiction in changing the words as long as the meaning remains unaffected, please bring it into accord with the proper [literary] standard. This was sent by Gendun Chopel while he was staying at Aluvihāra in Sri Lanka.

CHAPTER 15

Tibet's Glorious Past, from the *White Annals*

When Gendun Chopel returned to Tibet in 1945, he was working on the White Annals, *a political history of Tibet. He began work on the project in India, where he saw reproductions of ancient documents from the Tibetan monarchy that had been discovered in the Library Cave at Dunhuang in 1908. At least one of his motivations for returning to Tibet was to study the many ancient inscriptions found on pillars and steles across Tibet for the information they could provide about early Tibetan history. He was returning to Lhasa from a day of such research on the night of his arrest. He entrusted the unfinished manuscript to his student Horkhang and continued to provide instructions for its publication while he was in prison. Although he was instructed by the Tibetan government to continue work on the project after his release, he did not do so and the work was published unfinished. The opening poem and first paragraphs are translated here, providing ample proof of Gendun Chopel's patriotism.*

From the mouth of the Guide, flow waves of joy
Into the ocean of milk, good fortune of migrators.
Protect us with the light of your smile
Of forty perfect teeth, bright as the moon.

The descendants of the gods of clear light, endowed with the
light of the lineage's great pearl,
Ascending to the snowy midst of snowy mountains, dazzling
realm of the four domains,
Your happy subjects, protected by your word, followed you to a
happy land.
May the three ancestral kings, patriarchs of the realm, prevail,
endowed with the magic power of all knowledge.

How the one god Padmapāṇi, in the form of the lord of humans,
The great god, turned the wheel of the two systems;
How Songtsen Gampo, outshining the three worlds,
Brought the kingdoms in the four directions under his rule.

Compiling the available ancient writings
Setting forth authentic accounts and clear chronologies,
I have mustered a small degree of courage
To measure the breadth and might of the first Tibetan realm.

It is said that Tibet's army of red-faced demons,
Pledging their lives with growing courage
To the command of the wrathful Hayagrīva,
Once conquered two-thirds of the earth's circle.

Born of the lineage of the gods of the Heaven of Clear Light, those kings who manifested themselves as emperors ruling all of the vast earth with the golden wheel of the dual system of method and wisdom were in reality the noble and supreme protectors of the three lineages who simply came in the form of humans. Not only that, to the sight of ordinary beings, in terms of their territory, their dominion, and their military might, they were not inferior to the

Indian king Śrīharṣa, the Tang emperor Taizong, and the Persian king Yazdegerd.

In ancient times, there is no doubt that we had very extensive royal chronicles, accounts of what those kings and ministers did each day and month. However, beginning from the uprising against King Lang Darma, the seat of the royal family moved to many places and there was fear of the armies of upper and lower Mongolia two or three times. By the time of the various gains and losses in Kham, the royal chronicles had completely disappeared. In later times, it came to be that apart from histories of whatever deeds were done related to religion, nothing was left of everything else.

Therefore, there were many actual events of great importance: the Tibetan army arriving in India, capturing Kānyakubja, the capital of Magadha, and placing King Arjuna in prison, making about one hundred and eighty large and small towns vassals of Tibet; at a time in the past, Nepal remaining under Tibetan control for a little more than a generation; a large Tibetan army going beyond Wutaishan in China, deposing the emperor himself; and such places as Drugu, Khotan, and Yunnan also remaining under Tibet for more than a century. The parts of the royal chronicles that are able to touch on the truth have been forgotten. They are widely known among foreign historians, but for the most part the people of our country have come to the point where they have no knowledge of them.

The story of the invasion of India appears in detail in the *Testament of Ba*,[183] and [the account of] how the [Chinese] emperor fled from his capital is visible on the south face of the stone pillar at Zhol [at the base of the Potala]; this will be set forth below. Therefore, to that end I will discuss here the stories of the various deeds of those royal fathers and sons related to worldly governance; this will primarily describe how they went about increasing the area of their domains and kingdoms through fierce battle. Therefore, since they are widely known, I will not weary [the reader], giving just a small amount of the biographies of the extraordinary true natures of the royal fathers and mothers and how they made their mark on the excellent dharma.

Comparing the domains made by divine monarchs
As well as dates in royal chronicles,
This bride, based on three methods of calculation,
Is insistently offered to impartial scholars' sons.[184]

CHAPTER 16

On the Nature of Reality, from *Adornment for Nāgārjuna's Thought*

Gendun Chopel's most controversial work is his posthumously published Adornment for Nāgārjuna's Thought, *a work on Madhyamaka philosophy that is generally extolled by Nyingmas and Kagyus and excoriated by Geluks. Those who wish to praise Gendun Chopel but condemn this work claim that he did not write it, that it is instead the work of his Nyingma disciple Dawa Sangpo. However, there is clear evidence that it represents Gendun Chopel's thought.*

Many of the positions set forth in the text, especially on the question the nature of the ultimate and the conventional, resonate with those of earlier authors, including the renowned Sakya scholar Gorampa (1429–1489). However, Gendun Chopel presents his positions in his own inimitable way, writing in a conversational style, often inflected with irony. His knowledge of the world beyond Tibetan letters is also evident. The first text he mentions is the Koran; among the Buddhist authors that he cites is Buddhaghoṣa. Still, he clearly sees his work as participating in, rather than departing from, the venerable tradition of Tibetan explorations of emptiness.

Adornment *is divided into two parts. According to his friend and student Lachung Apo, Gendun Chopel wrote the first part in his own hand and gave it to him to cheer him up when he was sick. The second part is likely a compilation of notes made by Dawa Sangpo after Gendun Chopel's release from prison. The first part, ending with a long poem with the famous refrain "I am uncomfortable about positing conventional validity," is included here.*[185]

To the sharp weapons of the demons, you offered delicate flowers in return.
When the enraged Devadatta pushed down a boulder [to kill you], you practiced silence.
Son of the Śākyas, incapable of casting even an angry glance at your enemy,
What intelligent person would honor you as a friend for protection from the great enemy, fearful saṃsāra?

You are the eye of the world who displayed precise subtlety unerringly
Through your aspiration to the path of liberation, the source of the ambrosia of excellent virtue and soothing peace.
The assembled philosophers ever respect you without waxing or waning,
Saying, "This is the lord of the dharma, the supreme lion of speakers."

From the maṇḍala of the sun of your wisdom in the sky of Samantabhadra,
In the lotus garden of my heart of meager knowledge, innate or acquired,
[Grows] the glory of the smiling stamen of eloquent explanation, surrounded a thousandfold by the rays of reasoning.
May the bees of scholars of the three realms enjoy the sweet honey of the true transmission.

All of our decisions about what is and is not are just decisions made in accordance with how it appears to our minds; they have no other basis whatsoever. Therefore, when we ask, "Does it exist or not?" and the other person answers, "It exists," in fact we are asking, "Does this appear to your mind to exist or not exist?" and the answer is simply, "It appears to my mind to exist." In the same way, everything that one asks about—better or worse, good or bad, beautiful or ugly—is in fact merely asked about for the sake of understanding how the other person thinks. That the other person makes a decision and answers is in fact just a decision made in accordance with how it appears to his or her own mind; there is no other reason whatsoever. Therefore, as long as the ideas of two people are in disagreement with each other, they will argue. When they agree, the very thing that they agree upon will be placed in the class of what is, what exists, what can be known, and what is valid, and so on. Thus, the more people there are who agree, the more the point they agree upon becomes of great significance and importance. Contrary views are taken to be wrong views, mistaken perceptions, and so on.

Regarding the mode of agreement furthermore, occasionally agreement is based just on some scripture. For example, two Muslims argued about whether or not it is permissible to eat camel meat. Finally, when they saw that the Koran grants permission to eat camel meat, they agreed that it is permissible to eat it. Occasionally, the agreement of two people is based on the reasoning of the two disputants. For example, if there is an argument about whether or not there is a fire beyond a mountain pass, they agree when they see smoke at the summit of the pass. Whatever it may be, if they both see it directly, they agree without argument. This is the case for all common beings. Now someone may wonder whether it is infallible to accept a presentation of what can be known that is based on some universal agreement. It is not. For example, if one arrives in a place in which the eyes of all of the people in the land are afflicted by bile disease, all the people of that land will agree that a white conch is yellow, that there is no white. However, one cannot hold that a white conch is yellow due merely to that. Thus, the existence of that object is not decided by the mere agreement of some hundred people. It is not decided by the agreement of a thousand or ten thousand. It is not decided if all humans agree. It is not decided even by the agreement of all the common beings of the three realms. Therefore, all of our decisions about what exists and does not exist, what is and is not, are merely decisions in accordance with how it appears to our respective minds. When many hundreds of thousands of common beings to whose minds [things] appear similarly gather together, then the thing that they decide upon becomes firmly grounded and unchangeable, and those who speak in disagreement are proclaimed to be denigrators, nihilists, and so on.

Therefore, our statements about what does and does not exist are in fact classifications of what appears before our mind. Our statements that something does not exist or is impossible are classifications of what cannot appear before our mind. The reality (*dharmatā*) that is neither existent nor nonexistent does not belong to the former class, it belongs to the latter.

An amazing example of a majority in agreement dismissing the minority as false is set forth by the master Candrakīrti. Āryadeva's *Four Hundred* (*Catuḥśataka*) says, "Therefore, why is it incorrect to say that the whole world is insane?" The commentary on that [by Candrakīrti] says, "Once, in a country, there was an astrologer who went before the king and said, 'Seven days from now a rain will fall. All those whose mouths the water enters will go insane.' When the king heard that he carefully covered the mouth of his well of drinking water and none of the rain fell into it. His subjects were unable to do the same and so the water went into all of their mouths and they all went insane. The king was the only one whose mind remained normal. In that country the way of thinking and the way of speaking of all the people did not agree with the way of thinking and the way of speaking of the king. Therefore, they all said, 'The king is insane.' In the end, not knowing what else to do, the king drank the water, whereby he came to agree with everyone else."

Thus, due to the single great insanity from our having continually drunk the crazing waters of ignorance from time immemorial, there is no confidence whatsoever in our decisions concerning what exists and does not exist, what is and is not. Even though a hundred, a thousand, ten thousand, or a hundred thousand of such insane people agree, it in no way becomes more credible.

One may think, "We concede that our decisions are unreliable, but when we follow the decisions of the Buddha, we are infallible." Then who decided that the Buddha is infallible? If you say, "The great scholars and adepts like Nāgārjuna decided that he is infallible." Then who decided that Nāgārjuna is infallible? If you say, "The Foremost Lama [Tsong kha pa] decided it." then who knows that the Foremost Lama is infallible? If you say, "Our kind and peerless lama, the excellent and great so and so decided," then infallibility, which depends upon your excellent lama, is decided by your own mind. In fact, therefore, it is a tiger who vouches for a lion, it is a yak who vouches for a tiger, it is a dog who vouches for a yak, it is a mouse who vouches for a dog, it is an insect who vouches for a mouse. Thus, an insect is made the final voucher for them all. Therefore, when one analyzes in detail the final basis for any decision, apart from coming back to one's own mind, nothing else whatsoever is perceived.

But is it not appropriate to place one's confidence in that very decision which has been made by one's own mind? It is not the case. Sometimes this mind of ours seems mistaken, sometimes it seems correct. It is established by experience that it is always deceptive, like the divination of a bad soothsayer. Who can trust it? Many things that are decided to be in the morning are decided not to be in the evening. Things that are decided to be early in life are decided not to be later in life. Things that one hundred thousand Muslims decide are true are decided to be false by one hundred thousand Buddhists. Each is firmly based in their own scripture and reasoning, which are as immutable as a diamond. Each of them asserts that their teacher is the infallible final refuge.

But then who should decide what is true? Someone may say, "Since the mere agreement of the majority is not sufficient, it must be decided from the point of view of valid knowledge (*pramāṇa*)." Then what sort of thing is this so-called valid knowledge? Is this pillar that one vividly sees with the eyes established by valid knowledge and is the awareness that sees it in such a way a valid consciousness? If it is, how should one decide that this awareness is infallible? Until one decides whether or not the pillar exists, one does not know whether or not this awareness is a valid consciousness. Until one decides whether or not this awareness is a valid consciousness, one does not know whether or not the pillar exists. Therefore, when does one decide?

Someone may think, "The reason the pillar exists is that it can be seen by the eyes, touched by the hands, and can also be seen when looked at by a friend." As was said before, it is decided because the eye and the hand agree and, in addition, the friend agrees. What confidence is there in something like that? If it is possible for the eye to be mistaken, what is the reason it would be impossible for the hand and the friend to be mistaken as well? For two people with bile disease, a yellow conch can be seen with their eyes and touched with their hands, and they both agree that it is yellow. In fact, are they not all in error?

Therefore, having made hundreds of presentations of what exists and does not exist, what is and is not, you go on to make various grandiloquent statements that the person who decides these things is not me, it is the Buddha, it is Nāgārjuna, it is the Great Charioteers, and so on. However, in the final analysis the Buddha, Nāgārjuna, the Great Charioteers, and so on are decided by just this mind of ours, and no scholar asserts that our own mind is unmistaken. Hence, is not the root of everything now rotten?

Therefore, as long as we remain in this land of saṃsāra, it is true that there is no other method than simply making decisions, having placed one's confidence in this mind in which one can have no confidence in any of the decisions that it makes. However, is it not going too far by virtue of merely this to concoct a system of thought for the nature of the final reality (dharmatā) and for each and every one of all the inconceivable and unnameable supramundane qualities and, having given a name to each and every one of them, to then make decisions?

Therefore, regarding these conventional phenomena that have the nature of fictions, it comes down to the fact that there is nothing suitable other than a mere decision by this mind of ours, which is itself a source of fictions. However, those who strive wholeheartedly in search of the ultimate truth must understand at the outset that this fiction-making mind does not take you very far.

In brief, if a final reason for the unmistakenness and infallibility of this mind of ours could be demonstrated, then it would be possible to posit many other unmistaken and infallible things. However, the reason one's mind is unmistaken is nothing other than mere stubbornness and arrogance. Candrakīrti's *Commentary on the Entrance to the Middle Way* (*Madhyamakāvatārabhāṣya*) says, "Saying simply, 'It is true because it is true' does not make it true." In the same way, even if one would exert the greatest stubbornness in saying, "It is unmistaken because it is unmistaken," how could that make it unmistaken?

What is there to say about the mistaken mind of a vulgar fool? The venerable Buddhaghoṣa decided that external objects are truly established, but the master Asaṅga took them to be fictions. And Asaṅga himself decided that the imaginary lacks truth and that the dependent is truly established. The Madhyamaka masters, however, placed it in the category of fictions. Therefore, if there can be no confidence even in the minds of those scholars, in whose mind can there be confidence? Even in the case of someone like us, I would say:

If one analyzes with one's own experience,
One can understand how much our attitudes change
From the time we are children until we are old and decrepit.
How can one have confidence in today's conceptions?

But if there is no confidence in anything at all, what should one do? As stated before, as long as one abides in this world, there is nothing to do other than to remain believing in fictions, placing one's trust in fictions, making various presentations on the basis of fictions.

However, to think that the earth, stones, mountains, and rocks that we see now are still to be seen vividly when we are buddhas is very much in error. As long as consciousness remains in the body of a donkey, one is able to experience the delicious flavor of grass, but when it has left [the body of the donkey], the flavor is also completely lost. The knowledge of the rooster that the night has passed is completely lost when consciousness departs from the rooster's body. In our case as well, if we had some additional sense organs other than these present five, all external objects of knowledge also would increase. If these two eyes were stacked one on top of the other rather than on the right and left, it is certain that the shapes and colors of all external forms would be different. In whatever we decide, we have no means whatsoever other than deciding in dependence on these five sense organs. If it is not seen within these two eyes on the forehead, there is no other method to see forms. It is impossible to hear any sound that does not fit within this small hole of the ear. And so on. Therefore, to decide that all objects of knowledge are included within just this measure, based on these five weak senses, with the mistaken mind summoned to assist, and to remain content, saying that the mode of being which does not appear before our mind is nonexistent and impossible, is the door to all trouble.

That our sensory valid consciousnesses cannot be the criteria was also stated clearly by the Bhagavan himself. As it says in the *King of Meditations* [*Sūtra*]: "The eye, the ear, the nose are not valid; the tongue, the body, the mind are not valid. If these senses were valid, what could the noble path do for anyone?"[186]

Therefore, the ultimate purpose for cultivating the noble path is in order to newly understand what the mind did not perceive and the eyes did not see before. When we carefully examine all of these assumptions that we hold about supramundane qualities, they are merely fabrications from examples taken from the world and, within that, from the human realm alone. For example, due to the fact that we like jewels, the ground, houses, and so on in Akaniṣṭha are made of jewels. Similarly, the auspicious marks of a saṃbhogakāya are in fact things that are pleasing to our human eye.

It is known through detailed analysis that the attire of the saṃbhogakāya and of the gods is the attire of ancient Indian kings. These are not merely our concoctions but are stated in the sūtras. Indeed, they are merely set forth with skillful methods so that the qualities of the buddha level, which in reality cannot appear to our mind, can appear to our mind in order to create admiration and delight within us. For example, if the Buddha had been born in China, it would certainly be the case that the saṃbhogakāya of Akaniṣṭha would have a long shiny beard and would wear a golden dragon robe. Similarly, if he had been born in Tibet, there is no doubt that in Akaniṣṭha there would be fresh butter from wish-granting cows in a golden tea churn five hundred yojanas high, and there would be tea made from the leaves of the wish-granting tree. Therefore, all of this is merely the way that we common beings think. Regarding the actual domains of the Buddha himself, the master Candrakīrti said, "However, this secret of yours cannot be told."[187] It is certain that it is not suitable to be spoken in our presence or that, even though it were spoken, it is something that we could not understand. If one has just a little faith toward the inconceivable secret of the Buddha, then one should have some slight belief in all these deeds by the Buddha of making an aeon equal to an instant and an atom equal to a world.

But if this mind of ours is a valid consciousness, we conclude that an atom is the smallest material form and we conclude that a world is extremely vast. We conclude that the great does not fit inside the small. Therefore, no matter how great the magical powers and abilities of the Buddha may be, how is he able to destroy principles that are established by valid knowledge? If he is able to do so, is the power of the Buddha able to make all phenomena become truly established and capable of making all sentient beings into buddhas? If there is no reason why he cannot, other than because sentient beings are not buddhas and because all phenomena are not truly existent, then why can't they be transformed? If, when we say that an atom and a world do not differ in size, we denigrate the conventional and fall into nihilism, then could there be a sin more heavy than the Buddha's putting that very nihilism into practice when he actually makes them the same size? To decide that in general an atom and a world differ in size, but then to have to make many exceptions, such as saying that the Buddha's doing so is a special case, is in fact proof that the bag of our valid knowledge is leaking in all directions.

If this is understood well, the Buddha's making an atom and a world equal in size is not a case of making the unequal equal by reason of the immense power of the Buddha. Is it not because the mind of the Buddha, which has the nature of nondual wisdom, cannot be bound by this decision based on a conception that sees large and small to be contradictory for our minds? The Buddha sees large and small as of the same taste; large and small are in fact of the same taste. Therefore, it is an act of making what is, is. How could it be a magical display of turning what is not into what is?

To our conceptions, existence and nonexistence, is and is not, large and small, good and bad, and so on are all simply mutually exclusive. Therefore, a world not fitting into an atom is a great feat of magic conjured by this very conception of ours, which we choose to call valid knowledge. Thus, one must understand that we, and not the Buddha, are the real magicians.

In the colophon to the *Entrance to the Middle Way* it says that the master Candrakīrti "reversed attachment to things as being true by milking a picture of a cow..." If this appearance is established by valid knowledge, then because it is impossible for a picture of a cow to have intestines, lungs, udders, and so on, if he could milk some real milk from something like that, Candrakīrti would have greatly denigrated dependent origination. How would that reverse [attachment to] true establishment?

In the *Book of the Kadam*,[188] it says that Atiśa displayed various miracles, such as placing his entire body inside a small *tsha tsha* mold after which he said, "Everything we did today is counted as a contradiction by reason-advocating logicians. But if they count it [as such], let them count. I am ready to roam through India and Tibet, swearing that: 'The mode of being of phenomena is certainly not like that.'"

Therefore, we proclaim with a great roar such things as if something is not nonexistent it must be existent, if it is not existent, it must be nonexistent, that those two are explicitly contradictory and that something that is neither of those two is impossible. Similarly, [we proclaim that] if something is small it must not be large, if something is large it must not be small, and if there is no difference between them, then all categories of dependent origination will be destroyed. Statements like "The view that reality is free from the eight extremes of elaboration is great nihilism" are made because nothing can appear to our mind other than existence and nonexistence and because our mind does not recognize anything other than existence and nonexistence. But how can the inability of something to appear to our mind prove that it is impossible and does not exist?

For example, if you arrived in a region of the Northern Plain where the people had no familiarity with anything sweet other than milk, they would be stubbornly certain that "if something is sweet it must be milk; if it is not milk it is not sweet." To the sight of the people from that region, not being milk and being sweet is an ultimate explicit contradiction, and those who said something [to the contrary] are great nihilists who denigrate the conventional. Similarly, for example, if someone does not know anyone other than Namgyel and Tsering, then, in deciding that there is someone in a house, when he decides that Namgyel is absent, he decides that the person is Tsering. Because of not recognizing people other than those two, he would insist, "If it is not one, it must be the other."

It is true that, in the same way, our mind continually oscillates between existence and nonexistence. There is no method for abiding in something that is other than those two.

However, referring to the middle path as that which is in the center of existence and nonexistence is very clearly set forth by the Buddha himself. For example, in the *Kāśyapa Chapter* there are such statements as, "Kāśyapa, 'existence' is one extreme; 'nonexistence' is the second extreme. That which is in the center of those two is the inexpressible and inconceivable middle path." And it is stated very clearly in the *Pile of Jewels* [*Sūtra*]: "Existence and nonexistence are disputed. Pure and impure are also disputed. Suffering is not pacified by disputes. Being without dispute is the end of suffering." However, when scholars these days hear a scripture that refers to neither existence nor nonexistence, they first seek out the identity of the speaker of the scripture. If the scripture is a statement of an earlier Tibetan scholar, they dismiss it [saying]: "One who says something like that is a nihilistic fool." If the scripture is identified as a statement of the Buddha, Nāgārjuna, and so on, they patch it with words like "The statement 'does not exist' means 'does not truly exist,'" and "'Is not nonexistent' means 'is not conventionally nonexistent,'" so that it fits with their own desires. In fact, the only difference is that if they direct refutations at the Buddha, they fear being labeled evil persons with evil views, [whereas] if they are able to refute earlier Tibetans, they are labeled heroic scholars. Apart from that, there is no difference in the frequency of occurrence of expressions like "does not exist," "does not not exist," "inexpressible," and "free from elaboration" in the sūtras and Nāgārjuna's *Collections of Reasoning* [on the one hand] and the scriptures of the earlier Tibetan scholars [on the other]. Therefore, some refute the statements of the earlier Tibetan scholars that the mode of being is inexpressible and inconceivable, saying that they are fools and nihilists, and some show some slight respect, saying that there are no great errors in the thinking of those earlier Tibetan scholars and adepts—it is just that at the time that they spoke the fine points of someone like the Foremost Lama [Tsong kha pa] had not yet appeared. If that is true, there are no errors in the thinking of the Bhagavan himself, yet when he spoke he simply said such things as, "the perfection of wisdom, inexpressible by words or thoughts" and "When you use 'it is,' you use signs; when you use 'it is not,' you use signs." Those beautiful patches of the system of those of us from Ganden Mountain, such as, "When you use that which is truly established, you use signs," and "When you use what does not exist, you use signs," do not appear. [The Buddha] left them out. Thus, the way that the Buddha himself taught the doctrine is something that lacks fine points.

Therefore, if the earlier Tibetans and the Buddha are to be refuted, refute them equally. If they are to be affirmed, affirm them equally. Please do not be deceitful, turning your tongue in various ways and worrying about whether or not people will criticize you.

Thus, if one takes pains in analyzing the ultimate, one must accept that all our decisions are mere fabrications of the mind, with no basis whatsoever. When one thinks about things like this, a great fear is created, and this is the onset of the arising of fear of the view of emptiness. Otherwise, we leave our ideas of existence and nonexistence, is and is not, purity and filth, good and bad, buddha and sentient being, heaven and hell, and so on just as they are, saying that they are all infallible dependent arisings, and it would not be proper to refute those. If they are refuted, it is decided that one falls to such things as nihilism. Saying that one must refute some so-called true establishment which is not that is just the talk of some scholars who are skilled in dry words.

According to their system, this mind of ours that ordinarily thinks "I" is not the conception of self and therefore is not to be refuted. Therefore, this is how they identify the innate conception of "I": For example, when someone says, "You are a thief," you say, "How am I a thief?" The appearance of a freestanding "I" is the innate conception of "I". That is what they say.

If this ordinary mind that thinks "I" is valid, then the mind thinking "I" that is produced when someone says "You are a thief" would simply be more valid. How could this mean that it becomes the conception of true existence? If it is the conception of true existence, then when someone says [something equally false, such as], "The Buddha is not a refuge," then why is the mind which thinks, "How can he not be a refuge?" not the conception of true existence? Similarly, when someone says, "This is not a pot," then the mind that decides, "If it is not a pot, what else is it? It is a pot," is also a conception of the true existence of the pot. How is it valid? Therefore, according to their system, it seems that weak thoughts are valid, and when that very mind becomes stronger, like a shift in the wind, it turns into a conception of true existence. How strange!

"In order to understand the view, it is very important to identify the object of negation" is as well known in the mouths of everyone as their breath. If this is true, how is it possible to identify true establishment separately before understanding the view? For the Foremost Lama himself said, "Until one has understood emptiness, it is impossible to ever distinguish mere existence from true existence and, similarly, one cannot distinguish non-true existence from mere nonexistence," and, "That is the final reason why there is no commonly appearing subject for Prāsaṅgika and Svātantrika." Thus, how can one rely on that pretense of the identification of the object of negation?

Moreover, some say that when a valid form of awareness is produced that thinks, "A pot exists," a conception of true existence is simultaneously produced which thinks, "The pot exists as truly established," but that it is difficult to identify them separately.

Now, the so-called valid knowledge is the primary cause of attaining buddhahood, and the so-called conception of true existence is the root of all faults. It is very strange that they cannot be identified separately by reason of their being so similar to each other. If one is certain to arrive whenever the other arrives, then when they are refuted, they should be refuted equally. How is it possible to distinguish between them?

The mind that thinks, "It is dawn" is valid. The mind that thinks, "I am tying my belt" is valid. In the same way, if all the thoughts like "I am drinking tea" and "I am eating tsampa" are simply valid, then among all the thoughts that fill a day, there is not even one thing to refute. Thus, when is this object of negation, the so-called conception of true existence, produced? If it is the case that the mind which is the conception of true existence, grown accustomed to from time immemorial, does not occur more than a couple of times a day, then it is most amazing.

Thoughts of whatever you are most accustomed to are produced first. For example, as stated in the treatises on valid knowledge, when you see your father coming, who is also a Brahmin and a teacher, the first thought produced is, "My father is coming." Such thoughts as, "The teacher is coming" or "A Brahmin is coming," do not appear to the mind. Because we have become accustomed from time immemorial to this mind which is the conception of true existence, we must decide that when we see a pot, the mind that is produced first is the conception of the true existence of the pot. Therefore, no matter how much one verbally specifies the object of negation by reasoning, in fact, what is to be negated is that the pot must be negated, the pillar must be negated, existence must be negated, nonexistence must be negated. Leaving the pot aside, how could there be something to negate separately called a "truly established pot"? This approach is not simply that of the scholars of old. It was also clearly understood by scholars and adepts on the Geluk side who had [meditative] experience. There are unpleasant statements, like that of Jangkya Rinpoche: "Leaving this vivid appearance where it is, they search for something protruding to refute." Gungthang Tenpé Dronmé and Paṇchen Losang Chogyen also said the same thing.

Some fear that if pots and pillars are refuted by reasoning, it will create nihilism, the view that nothing exists. This is a pointless worry. How is it possible that the nihilistic view that this pot that he sees in front of him is utterly nonexistent will be produced in an ordinary common being?

Even if such an idea were produced, because he knows explicitly that the pot is something to be seen and something to be touched, the thought is spontaneously produced that "This pot is something that appears to me. However, it does not exist at all in the way that it appears." Such a thought is the Madhyamaka view of the composite of appearance and emptiness, which understands that although things appear, they do not exist in the way that they appear. How is this nihilism?

In brief, when one thinks that a pot is utterly nonexistent and sees it directly with the eyes, the illusion-like awareness is produced automatically. Thus, what danger is there of falling into nihilism? Thus, I would say:

When one decides that it does not exist with one's mind
And sees that it exists with one's eyes,
Even without being taught by the yellow hat abbot,
What can arise other than the awareness of illusion?

For example, if gold, earth and stones, plants, and so on are simultaneously and without differentiation burned in a fire, the flammable things will burn and the nonflammable things will remain. In the same way, even though all appearances are refuted by reasoning without differentiation, the illusory things are what is left. Being left, they are certain to remain. What need is there to separate out the illusion-like dependent arisings right from the very beginning, placing them where harm will not be inflicted upon them by reasoning?

"Without asserting that conventions are validly established, how is it that you do not lack confidence in dependent origination?" In general, this so-called "establishment by valid knowledge" is synonymous with what scholars call "establishment by the reasoning of the three modes," with their great need to construe coarse conventional appearances subtly and minutely. In fact, for the sake of the great need for there to be some distinction among the objects of the artificial ignorance, the logical reasoning of scholars construes [the conventional] with exceeding clarity. In general, apart from the difference of merely adding or not adding through logical reasoning expressions such as "validly established," "trustworthy," "infallible," "undeniable," and so on, there is nothing other than what merely appears through the changing orientations of this conventional consciousness, which occurs instinctively in the minds of all six types of transmigrators. We assert that it is infallible and undeniable that a child says, "Ouch!" when its hand meets fire. To give a reprimand that uses reasons, like the father saying, "Fire is hot. The hand is flesh. Therefore, if it touches the fire, why would it not be hot?" is the system of proving it with the valid knowledge of scripture and reasoning. Therefore, as long as these appearances of earth, stones, mountains, rocks, and so on do not vanish, there is no purpose in appearances such as the three jewels, cause and effect, and dependent origination also vanishing. If the necessary appearances vanish first and the unnecessary appearances remain behind, how could it be appropriate for anyone other than common beings of base nature who lack religion?

When one has arrived at the level which the tantric masters of the past described in their vocabulary as, "Phenomena have ceased, the mind has been transcended," these conventionalities of good, bad, and everything in between—like earth and stones, dependent origination, and the three jewels—completely vanish, and I wonder whether many things—like the union of body and mind, the union of the two truths, the union of good and bad, the union of virtue and sin—will not come in their place. At that time, I think that those billions of parts of the knowledge that sees the multiplicities all become the nature of the single knowledge that sees the mode of being.

In general, for us common beings, there are many beliefs, things that we believe willingly, things we believe unwillingly, and things that we believe with no choice, but their basis is nothing other than merely our own belief in our own perceptions. What is meant by "belief" is the mind being required to engage in a particular object involuntarily through the force of habit.

No one would assert that what appears in a dream is a validly established truth. However, we must believe involuntarily in the appearances and feelings of things like happiness, suffering, and fear that occur in a dream. For example, when dreaming that you are falling from the peak of a great rocky mountain down into an abyss, if you analyze with the reasoning of the three modes, there is no possibility other than death. But you fall into the abyss and then return. Again, with regard to all those appearances that are not proved by reasoning, such as flying in the sky, it is undeniable that a variety of experiences occur, such as fear when you fall into an abyss and joy when you are flying through the sky. In brief, a fish is carefree in water and a human dreads sinking in water. In both cases, the fish and the human must undeniably and involuntarily believe [this about water].

Therefore, regarding the difference in what is asserted for oneself and for others in the unique system of the Prāsaṅgikas, these things that must be asserted involuntarily by common beings who have not turned away from dualistic appearances are assertions for others. The fact that a yogin who understands reality does not assert as his own system even one among all objects in the way that they are perceived and conceived by a common being is the meaning of the Prāsaṅgikas not taking their own position. When one opponent who has assertions debates using scripture and reasoning with an opponent without assertions who abides in a state of meditative equipoise, free from verbalization, whatever answers the latter gives all become mere assertions. Thus, there is no place to fit this view of having no assertions within words, sounds, and, particularly, the reasoning of logicians.

In summary, if one asserts from the depths of the heart that earth exists, it is an assertion of one's own system. If one is compelled to assert, "Earth exists," it is an assertion for others. That the Tathāgata remained under the Bodhi tree for a week without closing his eyes is his own system, which is without assertions. His turning of the wheel of doctrine of the four truths so that this very view [of reality] could be understood is a presentation of assertions for others, which he entered into through the power of compassion. This way of understanding is not limited to the Prāsaṅgikas. It is not different in the other tenet systems that assert a presentation of the provisional and definitive and the two truths. [Dharmakīrti's] *Commentary on Valid Knowledge* says, "Thus, [the buddhas], endowed with equanimity on the meaning of reality, having gazed like elephants, posited external deeds."[189] It seems to be clear in the Indian commentaries that this is how the Bhagavan asserted how external objects exist when he explained the doctrine.

Each human has two ways of thinking, two ways of asserting, two ways of explaining—for oneself and for others. Who would believe in something like all the ways of perception and the ways of explanation of buddhas and sentient beings being wrapped up in one intention and one voice?

If one is frightened merely of being injured in the ordinary debates of today's debating courtyards, then one does not need any other answer [than "I have no assertion"] to whatever consequence that is presented. This mere answer of "I have no assertion, I have no assertion," can turn into a joke.

Logical reasoning of the three modes that takes as its foundation the misconceptions of common beings, when used simply as a method to destroy itself by itself, is good. But when it is used as a tool to damage the view of having no assertion, then there is no method for entering the dharmadhātu. This is very clearly stated by the master Dignāga in his *Compendium on Valid Knowledge* (Pramāṇasamuccaya). So I would say:

Objects of knowledge posited by the mind as existent and
 nonexistent;
Valid forms of knowledge dependent on objects true and false;
Having seen that the source of falsity in one is entrusted to the other,
I am uncomfortable about positing conventional validity.

The presentation of the unexamined, unanalyzed world;
The traditions of tenets that examine and analyze;
Having seen that the foundation of one rests on the other,
I am uncomfortable about positing conventional validity.

Illusions that are mere appearances to the mind;
The mode of being determined to be real;
Having seen that if one is true, the other is false,
I am uncomfortable about positing conventional validity.

The first opponent hides the mountain of his own faults;
The second opponent searches for the faults of the other with
 a needle;
Having seen that they take turns defeating each other,
I am uncomfortable about positing conventional validity.

The nonobservation of what is suitable to appear negates the
 extreme of existence;
The nonobservation of what does not appear abandons the
 extreme of nonexistence;
Having seen that the presentation of one is destroyed by the other,
I am uncomfortable about positing conventional validity.

Because there is no difference in the attachment produced
By the conception of true existence that holds a friend to be real and
By the valid knowledge which understands that friends are helpful,
I am uncomfortable about positing conventional validity.

Having seen no difference in the hatred produced
By the conception of real existence that holds an enemy to be true and
By the valid knowledge which determines that enemies are harmful,
I am uncomfortable about positing conventional validity.

Inferential valid knowledge is produced from direct awareness;
Inference analyzes whether direct perception is true or false;
Because the child is serving as the father's witness,
I am uncomfortable about positing conventional validity.

Analysis by reasoning depends on the founders' systems;
The founders are established [as such] by the power of reasoning;
If I can decide on my own, whom should I follow?
If I cannot decide, on whom can I rely?

Correct reasoning is found in the definitive scriptures;
The provisional and definitive are differentiated by stainless reasoning.
If one understands with reasoning, why search for the definitive meaning?
If one does not understand with reasoning, how does one find the definitive meaning?

Because of this way in which Maitreyanātha was seen as a female dog,
I do not believe in the unanalyzed, innate mind.
Because of this way in which the views and tenets of Madhyamaka and Cittamātra abbots contradict each other,
I do not believe in the minds of analytical scholars.

Vulgar people, having repeatedly followed what is right,
Find the innate conception of true existence; it is the root of all downfall.
Scholars, having repeatedly followed what is right,
Find the artificial conception of true existence; it is worse than that.

In this world in which the noise of debate about
Existence and nonexistence, is and is not, true and false resounds,
Whatever is constantly seen appears as an object of knowledge.
Whatever one has become continually accustomed to appears to be valid.

Whatever most people like appears as the truth;
Whatever most mouths agree on appears as a philosophical tenet.
Inside each person is a different valid form of knowledge,
With an adamantine scripture supporting it.

Beyond each mountain pass is a different religious sect
With thousands of scholars and fools who follow it, saying,
"Just this is true; this will not deceive you."
This self-authorization of one's own truth
Delights a group of similar beings;
When told to a group who does not agree, they are scornful.

Here in the capital of the six types of transmigrators who do not agree,
What is asserted by ten is not asserted by a hundred;
What is seen by humans is not seen by gods.
Therefore, who makes the laws for validating truth and falsity?

If even the mind of an abbot of tenets who has consumed his human life
By training in wisdom can be mistaken,
Then it is mistaken to place confidence
In the false perceptions of the fools of the world as conventionally valid.

All the things that appear to the mind to be useful and good
Are separated out and asserted to be valid.
Therefore, in the ruins of a magical city in an empty plain,
One finds the illusion of a pile of jewels once again.

This reflection of objects of knowledge, inconstant and changing—
By changing the face slightly, it changes,
By changing the mirror slightly, it also changes—
Is certain to vanish completely in the end.

Because analysis comes to this, I wonder whether it does not exist.
Because the hand touches a needle, I wonder whether it exists.
Because it is a direct experience, I wonder whether it happened.
Because perceptions can be mistaken, I wonder whether it did not happen.

Because we seek the root of existence, I wonder whether it does not exist.
Because we see the peak of nonexistence, I wonder whether it exists.
When we plant the seed of truth, we know it to be false.
When we taste the fruit of the false, it seems to be true.

Acknowledgments

I WOULD LIKE TO express my gratitude to a number of friends and colleagues for their assistance in the composition of this book. First, I would like to thank the editor of the series, Kurtis Schaeffer, for inviting me to write it. At Shambhala Publications, I have benefited from the counsel and editorial skills of Nikko Odiseos and Casey Kemp. For assistance in acquiring materials connected to the life of Gendun Chopel, I am grateful to Paul Hackett, Maya Joshi, Luc Schaedler, Vesna Wallace, and especially Isrun Engelhardt. Chapter 3, on Gendun Chopel's time in Sri Lanka, is adapted from my essay, "When Vehicles Collide: A Tibetan in Sri Lanka, 1941," found in Benjamin Bogin and Andrew Quintman, eds., *Himalayan Passages: Tibetan and Newar Studies in Honor of Hubert Decleer* (Wisdom Publications, 2014). The second section of this book contains selections from previously published translations, some translated by me, others by Thupten Jinpa and me. Excerpts from *The Madman's Middle Way: Reflections on Reality of the Tibetan Monk Gendun Chopel*, *In the Forest of Faded Wisdom: 104 Poems by Gendun Chopel*, *Grains of Gold: Tales of a Cosmopolitan Traveler*, and *The Passion Book: A Tibetan Guide to Love and Sex* are reprinted here by special arrangement with the University of Chicago Press; I am grateful to Randy Petilos for his assistance.

Notes

1. *ma yin dgag*.
2. *med dgag*.
3. *Thor bu gnyis pa*.
4. *sngags pa*; "tantric practitioner."
5. *gter ston*.
6. Kirti Rinpoche, *Dge 'dun chos 'phel gyi rab byed zhabs btags ma*, pp. 96–97. For an English translation, see Kirti Rinpoche, *Gendün Chöphel*, p. 50.
7. On Griebenow, see Paul Nietupski, *Labrang*.
8. *tha snyad pa*.
9. Kirti Rinpoche, pp. 95–96. For an English translation, see Kirti Rinpoche, *Gendün Chöphel*, p. 55.
10. On the period of warfare surrounding Labrang, see Nietupski, *Labrang*, pp. 81–93.
11. Gendun Chopel would publish a brief account of his journey (in English), entitled "My Journey from Khumbum to Lhassa" in the July 1940 issue of *The Maha-Bodhi*. There, on page 241, he writes, "So at dawn on the 6th day of the month of the Dragon (March) in the year of the Dragon (1927 A.D.) our caravan left Khumbum, in a cheerful mood, on its long pilgrimage." The third month of the Tibetan calendar would fall around May; the year of the Dragon was 1928, rather than 1927.
12. Gendun Chopel, *In the Forest of Faded Wisdom*, pp. 44–45. The poem is based on the Pabongkha's personal name, Jampa Tenzin Tinley Gyatso, literally "Kindness, Upholder of the Teaching, Deeds, Ocean," terms that appear in order in the four lines of the poem.
13. For a biography of Sankrityayan, see Alaka Atreya Chudal, *A Freethinking Cultural Nationalist*.
14. Rahul Sankrityayan, *Meri Jeevan Yatra*, p. 160.
15. Gendun Chopel, *Grains of Gold*, pp. 31–32.

16. Ibid., pp. 29–57.
17. Ibid., p. 39.
18. Ibid., p. 57.
19. Gendun Chopel, *In the Forest of Faded Wisdom*, p. 117.
20. *Rgya gar gyi gnas chen khag la 'grod pa'i lam yig*. For an edition and fully annotated translation of the text, with a detailed introduction, see Toni Huber, *The Guide to India*.
21. *dag snang*.
22. For an excellent study of India and pilgrimage to India in the Tibetan imagination, see Toni Huber, *The Holy Land Reborn*. An insightful analysis of Gendun Chopel's *Guide to the Sacred Sites of India* appears on pp. 317–35.
23. Ibid., pp. 322–24.
24. Huber, *The Guide to India*, p. 101.
25. Ibid., p. 86; my translation.
26. Gendun Chopel, *Grains of Gold*, p. 111.
27. Huber, *The Guide to India*, pp. 42 and 44; my translation.
28. Ibid., p. 86; my translation.
29. Ibid., p. 104; my translation.
30. *'bras ljongs skad*.
31. Gendun Chopel and Rakra Trathong, *Gsar bsgyur Rā ma yā ṇa'i rtog brjod*.
32. Gendun Chopel translated the second, third, fourth, and twelfth chapters, with the twelfth chapter being published in a bilingual Tibetan-Sanskrit edition in 1941 by the Ramakrishna Vedanta Ashrama in Darjeeling. See *The Gita: Bhakti-Yoga Chap. XII*. I am grateful to Paul Hackett for providing me with one of the few surviving copies of this publication. For a description of how he found it, see Paul Hackett, "Looking for a Lost Gītā," pp. 41–45.
33. *Legs sbyar bang mdzod*.
34. See Gendun Chopel, *In the Forest of Faded Wisdom*, p. 77.
35. See Richard Davis, *The Bhagavad Gita*.
36. See Huber, *The Holy Land Reborn*, p. 323.
37. *dbu can*.
38. *Yul phyogs so so'i gsar 'gyur me long*.
39. This was the *La dwags kyi āg bar*, published by the Moravian missionary, August Hermann Francke, from 1904 to 1907. For a study, with facsimiles of the issues, see Hartmut Walravens, ed., *The First Tibetan Serial*.
40. *Melong*, vol. 8, no. 3–4, p. 3.

41. Gendun Chopel also copied a number of Dunhuang documents related to Tibetan history. They are published in his collected writing as *Dge 'dun chos 'phel gyis bsdu rub gnang ba tun hong yig cha* (*Dunhuang Documents Assembled by Gendun Chopel*). See *'Dzam gling rig pa'i dpa' bo mkhas dbang dge 'dun chos 'phel gyi gsung 'bum*, vol. 1, pp. 243–308.
42. *Deb ther dkar po.*
43. See Paul Hackett, *Theos Bernard, the White Lama*, pp. 135–36. The discussion of Bernard that follows is drawn from Hackett's meticulously researched biography of Theos Bernard.
44. Cited in Ibid., p. 323.
45. For an English translation of his Hindi account, see Rahul Sankrityayan, *My Third Expedition to Tibet*. Another account was published in two parts in *The Maha-Bodhi*. The first, called "On Way to Tibet," appeared in vol. 44, nos. 10 and 11 (October–November 1936): 82–113. The second part was called "On the Way to Tibet" and appeared in vol. 45, no. 1 (January 1937): 141–54.

    Rahul Sankrityayan made a total of four trips to Tibet, contributing scholarly reports on the second, third, and fourth to *The Journal of the Bihar and Orissa Research Society*. The first, describing the expedition during which he first met Gendun Chopel, is Rāhula Sānkṛityāyana, "Sanskrit Palm-leaf MSS. in Tibet," in *The Journal of the Bihar and Orissa Research Society*, vol. 21, part 1 (March 1935): 21–43. The second, describing an expedition that began on February 16, 1936 (in which Gendun Chopel did not participate), is Rāhula Sānkṛityāyana, "Second Search of Sanskrit Palm-Leaf MSS. in Tibet," in *The Journal of the Bihar and Orissa Research Society*, vol. 23, part 1 (1937): 1–57. The third describes the expedition that began on May 4, 1938, and included Gendun Chopel; he writes on the opening page, "At the beginning our party consisted of three members viz.—the Tibetan Scholar Gendun Chhomphel, the photo-artist Mr. Fany Mockerjee and myself." See Rāhula Sānkṛityāyana, "Search for Sanskrit Palm-Leaf MSS. in Tibet," in *The Journal of the Bihar and Orissa Research Society*, vol. 24, part 4 (1938): 137–63.
46. See Sir Edwin Arnold, *East and West*, p. 311.
47. For a biography of Dharmapala, see Steven Kemper, *Rescued from the Nation*.
48. The articles are "Kumbum, the Mystic City" (August 1939), "Lhassa, The Capital of the Land of Snow" (April 1940), "My Journey from Khumbum

to Lhasa" (July 1940), "An Ill-Starred Dalai Lama" (October 1940) about the Sixth Dalai Lama, and "Two Famous Bengali Pandits in Tibet" (January 1941) about Śāntarakṣita and Vanaratna. The four poems all appear in the August 1941 issue.

49. "Lama Geshe Chompell," p. 3.
50. *Deb ther sngon po*.
51. See Gendun Chopel, *In the Forest of Faded Wisdom*, p. 69.
52. Ibid., p. 107. The final two stanzas seem to describe the experience of watching a motion picture. The "golden haired monkeys" are the British.
53. Gendun Chopel, *The Passion Book*, p. 112.
54. An important exception in this case, both for the detail it provides and for the fact that it was composed by a woman, is the autobiography of Sera Kandro (1892–1940). See Sarah Jacoby, *Love and Liberation*.
55. Gendun Chopel, *In the Forest of Faded Wisdom*, pp. 65–67.
56. See Donald S. Lopez Jr., *Gendun Chopel*, p. 46.
57. Gendun Chopel, *In the Forest of Faded Wisdom*, p. 79.
58. Ibid., p. 71.
59. See, for example, the recollections of Gendun Chopel's sometime traveling companion, Golok Jigme, in Luc Schaedler's 2005 documentary *Angry Monk*.
60. Gendun Chopel, *In the Forest of Faded Wisdom*, p. 69.
61. Those paintings have been published in Lopez, *Gendun Chopel*.
62. Gendun Chopel, *Grains of Gold*, p. 414 and Gendun Chopel, *In the Forest of Faded Wisdom*, pp. 80–83.
63. "Lama Geshe Chompell," p. 3.
64. Gendun Chopel, *Grains of Gold*, pp. 344–45.
65. Ibid., p. 346.
66. *sbom po'i ltung ba*.
67. *Thun drug gi rnal 'byor*, p. 31.
68. See George Roerich, *Biography of Dharmasvāmin*, pp. 18–19. My translation.
69. *grub mtha'*.
70. *phar phyin*.
71. *dge 'dun nyi shu*.
72. See Jacob Dalton, *The Gathering of Intentions*.
73. See, for example, Benjamin Bogin, "Locating the Copper-Colored Mountain," pp. 3–17.
74. Gendun Chopel is referring here to the famous Pānadure Debate of

1873. The Buddhists were represented by Migeṭṭuwattē Guṇānanda Thera (1823–1890), whom Gendun Chopel mistakenly calls Guṇaratna.

75. Gendun Chopel, *Grains of Gold*, pp. 343–44.
76. Gendun Chopel, *In the Forest of Faded Wisdom*, p. 79. This is the second colophon to his translation of the *Dhammapada*, added when the blocks were carved in Sikkim in 1945.
77. Quoted in the biography of Gendun Chopel by his friend Lachung Apo, also known as Shes rab rgya mtsho. See Shes rab rgya mtsho "Dge 'dun chos 'phel," pp. 639–40.
78. Gendun Chopel, *Grains of Gold*, p. 347.
79. Ibid., pp. 313–14.
80. Ibid., p. 318.
81. See Bkras mthong thub bstan chos dar, *Dge 'dun chos 'phel gyi lo rgyus*, p. 57.
82. Gendun Chopel, *In the Forest of Faded Wisdom*, pp. 117–23.
83. Bkras mthong thub bstan chos dar, *Dge 'dun chos 'phel gyi lo rgyus*, p. 56.
84. Gendun Chopel, *Grains of Gold*, pp. 319–20.
85. Ibid., pp. 346–47.
86. Stephen Wootton Bushell, "Early History of Tibet from Chinese Sources," pp. 435–541. Gendun Chopel translated substantial Chinese materials related to Tibet into Tibetan. These appear in his collected writings as *Rgya'i lo rgyus las byung ba'i bod kyi rgyal rabs skor* (*On the Dynastic History of Tibet That Appears in Chinese Histories*). See *'Dzam gling rig pa'i dpa' bo mkhas dbang dge 'dun chos 'phel gyi gsung 'bum*, vol. 3, pp. 185–282. The last of these is signed and dated the twenty-fifth day of the third Tibetan month of 1943.
87. The story appears in an unpublished brief biography of Gendun Chopel by Hor khang bsod nams dpal 'bar, dated 1990, entitled "Mkhas pa'i dbang po dge 'dun chos 'phel gyi rnam thar yang zhun gser gyi thigs pa," pp. 7–8.
88. Gendun Chopel, *In the Forest of Faded Wisdom*, p. 143.
89. For a translation, see Gedun Chos-'phel, *The White Annals (Deb-ther dkar-po)*. For Hugh Richardson's review of the translation, see "Dge-'dun chos-'phel's 'Unfinished'" in Hugh Richardson, *High Peaks, Pure Earth*, pp. 82–88. As Richardson notes, Samten Norboo's translation contains many errors.
90. Shes rab rgya mtsho, "Dge 'dun chos 'phel," p. 644. See also Irmgard Mengele, *dGe-'dun-chos-'phel*, pp. 33, 62.
91. Ibid., pp. 647–48. See also Mengele, pp. 36–37, 65–66.

92. *Dge bshes chos kyi grags pas brtsams pa'i brda dag ming tshig gsal ba*, 1949.
93. Harrer's papers are found in the Himalayan Collection of the Ethnographic Museum of the University of Zurich (Völkerkundemuseum der Universität Zürich). At the present time, his diaries have no shelf number. I am most grateful to Isrun Engelhardt for locating this diary entry and providing a translation.
94. *Ngo mtshar rin po che'i phreng ba*.
95. Sir Charles Bell, *Portrait of the Dalai Lama*, p. 16.
96. Heather Stoddard, *Le mendiant de l'Amdo*, p. 102 and note 162.
97. Harrer papers, Völkerkundemuseum der Universität Zürich, diary entry of November 26, 1946.
98. A biography of Kashöpa by his son, in which this story does not appear, portrays the famous figure as a constant admirer and friend of Gendun Chopel, who did not intercede after his arrest for political reasons, reporting that Kashöpa instructed Gendun Chopel's jailers to flog him in such a way that he was not injured. See Jamyang Choegyal Kasho, *In the Service of the 13th and the 14th Dalai Lamas*.
99. Cited in Melvyn C. Goldstein, *A History of Modern Tibet*, p. 459. See pp. 449–63 for a detailed discussion of the Tibet Improvement Party and its demise; the full document cited here appears in pp. 458–59.
100. Alexandre Andreyev, *The Myth of the Masters Revived*, p. 200.
101. Kirti Rinpoche, *Dge 'dun chos 'phel gyi rab byed zhabs btags ma*, pp. 252–53. For an English translation, see Kirti Rinpoche, *Gendün Chöphel*, p. 134.
102. Ibid., 253–54; English translation, p. 135.
103. This report occurs twice in the "Declassified Files of Ministry of External Affairs" (EAD) of the National Archives of India (NAI), North Eastern Frontier (NEF), under ID 30308 and ID 30311. "Ceishe Cholak" is the Mongolian monk Geshé Chodrak. Both documents carry the title "Reports regarding Gedun Chompel La, alleged to be a Communist and al. Agent of Soviet Russia and Ceishe Cholak of Tibet." Gendun Chopel figures in another report in the same archive, again appearing twice, under ID 32952 and ID 36466. Both documents carry the title (original spelling preserved), "Reports regarding Gedun Chhompallal, Alleged to be a Communist and an Agent of Soviet Russ a regent to P.O. in Siim to keep an eye on him." "P.O. in Siim" refers to "Political Office in Sikkim." This report is dated 1949, when Gendun Chopel was in Lhasa and likely still in prison.

104. Kirti Rinpoche, *Gendün Chöphel*, p. 145.
105. Goldstein, *A History of Modern Tibet*, p. 462. The date of the letter from J. E. Hopkinson is July 11, 1946, but he is quoting a letter from Richardson to Gould of January 4, 1946. I am grateful to Isrun Engelhardt for pointing this out to me.
106. *srid lugs*.
107. *Btson nas hor khang la gnang ba'i phyag bris*, in *'Dzam gling rig pa'i dpa' bo mkhas dbang dge 'dun chos 'phel gyi gsung 'bum*, vol. 5, p. 82.
108. Gendun Chopel, *In the Forest of Faded Wisdom*, p. 147.
109. Ibid., p. 91. See note 49 on that page for the poem that he committed to memory.
110. Sankrityayan, *My Third Expedition to Tibet*, pp. 6–7.
111. Sankrityayan, *Meri Jeevan Yatra*, p. 168.
112. The Japanese spy Kimura Hisao, who traveled in Tibet disguised as a Mongolian monk named Dawa Sangpo, says that he met Gendun Chopel in 1948, delivering a letter from Dorje Tharchin. He states in his account of his travels in Tibet that Gendun Chopel "was only in prison for a year, but sometime during that year his brilliant but always erratic mind snapped." See Hisao Kimura, *Japanese Agent in Tibet*, p. 194.
113. In Luc Schaedler's documentary *Angry Monk*, Gendun Chopel's wife, Tseten Yudron, says that he lived for two years after his release. However, Tharchin's obituary of Gendun Chopel in *Melong*, published on December 1, 1951 (and translated in full at the end of this chapter) states that he was released one year ago, thus supporting the November 1950 date.
114. The story appears in Lachung Apo's biography of Gendun Chopel. See Shes rab rgya mtsho, p. 651, and Mengele, pp. 40 and 69. See also Gendun Chopel, *In the Forest of Faded Wisdom*, p. 107.
115. *Rten 'brel bstod pa*.
116. *'Jam dpal rdzogs pa chen po gzhi lam 'bras bu dbyer med pa'i don la smon pa*.
117. Gendun Chopel, *Grains of Gold*, p. 352.
118. *phyi rol mu stegs pa*.
119. Gendun Chopel, *Grains of Gold*, p. 100.
120. Ibid., p. 104.
121. Ibid., p. 402.
122. Ibid., pp. 265–68.
123. Ibid., pp. 150–51.
124. Ibid., p. 143.

125. Ibid., p. 276.
126. Ibid., pp. 246–47.
127. Ibid., p. 318.
128. Gendun Chopel, *In the Forest of Faded Wisdom*, p. 25.
129. See Kirti Rinpoche Lobsang Tenzin, *Dge 'dun chos 'phel gyi rab byed zhabs btags ma*, p. 93. For an English translation, see Kirti Rinpoche, *Gendün Chöphel*, pp. 48–49.
130. See, for example, Huber, *The Guide to India*, p. 87.
131. *Sems tsam pa'i grub mtha'i rnam bzhag.*
132. *Dbu tshad kyi dka' ba'i gnad.*
133. *Shin tu dka' ba'i rigs lam.*
134. For a useful annotated list of Gendun Chopel's works, both published and rumored, see Irmgard Mengele, *dGe-'dun-chos-'phel*, pp. 85–113. The list of his "Attributed and Unpublished Works" begins on p. 105.
135. David Jackson, *A Saint in Seattle*, p. 179.
136. *'Jam dpal dgyes pa'i gtam gyis rgol ngan phye mar 'thag pa reg gcod ral gri'i 'phrul 'khor.* Cited in Kirti Rinpoche, *Dge 'dun chos 'phel gyi rab byed zhabs btags ma*, p. 3.
137. *Dbu ma'i zab gnad snying por dril ba'i legs bzhad klu sgrub dgongs rgyan.*
138. Donald S. Lopez Jr., *The Madman's Middle Way*, p. 53.
139. *bsam gyis mi khyab pa.*
140. Gendun Chopel, *Grains of Gold*, p. 36.
141. Lopez, *The Madman's Middle Way*, pp. 48–49.
142. *blo ldan.*
143. Ibid., p. 69.
144. Ibid., p. 68.
145. Gendun Chopel, *The Passion Book*, p. 105.
146. The translation is taken from Gendun Chopel, *Grains of Gold*, pp. 29–32.
147. Ibid., pp. 59–62.
148. Translated from the Tibetan text in Huber, *The Guide to India*, pp. 44–48.
149. Huber, *The Guide to India*, pp. 56–58.
150. For the original Tibetan, see "'Jigs rten ril mo 'am zlum po," in *'Dzam gling rig pa'i dpa' bo mkhas dbang dge 'dun chos 'phel gyi gsung 'bum*, vol. 5, pp. 299–300.
151. Gendun Chopel, *In the Forest of Faded Wisdom*, pp. 22–25. This collection of Gendun Chopel's poetry provides information about the poem in

the note at the end of each poem. See those notes for this poem and the others in this chapter.

152. Ibid., pp. 26–29.
153. Ibid., pp. 32–33.
154. Ibid., pp. 34–35.
155. Ibid., pp. 36–37.
156. Ibid., pp. 42–45.
157. Ibid., pp. 46–47.
158. Ibid.
159. Ibid.
160. Ibid., pp. 48–49.
161. Ibid., pp. 58–61.
162. Ibid., pp. 64–67.
163. Ibid., pp. 66–71.
164. Ibid., pp. 72–75.
165. Ibid., pp. 76–77.
166. Ibid., pp. 83–87.
167. Ibid., pp. 98–101.
168. Ibid., pp. 162–65.
169. Ibid., pp. 137–39.
170. The translation is taken from Gendun Chopel, *The Passion Book*. Stanza numbers are provided for ease of reference.
171. The translation is taken from Gendun Chopel, *Grains of Gold*, pp. 268–74.
172. Ibid., pp. 311–25.
173. Pāli: Udena and Vāsuladattā.
174. Pāli: Ambapālī.
175. Pāli: Padumāvatī in Ujjenī.
176. Pāli: Jīvaka Komāra and Sirimā.
177. The translation is taken from Gendun Chopel, *Grains of Gold*, pp. 397–416. Please see this version for annotations to the translation.
178. *Pramāṇavārttika*, chapter 1, verse 221.
179. Illustration is not extant.
180. *gaṇacakra*.
181. *dhūtaguṇa*.
182. *ekāsanika*.
183. *Rba bzhad*.

184. For the Tibetan text, see *'Dzam gling rig pa'i dpa' bo mkhas dbang dge 'dun chos 'phel gyi gsung 'bum*, vol. 1, pp. 168–70.
185. The translation is taken from Lopez, *The Madman's Middle Way*, pp. 47–64. See that translation for annotations.
186. *Samādhirāja Sūtra* IX.23.
187. *Madhyamakāvatāra* XII.39d.
188. *Bka' gdams glegs bam.*
189. *Pramāṇavārttika* III.219.

Bibliography of Works Cited

Andreyev, Alexandre. *The Myth of the Masters Revived: The Occult Lives of Nikolai and Elena Roerich.* Leiden: Brill 2014.

Arnold, Sir Edwin. *East and West: Being Papers Reprinted from the "Daily Telegraph" and Other Sources.* London: Longmans, Green, and Co., 1896.

Bell, Sir Charles. *Portrait of the Dalai Lama.* London: Collins, 1946.

Bkras mthong thub bstan chos dar. *Dge 'dun chos 'phel gyi lo rgyus.* Dharamsala: Library of Tibetan Works and Archives, 1980.

Bogin, Benjamin. "Locating the Copper-Colored Mountain: Buddhist Cosmology, Himalayan Geography, and Maps of Imagined Worlds." *HIMALAYA, the Journal of the Association for Nepal and Himalayan Studies* 34.2 (2014): 3–17.

Bushell, Stephen Wootton. "Early History of Tibet from Chinese Sources." *Journal of the Royal Asiatic Society of Great Britain and Ireland* Vol. XII, No. 4 (October 1880): 435–541.

Chudal, Alaka Atreya. *A Freethinking Cultural Nationalist: A Life History of Rahul Sankrityayan.* New Delhi: Oxford University Press, 2016.

Dalton, Jacob. *The Gathering of Intentions: A History of Tibetan Tantra.* New York: Columbia University Press, 2016.

Davis, Richard. *The Bhagavad Gita: A Biography.* Princeton: Princeton University Press, 2014.

Dge bshes chos kyi grags pa. *Dge bshes chos kyi grags pas brtsams pa'i brda dag ming tshig gsal ba.* Lhasa: 1949; Peking: 1957.

Dge 'dun chos 'phel. *'Dzam gling rig pa'i dpa' bo mkhas dbang dge 'dun chos 'phel gyi gsung 'bum*, 5 vols. Hong Kong: Zhang kang gyi ling dpe skrun khang, 2006.

Dze smad Blo bzang dpal ldan bstan 'dzin yar rgyas. *'Jam dpal dgyes pa'i gtam gyis rgol ngan phye mar 'thag pa reg gcod ral gri'i 'phrul 'khor.* Delhi: D. Gyaltsan and K. Legshay, 1972.

Gedun Chos-'phel. *The White Annals (Deb-ther dkar-po)*. Translated by Samten Norboo. Dharamsala, India: Library of Tibetan Works and Archives, 1978.

Gendun Chompell, Lama. "Kumbum, the Mystic City." *The Maha-Bodhi* Vol. 47, No. 8 (1939): pp. 355–58.

Gendun Chopel. *Grains of Gold: Tales of a Cosmopolitan Traveler*. Translated by Thupten Jinpa and Donald S. Lopez Jr. Chicago: The University of Chicago Press, 2014.

———. *In the Forest of Faded Wisdom: 104 Poems by Gendun Chopel: A Bilingual Edition*. Edited and translated by Donald S. Lopez Jr. Chicago: University of Chicago Press, 2009.

———. *The Passion Book: A Tibetan Guide to Love and Sex*. Translated by Donald S. Lopez Jr. and Thupten Jinpa. Chicago: The University of Chicago Press, 2018.

Gendun Chopel and Ra kra bkras mthong. *Gsar bsgyur Rā ma yā ṇa'i rtog brjod*. Beijing: Mi rigs dpe skrun khang, 2005.

Geshe Chompell, Lama. "Lhassa, the Capital of the Land of Snow." *The Maha-Bodhi*, Vol. 48, No. 4 (1940): pp. 115–19.

———. "Two Famous Bengali Pandits in Tibet." *The Maha-Bodhi* Vol. 49, No. 1 (1941): pp. 31–32.

———. "An Ill-starred Dalai Lama." *The Maha-Bodhi* Vol. 48, No. 10 (1940): pp. 370–74.

Geshe Chomphell, Lama. "My Journey from Khumbum to Lhassa." *The Maha-Bodhi* Vol. 48, No. 7 (1940): pp. 241–43.

The Gita: Bhakti-Yoga Chap. XII. Translated by Lama Gendun Chhophel La in collaboration with Swami Prabuddhananda. Darjeeling: Ramakrishna Vedanta Ashrama, 1941.

Goldstein, Melvyn C. *A History of Modern Tibet: The Demise of the Lamaist State*. Berkeley: University of California Press, 1989.

Hackett, Paul. "Looking for a Lost Gītā." *Nāmarūpa* (Fall 2007): 41–45.

———. *Theos Bernard, the White Lama: Tibet, Yoga, and American Religious Life*. New York: Columbia University Press, 2012.

Hor khang bsod nams dpal 'bar. "Mkhas pa'i dbang po dge 'dun chos 'phel gyi rnam thar yang zhun gser gyi thigs pa." Unpublished.

Huber, Toni. *The Guide to India: A Tibetan Account by Amdo Gendun Chöphel*. Dharamsala: Library of Tibetan Works and Archives, 2000.

———. *The Holy Land Reborn: Pilgrimage and the Tibetan Reinvention of Buddhist India*. Chicago: The University of Chicago Press, 2008.

Jackson, David. *A Saint in Seattle: The Life of the Tibetan Mystic Dezhung Rinpoche.* Boston: Wisdom Publications, 2004.

Jacoby, Sarah. *Love and Liberation: Autobiographical Writings of the Tibetan Buddhist Visionary Sera Khandro.* New York: Columbia University Press, 2015.

Jamyang Choegyal Kasho. *In the Service of the 13th and the 14th Dalai Lamas: Choegyal Nyima Lhundrup Kashopa, Untold True Stories of Tibet.* Frankfurt: Tibethaus Verlag, 2015.

Kemper, Steven. *Rescued from the Nation: Anagarika Dharmapala and the Buddhist World.* Chicago: The University of Chicago Press, 2015.

Kimura, Hisao. *Japanese Agent in Tibet: My Ten Years of Travel in Disguise.* London: Serindia Publications, 1990.

Kirti Rinpoche Lobsang Tenzin. *Dge 'dun chos 'phel gyi rab byed zhabs btags ma: Mdo smad pa mkhas dban Dge 'dun chos 'phel gyi nag rgyun lo rgyus sogs dpyad gzhi'i yig cha phyogs bsgrigs.* Dharamsala: Kirti Jepa Datsang Institute of Tibetan Higher Studies, 2003. English translation: Kirti Rinpoche, *Gendün Chöphel: Portrait of a Great Thinker.* Translated by Yeshi Dhondup. Dharamsala, India: Library of Tibetan Works and Archives, 2013.

"Lama Geshe Chompell," *The Maha-Bodhi* 49 (August 1941): 3.

Lopez, Donald S., Jr. *Gendun Chopel: Tibet's First Modern Artist.* Chicago: Serindia Publications, 2013.

———. *The Madman's Middle Way: Reflections on Reality of the Tibetan Monk Gendun Chopel.* Chicago: The University of Chicago Press, 2006.

Mengele, Irmgard. *dGe-'dun-chos-'phel: A Biography of the 20th-Century Tibetan Scholar.* Dharamsala: Library of Tibetan Works and Archives, 1999.

Nietupski, Paul. *Labrang: A Tibetan Buddhist Monastery at the Crossroads of Four Civilizations.* Ithaca, NY: Snow Lion Publications, 1999.

Richardson, Hugh. *High Peaks, Pure Earth: Collected Writings on Tibetan History and Culture.* Edited by Michael Aris. London: Serindia Publications, 1998.

Roerich, George. *Biography of Dharmasvāmin (Chag lo tsa-ba Chos-rje-dpal), A Tibetan Monk Pilgrim.* Patna: K. P. Jayaswal Research Institute, 1959.

———, ed. and trans. *The Blue Annals*, second ed. Gos Lo-tsa-ba Gzon-nu-dpal. Delhi: Motilal Banarsidass, 1976.

Sankrityayan, Rahul. *Meri Jeevan Yatra.* Second edition. Delhi: Radhakrishna Prakashan, 2002.

———. *My Third Expedition to Tibet.* Dharamsala, India: Library of Tibetan Works and Archives, 2015.

Sānkṛityāyana, Rāhula. "Sanskrit Palm-leaf MSS. in Tibet." *The Journal of the Bihar and Orissa Research Society* Vol. 21, Part 1 (March 1935): 21–43.

——. "Search for Sanskrit Palm-Leaf MSS. in Tibet." *The Journal of the Bihar and Orissa Research Society* Vol. 24, Part 4 (19.8): 137–63.

——. "Second Search of Sanskrit Palm-leaf MMS. in Tibet." *The Journal of the Bihar and Orissa Research Society.* Vol .23, Part 1 (1937): 1–57.

Shes rab rgya mtsho. "Dge 'dun chos 'phel." In *Biographical Dictionary of Tibet and Tibetan Buddhism, Volume 4: The Rñiṅ-ma-pa Tradition (Part Two).* Edited by Khetsun Sangpo, pp. 639–40. Dharamsala: Library of Tibetan Works and Archives, 1973.

Stoddard, Heather. *Le mendiant de l'Amdo.* Paris: Société d'ethnographie, 1985.

Thun drug gi rnal 'byor. In *Bla ma'i rnal 'byor dang yi dam khag gi bdag bskyed sogs zhal 'don gces btus bzhugs.* Dharamsala: Tibetan Cultural Printing Press, 1992.

Walravens, Hartmut, ed. *The First Tibetan Serial: August Hermann Francke's* La-dvags-kyi ag-bâr *(1904–1907).* Berlin: Staatsbibliothek zu Berlin, 2010.

Index

LIBRARY OF CONGRESS CATALOGING-IN-PUBLICATION DATA
Names: Lopez, Donald S., Jr., 1952– author. |Dge-'dun-chos-'phel, A-mdo, 1903–1951.
Title: Gendun Chopel: Tibet's modern visionary / Donald Lopez.
Description: Boulder, Colorado: Shambhala, 2018. | Series: Lives of the masters | Includes bibliographical references and index.
Identifiers: LCCN 2017029910 | ISBN 9781611804065 (paperback)
Subjects: LCSH: Dge-'dun-chos-'phel, A-mdo, 1903–1951. | Lamas—China—Amdo (Region)—Biography. | Scholars—China—Amdo (Region)—Biography. | Amdo (China: Region)—Biography. | BISAC: RELIGION / Buddhism / Tibetan. | BIOGRAPHY & AUTOBIOGRAPHY / Religious. | HISTORY / Asia / India & South Asia.
Classification: LCC BQ950.G38 L67 2018 | DDC 294.3/923092 [B]—dc23
LC record available at https://lccn.loc.gov/2017029910